Ordinary Poverty

In the series
Labor in Crisis
edited by Stanley Aronowitz

Ordinary Poverty

A Little Food and Cold Storage

WILLIAM DiFAZIO

Temple University Press

Philadelphia

WILLIAM DiFAZIO is Professor of Sociology at St. John's University. He is the author of *Longshoremen: Community and Resistance on the Brooklyn Waterfront* and co-author, with Stanley Aronowitz, of *The Jobless Future: Sci-Tech and the Dogma of Work*. He is the host of the weekly radio show "CityWatch" on WBAI–99.5FM in New York City with Deena Kolbert.

Temple University Press
1601 North Broad Street
Philadelphia PA 19122
www.temple.edu/tempress

∞ The paper used in this publication meets the requirements of the American National Standard for Information Sciences—Permanence of Paper for Printed Library Materials, ANSI Z39.48-1992

Library of Congress Cataloging-in-Publication Data

DiFazio, William.
Ordinary poverty: a little food and cold storage / William DiFazio.
     p.   cm.—(Labor in crisis)
Includes bibliographical references and index.
Contents: Introduction: ordinary poverty—Soup kitchen blues, 1988–1993—Beggars can't be choosers, 1993–2000—The dialectic of Sister Bernadette: the limits of advocacy—Forgetting poverty: a Seder for everyone—Conclusion: making poverty extraordinary.
ISBN 1-59213-014-3 (cloth : alk. paper)—ISBN 1-59213-458-0 (pbk. : alk. paper)
1. Poverty—United States.   2. Poor—United States—Case studies.
3. St. John's Bread and Life (Soup kitchen).   4. United States—Economic policy.
5. United States—Social policy.   6. Social justice—United States.
I. Title.   II. Series.

HC110.P6D54 2006
362.5'0973–dc22

                                                                    2005050595

2 4 6 8 9 7 5 3 1

Contents

For Sister Mary Bernadette Szymczak, D.C., Patricia Johnson, William Baker, Jose Nicolau, and Hossein Saadat

Acknowledgments

THERE ARE MANY FAILURES to write about when you are writing about poverty in the United States and the tens of millions of people who are poor in the richest country in the world. The first and most important failure is that of the free market, which has been totally unsuccessful in eradicating the daily misery of the poor. Congress has failed as well. Welfare reform is just the application of free market capitalism to social policy and just a continuation of the failure of the economy to develop a political remedy for poverty. President Ronald Reagan's disastrous budget cuts and the Omnibus Budget Reconciliation Act of 1981 (OBRA) created massive homelessness and hunger. In response, a nationwide voluntary network was developed to patch the holes in the social safety net with a combination of direct services and political advocacy for those who seemed unable to speak for themselves. But the safety net itself is a measure of the failure of social policy, since all it does is establish a minimum of squalor that no poor person was supposed to fall below. In the early 1980s, too many people were falling below that minimal standard.

The advocates who emerged in this period were a mixture of well-meaning religious and secular people, some veterans of the war against poverty, some community activists. Political struggles were put on hold as people were fed and given temporary protection from the elements. As the United States became more conservative politically, these temporary and emergency measures became permanent, and the advocates became bureaucrats in the organizations that they had created.

In 1988 my students in the Sociology Club at St. John's University, under the direction of Father Brian J. O'Connell, C.M., took me to St. John's Bread and Life soup kitchen in the Bedford-Stuyvesant neighborhood of Brooklyn. The soup kitchen was in St. John the

Baptist Church. The pastor was Father Thomas Hynes, but the kitchen itself was under the direction of Sister Mary Bernadette Szymczak, D.C., who provided the spiritual care that was as important to the hundreds of poor people who came to the kitchen as the food and services offered. I was soon a regular volunteer, and this book is the result of that participant observation. Hossein Saadat became the kitchen's executive director soon after I started to volunteer. Seeing me as part of his meager staff, he immediately got me involved with fundraising and recruiting volunteers. Hossein and his assistant, Anne Sukhan-Ramdhan, administered one of the largest programs in New York City, serving over a thousand people a day, run on fewer funds than it needed, and, like others, in a continuous financial crisis.

In the 1990s, as St. John's Bread and Life provided more services, fundraising demanded more of Hossein's time, and he began using me as his political surrogate within New York City's antipoverty and antihunger community. I was sent to City Hall to testify before the City Council on antihunger and employment policy. At the monthly meetings of the New York City Coalition Against Poverty (NYCCAH), I met Executive Director Judith Walker and the board chair, Father John Bucki. I soon became active in NYCCAH. Through one of its programs, Interfaith Voices Against Hunger (IVAH), I met Rabbi Ellen Lippman, the Reverend Ozzie Edwards, and Rob Schwartz, among many others, and participated in their monthly prayer vigils at City Hall. I soon become a member of the NYCCAH Board and met Reverend Elizabeth Maxwell from Holy Apostle Church, the largest soup kitchen in New York City, and Lorraine Lett and Bev Chevront, all-important antipoverty and antihunger advocates. Through these contacts I was introduced to Kathy Goldman, Jan Poppendieck, and Liz Krueger of the Community Food Resource Center (CFRC), Lucy Cabrera from the Food Bank, and Mark Dunlea from Hunger Action Network New York State (HANNYS). Through Judith Walker, I was introduced to the advocacy community in New York City.

We created a board at St. John's Bread and Life as a way of dealing with our continuing fundraising problems. I became a member of the

board of HANNYS, the board of Neighbors Together Soup Kitchen in
Brownsville, Brooklyn, and the steering committee of the Same Boat
Coalition. I was helping to provide direct services, educational services, and political services to people in New York City. I too had
become an advocate and a bureaucrat.

I would never argue that these services aren't necessary, but the
price of advocacy and organization building is that activism and
movement building become a very low priority. We ameliorated the
misery of the poor but did little to end it. This book is about this
specific failure to end poverty through direct service and advocacy. I
am not concerned merely with describing the ordinary lives of the
poor or evaluating direct service and advocacy. Description is not
enough, nor is theory—but at least theory gives us a way of going
beyond the immediacy of their everyday life and of the well-meaning
programs of advocates. This book is above all about the types of
struggle that are necessary to end poverty in the United States. It is in
the theoretical work of this book that the possibility of ending poverty in the United States is envisioned. And if poverty cannot be
ended in the richest country in the world, then the future is very grim
for the world's poor, especially in those countries where too many
people live on less than one or two dollars a day.

IN ALL THESE YEARS of researching and writing this book, I have met
many fine people who were generous with both their time and their
support for this project, even though many of them will not agree
with all of my conclusions.

I want to thank Bertha Lewis, the executive director of the Association of Community Organizations for Reform Now (ACORN),
and Jose Nicolau and Skip Roseboro, who are also from ACORN. I
was honored to participate in many ACORN actions. I am grateful to
the board of St. John's Bread and Life, and especially Father James
Maher, C.M., and Neil Sheehan; to the board and staff of HANNYS,
especially Executive Director Bich Ha Pham and Associate Director
Kim Gilliland; to members of the Same Boat Coalition, especially
Ed Ortiz; and to the board of Neighbors Together. And of course
this book would not be possible without the people who used the

programs at St. John's Bread and Life and who let me into their lives, especially Patricia Johnson and Bill Baker, who taught me the ways of life of the soup kitchen.

I write these acknowledgments just after coming from a meeting of the Marx study group at Mike Brown's loft. This group began in 1974 and met regularly into the 1990s. We have started it up again, and it is great that I can still meet with Eric Lichten, Meryl Sufian, Dawn Esposito, Jose Figueroa, Martha Ecker, George Snedeker, and Mike Brown, all of whom have been important in the formation of my intellectual and sociological thinking. The Margaret Yard Friday study group was important in the early theoretical work for this book, and the editorial collective of *Situations: Project of the Radical Imagination* was very helpful in finishing it. I thank the people who read all or part of the manuscript: Lynn Chancer, Ellen Willis, Judith Walker, Judith Desena, Heather Gautney, Paul McInerney, David VanArsdale, Randy Martin, and the members of *Situations* and both study groups. Most important has been the constant feedback of my wife, Susanna Heller, and my daughter, Liegia S. DiFazio. They have been my most loyal critics.

Working on the radio show *CityWatch* with my partner Deena Kolbert provided a continuous venue to talk about issues related to poverty in New York City. *CityWatch* began in 2000 as a short segment on *Wake-up Call* and later became a regular one-hour show on WBAI (99.5 FM). The show gave me access to New York City's elected officials and to many community organizations and eventually led to direct involvement in community struggles. Of these, the struggle to reopen Fire Engine Company 212 in Williamsburg, Brooklyn, was the most meaningful. In particular I want to thank Bernard White, the program manager of WBAI, and our engineer, Errol Maitland.

As a professor at St. John's University, I have been lucky enough over the years to have such fine colleagues as Father Brian O'Connell, Richard Harris, Henry Lesieur, Judith Desena, Dawn Esposito, and Rod Bush. My graduate assistants David VanArsdale and Felice Lee-Jones helped with the field research for this book. I am grateful also for the library research of Maureen Eliott, Bora Pajo, and Christian

Trans. The deans of St. John's College provided me with regular research reductions that helped to make the research and writing possible.

These are hard times in academia as the corporate boards that tend to control universities throughout the United States increasingly encroach on the intellectual aspects of learning and research. Most of these boards have little understanding of the work of teaching college students or the varieties of scholarly research. Thus, I want to thank Frank Leveness, John Greg, Bernie Cassidy, and Theresa Barz, the members of the St. John's University negotiating team of the American Association of University Professors (AAUP). I am proud to have been part of this negotiating team for two contracts.

I thank my agent, Neeti Madan at Sterling Lord Literistics; my visionary editor, Micah Kleit at Temple University Press; and the series editor, Stanley Aronowitz. Jane Barry's hard work editing the manuscript is appreciated. All of them have had major roles in making this book readable.

The breadth of Stanley Aronowitz's knowledge and his openness to theorizing in new ways encouraged me to move beyond the margins of my own empirical research. My friendship with him and with Ellen Willis has been an important part of my life for 30 years.

I am very lucky to still see many of my friends from grade school—P.S. 194 in Brooklyn. I can always depend on them for total support and lots of laughter. My lifelong friend Bruce Vanacour's constant help kept my 10-year-old Gateway computer running.

I am fortunate enough to have a wonderfully loving and supportive family: my mother, Sylvia DiFazio; my daughter, Liegia S. DiFazio; and my wife, Susanna Heller. The most difficult part of researching and writing this book was the loss of too many during the early years of the AIDS epidemic. At times it seemed as if I was always at a memorial for some soup kitchen guest. There were also losses from other causes. The death of my mentor George Fischer and the deaths of Father Brian J. O'Connell, C.M., Bill Baker, and Jose Nicolau were terribly upsetting to all who knew them. Sister Mary Bernadette Szymczak, D.C., made it hard for me to be cynical as she persisted in helping the poor no matter how difficult it became. She was a bold and courageous woman. The most difficult loss was the death of my father, Sebastian DiFazio, the main role model for my life and a very kind, open-minded, and fun-loving man. I continue to model the spirit of my life on his, and it was in this spirit that this book was written.

PARTS OF THIS BOOK appeared in earlier forms in the following books and journals: "Soup Kitchen Blues: Postindustrial Poverty in Brooklyn," in *The Other City: People and Politics in New York and London,* ed. Susanne MacGregor and Arthur Lipow (Atlantic Highlands, N.J.: Humanities Press, 1995); "Why There Is No Movement of the Poor," in *Post-Work,* ed. Stanley Aronowitz and Jonathan Cutler (London: Routledge, 1998); "Poverty, the Postmodern and the Jobless Future," *Critical Perspectives on Accounting* 9, no. 1 (February 1998); "Time, Poverty and Global Democracy," in *Implicating Empire: Globalization and Resistance in the 21st Century World Order*, ed. Stanley Aronowitz and Heather Gautney (New York: Basic Books, 2003); "Purposely Forgetting Poverty," *Situations: Project of the Radical Imagination* 1, no. 1 (April 2005).

1 Introduction

Ordinary Poverty

The ideas which are here expressed so laboriously are extremely simple and should be obvious. The difficulty lies not in the new ideas, but in escaping from the old ones.
     —J. M. Keynes, *The General Theory of Employment, Interest and Money*

AFRICAN AMERICAN WOMAN, 38 years old. She has lost her benefits and explains what she now does to get housing:

> My friend helps me. I live some of the time with him. I eat here [at St. John's Bread and Life soup kitchen] whenever I can.
>
> [Is it getting harder to make ends meet?] Yes it is. I can't survive; I need medical assistance and I'll do anything. I have to ask people to stay at their house. I have to do favors. I provide sexual favors [she points at her friend]. He only lets me stay with him for sex.

White man, 40 years old, a warehouse manager with 20 years of experience. He hasn't worked in a year:

> You should see the people I have to compete with. I am waiting for a job interview with a moving company. Beautiful operation. They liked me but they said they didn't want to train me. It's not because I'm obese. At least not this time. It's a computerized operation, and I would have to be trained on the computer. But I'm sitting waiting for the interview, the other guy sitting to be interviewed is an MBA, also my age. Knows how to use computer. Laid off from Wall Street, $80,000-a-year job. He's competing with me. I told him I just applied for a warehouse job at Busch Terminal. He asks me for the information and if I mind that he'll apply for the job. I give him the address. He's

1

more desperate than I am. How am I going to get a job? I have all on-the-job experience and only a two-year college degree. How can I compete for warehouse jobs with MBAs? And it happens all the time.

African American man, 49 years old. He doesn't have any benefits:

I live between a rock and a hard place. I'm homeless, but I have a basement that they let me sleep in for taking care of it. I don't have my own home. . . . It's truly a shame that I can't get a job. . . . I have an associate's degree in accounting. I was working in a beverage place that reclaims bottles and cans. It took me less than a minute to fill the boxes. I pride myself at my speed at work. They're paying me three dollars an hour. Working 10 hours a day, how can I live? Then they laid me off because they weren't busy. Its pitiful out there.

White man, January 20, 1989. President George H. W. Bush's inaugural address:

It is to make kinder the face of the nation and gentler the face of the world. My friends, we have work to do. There are homeless, lost and roaming. There are children who have nothing, no love, no normalcy. There are those who cannot free themselves of enslavement to whatever addiction—drugs, welfare, the demoralization that rules the slums. There is crime to be conquered, the rough crime of the streets. There are young women to be helped who are to become mothers of children they can't care for and might not love. They need our care and guidance, though we bless them for choosing life. . . . I have spoken of a Thousand Points of Light, of all the community organizations that are spread like stars throughout the nation, doing good. We will work hand in hand, encouraging, sometimes leading, sometimes led, rewarding. We will work on this in the White House, in the Cabinet agencies. I will go to the people and the programs that are the brighter points of light, and I'll ask every member of my government to become involved. The old ideas are new again because they are not old, they are timeless: duty, sacrifice, commitment and a patriotism that finds its expression in taking part and pitching in.[1]

White man, February 17, 1993. President Bill Clinton's economic address to a joint session of Congress:

> Later this year we will offer a plan to end welfare as we know it. I have worked on this issue for the better part of a decade and I know from personal conversations with many people, that no one—no one wants to change the welfare system as badly as those who are trapped in it. I want to offer the people on welfare the education, training, the child care, the health care they need to get back on their feet, but say after two years they must get back to work, in private business if possible, in public service if necessary. We have to end welfare as a way of life and make it a path of independence and dignity.[2]

Latino man from the Bronx. He is in the Work Experience Program (WEP):

> I don't understand, I work 35 hours per week and I get $68.50 every two weeks. I'm a single man so I get less for working the same jobs as someone who has kids. That's not fair; I'm doing the same work. I sweep the park at my site on Arthur Avenue. It's not enough to live on. With my food stamps I get four dollars a day for food, so I use the three dollars a day that I get to go to work every day for my food too. My rent is $270 but welfare only gives me $215, so I have to get the other $55 from my grants. So I walk everywhere. I walk an hour back and forth to work. I walk all over the Bronx and Manhattan, more than two hours each way. I'm in good shape. I like orange juice, but a container costs three dollars, so if you buy a container, I have almost nothing left for food for the day. I don't know what to do. Still I don't understand why I get so little for working, sweeping leaves in the park.

African American man, begging on the G train in Queens:

> You look at me and you say I should get a job. That I'm a bum. Why am I bothering you? But I just want some change so I can

get something to eat, a room for the night. You know that there's people doing drugs, killing each other, raping children, doing all kinds of terrible things. I'm just asking you for some money. And you say I should get a job. Well, let me tell you, there aren't any jobs out there. If there were jobs in Brooklyn and Queens, there wouldn't be people on this train going to Manhattan to work. And every time they advertise a job, there wouldn't be 150 people waiting for that job. There aren't any jobs out there. It's a lie that there are jobs for everyone. And that's why people are robbing, stealing, doing drugs, murdering. There aren't any jobs out there. So please give me some change. God bless you.

These are dramatic accounts but poverty is not dramatic—it is ordinary. Two of the accounts are by presidents of the United States who do not necessarily understand the daily lives of the poor but who have the power to change their lives. They will, in fact, change the lives of poor people dramatically. When President Clinton signs the welfare reform bill in 1996, he cuts their benefits on the premise that welfare recipients will get jobs. But most of the jobs pay poverty-level wages, and he succeeds only in increasing their misery. The man on the G train, who understands too well the lives of the poor, also wants some change. Sure, he wants a little money to purchase what he needs, but if his misery is going to end, he needs some social change as well.

Social change for the poor was rare in the 1990s and is still rare at the start of the twenty-first century. Welfare rolls are down, but poverty has not been reduced. In our free market system there are always a few winners, but most lose, and poverty just increases. Unemployment is low, under 5 percent, but jobs that pay well are declining, wages have not increased, and the poor face a choice between workfare and reduced benefits. Public funding for the poor has been cut (27.9% in aid for single mothers with children from 1979 to 1989).[3] The poor keep losing ground, and neither President Bush's "Thousand Points of Light" nor President Clinton's "welfare reform" has reduced their daily misery. Democrats and Republicans have agreed that workfare is the full-employment program for the United States: "Jobs for All," but at a rate that means indentured servitude for the poor. The politicians all speak the same language—jobs will reduce poverty—but there aren't enough jobs. New technologies are destroying the older job sectors without producing enough good new jobs, and most of the new jobs that have been created pay low, even poverty-level wages. To end poverty, jobs would have to pay above poverty level wages. They don't; instead, we have the end of welfare replaced by workfare, as the poor are forced to work for limited public assistance that just guarantees their continued poverty.[4] Poverty grows throughout the United States. It seems unchangeable. As a young homeless man in a soup kitchen says about his life, it's "a little food and cold storage." The hopelessness of the poor has become ordinary.

A Vocabulary Shift

The vocabulary of social policy has shifted over the decades, and the metaphors of the conservatives have become dominant.[5] In the mid-1970s, with the continuous increase in poverty, the recession, the oil crisis, and the fiscal crisis, the language of "community control" and "black power" and activism to "end poverty" gave way to the language of "benign neglect," "culture of poverty," and the "failure of social programs." The poor became "pathetic victims," "junkies," "the homeless." Such changes reflect the political shifts of the 1970s and 1980s. First, the language of social change mutated into the liberal language of advocacy. The poor could no longer speak for themselves; they were no longer part of dynamic social movements, and experts would speak for them. By the eighties, liberal social policy had been reduced to a holding action, and the only question was how much of the safety net could be saved. Next, as the practical, liberal language of advocacy gave way to the new conservative hegemony, the goal was to "end welfare." The language of possibility faded, and the conservative language of "individual achievement" and "personal responsibility" came to center stage. This shift excluded the poor.

Though the Reagan administration guaranteed that the "truly needy" would be provided for by the "social safety net," social welfare programs were slashed in the 1980s and 1990s. Poverty, hunger, and homelessness reached a level unknown in the United States since the Great Depression. The first President Bush reacted to this new poverty, not by redirecting federal money to the poor, but by promising that the private sector would make up the difference through the mobilization of volunteers, the "Thousand Points of Light."

William Jefferson Clinton started his presidency in 1992 with a pledge to "end welfare as we know it." Some hoped that this was merely a campaign promise, and that his administration would turn around the Reagan-Bush assault on welfare. Ultimately, however, Clinton spoke the same conservative language, even if he seemed to have more compassion for children. In 1996 the Democrats, originally reluctant, joined the Republicans in passing welfare reform, ending Aid to Families with Dependent Children (AFDC) and replacing it with Temporary Assistance to Needy Families (TANF).[6] On January 25, 1999, during his impeachment, Clinton boasted that because of his welfare reform program, there were fewer than 8 million Americans on welfare, down 44 percent from 14.3 million in 1994.[7] He left out some significant data. First, there were still 35.5 million people living below the poverty level in 1997, down only 0.5 percent since 1995.[8] Second, typical welfare recipients who found jobs through welfare-to-work programs across the United States earn between 65 and 70 percent of the federal poverty level.[9]

The language of possibility has become a one-dimensional language of the free market—a "final vocabulary," to use Richard Rorty's term: "It is final in the sense that if doubt is cast on the worth of these words, their user has no non-circular argumentative recourse. Those words are as far as he can go with language: beyond them there is only helpless passivity or a resort to force."[10] In this sense the final vocabulary of conservative social policy ends debate. Its key terms are "work," "productivity," "moral," "duty," "responsibility," "achievement," "free market," "competition," and "patriotism."

Both conservative and liberal politicians and social scientists have been affected by the conservative vocabulary shift. The victory of conservative policy makers means not just that their views have become dominant but that liberal social scientists and policy makers now speak the language of limitations of the free market. Plans for economic redistribution through a higher minimum wage, taxation, and government intervention against homelessness and hunger have been severely restricted by the forced austerity of budget cuts. Thus, the "economic boom" of the Clinton years did not mean a new era of possibility in the fight to end poverty but a continuation of the conservative vocabulary, with some new words added: "workfare," "time limits," "block grants," "sanctioning," and the "ending of entitlements."

With the policy shift to the right, the programs for the poor are determined not by their needs but by market forces. The new poverty advocates speak the language of accommodation, survival, and maintenance. Two government policies concerning poor children in the early 1990s demonstrate the conservative hegemony over poverty policy. First, the America 2000 Excellence in Education Act proposed to reform education in the United States by creating "New American School Communities" in which federal money would be allocated to public schools based on standards of excellence.[11] Schools in poor districts, already underfunded, would have to compete with well-funded schools in middle-class and wealthy districts. "The Bush administration argued that the competition would make the poor schools shape up or shut down."[12]

Second, a study entitled *Beyond Rhetoric: A New American Agenda for Children and Families*, by the National Commission on Children, reported on the condition of poor, battered, unhealthy, homeless, and hungry children in the United States. "The National Commission on Children calls on all Americans to work together to change the conditions that jeopardize the health and well being of so many of our youngest citizens and threaten our future as an economic power, a democratic nation and a caring society. Our failure to act today will only defer to the next generation the rising social, moral and financial costs of our neglect. Investment in children is no longer a luxury, but a national imperative."[13]

The commission proposed "52 billion to 56 billion in new federal funds in the first year."[14] This expenditure is not feasible in the current austere fiscal condition. It is not cost-effective. It will increase taxes. It will hinder American competitiveness in the global market. The language of possibility is quickly muted. Liberals must accommodate or become silent. The poor do not have a voice; without a social movement, they are spoken for. Advocates, though well meaning, are isolated and impotent. They cannot speak the vocabulary of social change. They "settle for"; they "do the best they can." Without power, they engage in piecemeal struggles. They do not struggle for new housing but for the right of the homeless to have a shantytown in Tompkins Square Park on the Lower East Side of Manhattan. Instead of struggling for a guaranteed middle-class income for all, they put all their energy into saving an inadequate safety net. These struggles yield some victories, but over the 13 years that this book deals with, failure was more common and the conditions of poor people have gotten worse. The vocabulary of advocacy is never a transformative vocabulary. In the name of practicality, advocates rule out social movement, change, and possibility. Ultimately, they support the status quo, and for the poor this means that their poverty is permanent.

POLICY AND DAILY LIFE IN BEDFORD-STUYVESANT

September 13, 1991. I am walking down Stuyvesant Avenue in Bedford-Stuyvesant, Brooklyn, surrounded by crumbling buildings and crumbling people. A man is collecting bottles, pushing a shopping cart draped with a green lawn-and-leaf bag. The bag is full of bottles and cans, which he can redeem at the supermarket for a nickel apiece. This is another example of the Protestant work ethic and free enterprise in Bedford-Stuyvesant. In my own Brooklyn neighborhood, Greenpoint, the bottle redemption center is next to a Key Food supermarket. Men and women line up daily with trash bags full of bottles and cans. Nickels for bottles: the fair exchange for their hard work. Many of the men in line at the Greenpoint Men's Shelter earn their living in this way. They keep the streets clean. They are underpaid.

The director of Catholic Charities says to me, "It's very depressing—the age of these people. They're young. They're not old and disabled—these are physically able people. It's very depressing."

Today at St. John's Bread and Life soup kitchen in Bedford-Stuyvesant, I am serving cookies. I take a handful, wrap them in a napkin, and give them out. I talk to Jerry, who works in the kitchen. He's living at the Glenwood Hotel on Broadway and Havermeyer Street in Williamsburg, Brooklyn, down the hall from John, who also works in the kitchen. John was forced to leave the Greenpoint shelter because of budget cuts about a year ago. "The hotel is a fleabag," he says. "It's shit, but it's better than the shelter. It's $6.50 a night, and welfare pays."

"The hotel is hell," Jerry says, "but I couldn't live on the streets. I've been worried about living on the street since my sister-in-law don't want me staying in the basement at their house. She says she wants to rent it and she can get more than I pay. I'm too old to be in the streets. It would kill me."

John interrupts, "We did it. We spent a whole winter in the streets, and then a long time at the shelter."

Jerry: "It would really kill me now. I could never do it again." He laughs: "Do you remember, you spent the whole winter without a coat? That was our project, to get you a warm coat."

John: "I don't know how I survived that whole winter without a coat."

Jerry: "We finally got him a coat, but it was February."

John: "It's great having Jerry down the hall."

All of these poor people are trying to cope with an unbearable situation. Politicians and policy makers make decisions about them, mostly without much knowledge of their daily lives. Here conservatives and liberals are the same, congratulating themselves even though their policies decrease funding and make the lives of poor people harder. It is important to analyze these policies and try to understand how they have failed to help poor people who are "living the experience" of poverty, increasing immiseration amidst prosperity.

On this same day, Professor E tells me that they are always "be-tween a rock and a hard place." Professor E is a West Indian who took it upon himself to educate me on the realities of "Bed-Stuy." I remember what Professor E said to me about the shortcomings of the first President Bush's solution to poverty: "If President Bush was serious, he would know that a thousand points of light ain't enough. At least a million is necessary."

TWO EXEMPLARS OF FREE MARKET SOCIAL POLICY

The Conservatives

Charles Murray's *Losing Ground* is the basic statement of the con-servative position on poverty and social welfare.[15] Murray's study was the bible of the Reagan and Bush administrations' poverty pol-icy[16] and an influential text even during the Clinton era. His discourse on poverty, framed in the language of the free market, launched the essential vocabulary shift and the new dogma that government social welfare programs are the problem. (Later, in the nineties, Michael Tanner, would echo Murray's account of the poor being enticed into welfare by a failed liberal welfare state.)[17] According to this narrative, the behavior of the disadvantaged is independent of social and psychological factors and determined by economically motivated rational choices. Social welfare programs create a context in which the rational choices of the disadvantaged are "not to enter the la-bor force," "not to get an education," and "not to get married." In short, the social welfare programs of the 1960s and 1970s failed be-cause "we made it profitable to be poor."[18]

Murray claimed that poverty increased in spite of the federally funded social programs of the 1960s and 1970s because those pro-grams decreased incentives for disadvantaged young blacks to enter the labor force, take available jobs (even at low wages), and continue working. Thus, these programs increased black unemployment. They also increased the proportion of black female-headed families be-cause benefits provided disincentives for marriage. Though his data was unconvincing, and he had many critics, his argument became dominant.[19] That was because his argument was based not on his data but on thought experiments, the most important of which was the case of Harold and Phyllis.

Harold and Phyllis have low-income parents, are not well educated, and have no special vocational skills. Phyllis is pregnant.[20] Harold and Phyllis are the children of AFDC, the most extensive public assistance package in the United States until it was ended in 1996. In Murray's view, it destroyed the motivation of Harold and Phyllis to form a family and to struggle at low-wage jobs. AFDC made it more advantageous for Phyllis to live off her welfare package and for Harold to work only enough to collect unemployment benefits. They cohabit out of wedlock because they would lose benefits if they got married. For Murray, social welfare programs have made this strategy the norm of economic advantage. It is not economically rational to work hard at a low-paid job and get married. Social welfare programs have made the personal dignity of both partners an economic disadvantage.

> When economic incentives are buttressed by social norms, the effects on behavior are multiplied. But the main point is that social factors are not necessary to explain behavior. There is no "breakdown of the work ethic" in this account of rational choices among alternatives. There is no shiftless irresponsibility. It makes no difference whether Harold is white or black. There is no need to invoke the spectres of cultural pathologies or inferior upbringing. The choices may be seen more simply, much more naturally, as the behavior of people responding to the reality of the world around them and making the decisions—legal, approved, and even encouraged decisions—that maximize the quality of life.[21]

Murray assumes that both Harold and Phyllis could work at low-wage jobs if they wanted to, that they could get married if they wanted to, but that social welfare programs have made it easier for them to live off the tolerable misery of public assistance. This is especially true because from 1965 through the early 1970s subsidies increased, altering the structure of incentives for the poor:

> It was easier to get along without a job. It was easier for a man to have a baby without being responsible for it, for a woman to have a baby

without having a husband. It was easier to get away with crime, it was easier to obtain drugs. Because it was easier to get away with crime, it was easier to support a drug habit. Because it was easier to get along without a job, it was easier to ignore education. Because it was easier to get along without a job, it was easier to walk away from a job and thereby accumulate a record as an unreliable employee.[22]

All of this was, for Murray, the result of increasingly generous social welfare programs: AFDC, food stamps, Medicaid, housing subsidies. These programs degrade the poor. If it were not for these programs, Harold and Phyllis would have chosen an alternative path. They would have married. Harold would have worked at a low-wage job, which, after years of hard work, would have provided them with a decent life. Independent of welfare, they would have personal dignity. "Work hard, stick to the job no matter how bad it is, and you will probably climb out of poverty, but not very far out."[23]

Murray's underlying assumption is that low-wage jobs are available if you are willing to work. Cut social programs severely, and the poor will become motivated to take these jobs. It is the logic not only of Newt Gingrich and Dick Armey's *Contract With America*,[24] but of President Clinton's policies as well. Murray's work was powerfully influential because he successfully combined the concept of the "culture of poverty," with its emphasis on the family structure of the black underclass, with free market capitalism. The Clinton economic boom of the nineties merely reinforced Murray's position. Capitalism is no longer the problem, nor are the inequities of class, because the problem is the behavior of poor people who refuse to work because they can successfully live off welfare.

The liberal Mickey Kaus exemplifies the range of Murray's influence. In *The End of Equality*, Kaus argues that an underclass—built on the dependency programs of "money liberalism"—has undermined the public sphere that makes civil society possible in the United States. The two key money liberal programs, AFDC and food stamps, "throw money" at poverty and have had the unintended consequence of supporting welfare over work. This must be corrected if a more egalitarian society is to be built. Kaus's answer is civic liberalism and the expansion of the public sphere as a means of creating more equality in American capitalist society. For Kaus, money liberalism fails to recognize the practical limitations of the redistribution of wealth through tinkering with capitalism. "Civic liberalism," on the other hand, "pursues social equality directly through government action, rather than by manipulating the unequal distribution of income generated in the capitalist marketplace."[25]

If the civic liberal program is followed, we can have the peaceful, civil society of the 1950s—"a society in which the various classes use the same subways and drop off their kids at the same daycare centers and run into each other at the post office. We don't have to repeal capitalism or abandon meritocracy to do these things. We don't have to equalize incomes or make incomes more equal or even stop incomes from getting more unequal to do these things. We just have to do them."[26] A more powerful public sphere will increase the possibility of egalitarianism by creating a society in which money counts for less and in which class mixing can occur.

Ultimately, Kaus's solution is the same as Murray's in that he puts the emphasis on the values of work and family. Here, political and economic change isn't necessary, only cultural change. The solution to the problem of poverty isn't eliminating structural inequality in American society but abolishing the culture of poverty and the behavior of the nonworking poor.

The extremely poor—the poorest 2.5 million of the 32 to 39 million who were estimated to be officially poor by the Bureau of the Census in the 1990s—are, for these thinkers, the ghetto underclass that has sabotaged the civility of the public sphere in the United States. They have degraded the country because they do not share the universal American values of work and family. Everyone should share these values even if they are stuck in low-wage, subsistence-wage, poverty-maintaining-wage jobs. The urban underclass isn't like Marx's proletariat; it "is the villain rather than the hero. It is a class whose values are so inimical to America's universal culture that its negation, and transformation, will allow those universal values to flower."[27]

This underclass stays poor for a long time. It consists of women who have out-of-wedlock births and receive AFDC, of men who won't work and are prone to criminal behavior and drug abuse. They

are mostly black. Kaus tells us, "I am saying what every urban res-
ident knows to be true, and what statistics know to be true, which is
that underclass areas are awful environments that produce a large
subculture of criminality, often violent criminality."[28] Kaus, like
Murray, bases his arguments on very selective evidence and, for
the most part, on what everyone "knows to be true." Thus he can state
that a black underclass who won't work and who are part of a large
criminal subculture are the villains who are destroying American
cities. This is ridiculous or worse, and yet his work is taken seriously.

Consider criminality. In actuality the costs of corporate crime are
much greater than that of the urban underclass. In 1992 white-collar
crime was estimated at $250 billion, whereas "the monetary costs to
all victims of personal crimes (e.g., robbery, assault, larceny) and
household crimes (e.g., burglary, motor vehicle theft) totaled $17.6
billion in that year."[29] The Savings and Loan scandal cost taxpayers
$500 billion, compared with the $35 million stolen in all the bank
robberies in 1992. Clearly the outrage over street crime is out of
proportion to its costs.[30]

The claim that teenage AFDC mothers have more out-of-wedlock
births is crucial because, if true, it attests to the degradation of the
black underclass family. Kristin Luker in *Dubious Conceptions: The
Politics of Teenage Pregnancies* finds that teens are less likely than older
women to have unwed births and abortions.[31] Mark Robert Rank has
shown that birth rates in the general population are higher than those
for welfare mothers.[32] But data isn't crucial to either Murray or Kaus
because their argument isn't scientific but ethical. It is an ethics based
on the shared charge that the underclass lacks the values of work and
family. Work is so important that Kaus has no difficulty in calling for
only "work-tested" programs and a new Works Progress Administration (WPA) offering subminimum-wage jobs to the extremely
poor.[33] This WPA-style workfare would only maintain poverty, but
these would be a more moral poor. Work and family values will
reduce the evils of welfare dependency. The success of this argument
is based neither on facts nor on results but on its broad acceptance
throughout the political realm. It is not a contradiction that the
conservative Murray and the liberal Kaus share the same closed

discourse, or that workfare has become commonsense policy for people of all political persuasions, translated directly into state and local politics throughout the United States. In New York City, Mayor Giuliani made it difficult for the poor to apply for food stamps, forcing them to spend two days being screened before applications are even given to them. (This is in violation of federal law, and the Department of Agriculture filed a suit against New York City, stating that "city officials routinely violate the law by denying poor people the right to apply promptly for food stamps.") But for Mayor Giuliani, making food stamps harder to get is good for poor people, whereas under the Department of Agriculture's "user friendly" program, "foodstamps have sometimes been used to buy drugs."[34]

In the same vein, New York City's Human Resources Administration (HRA) Commissioner Jason Turner bemoaned the fact that people who have been sanctioned off welfare can still find shelter from providers and still receive food from soup kitchens and food pantries. He said, "We need to create, if you will, a personal crisis in individual lives."[35] This is consistent with the final vocabulary of conservatives. Both Giuliani and Turner believe, as does Charles Murray, that harsh policies against public assistance will make the poor self-reliant, and that a "personal crisis" will force the poor to change their lives and become willing to work at low-wage jobs. The proof that conservatives are right about ending entitlements is "the 43 percent drop in welfare rolls" since the Personal Responsibility and Work Opportunity Reconciliation Act (PRWORA) was passed.[36] The success and power of the conservative vocabulary shift in poverty policy has been operationalized in welfare reform and has become the common sense behind the continued discourse on how to deal with the poor. For if a black underclass is subversive to the central American values of work and family, it is in the interest of national survival to end entitlements and incarcerate the large underclass criminal element.[37] Ending welfare is ultimately in the interest of the poor: "hard love." Abolishing AFDC, cutting food stamps, and imposing work requirements motivate the nonworking poor to take low-wage jobs. The conservative solution is a job solution.

The Liberals

William Julius Wilson embodies the liberal response to Murray, asking "why the behavior patterns in the inner city today differ so markedly from those of three decades ago."[38]

For Wilson, the social welfare programs of the 1960s and the race-specific programs of the 1970s succeeded in enlarging the black middle class. As this class became more affluent, it moved out of the inner-city ghetto, increasing the concentration of underclass blacks there: "150,000 blacks departed these communities during this ten year period (1970–1980) leaving behind a much more concentrated poverty population."[39]

Wilson is concerned about the increasing proportion of underclass blacks in the inner city. For many, his use of *underclass* is problematic and controversial: Bob Blauner proposes that social scientists stop using the term because "it suggests a group of people who are permanently outside of the class structure" and "calls up images of black people who whites find both frightening and morally irredeemable."[40] Wilson understands the problems with the term but uses it because he wants to move away from "race" as the dominant concept for explaining the continuation and overrepresentation of blacks among the poor. He doesn't deny that blacks are a highly stigmatized group, but he believes that *underclass* is a better term for describing the profound economic and social dislocations of the inner-city ghetto.[41]

Crucial for understanding these dislocations is the deindustrialization of the American economy and the loss of union jobs. Blacks have been disproportionately hurt by these changes. It is with an analysis framed by these economic transformations that Wilson confronts Murray's major contentions that black unemployment and the breakup of poor people's families (as indicated by an increase in female-headed households) are the result of social welfare programs. For Wilson, the problem is joblessness.

Responding first to Murray's contention that the increase in welfare benefits has led Harold and Phyllis to choose welfare over full employment, Wilson argues:

Real benefits in fact have fallen dramatically since the early 1970's. . . .
[B]y 1980 the real value of the AFDC plus food stamps has been
reduced by 16 percent from their 1972 levels. By 1984 the combined
payments were only 4 percent higher than their 1960 levels and 22
percent less than 1972. In the words of Greenstein, no other group in
American society experienced such a sharp decline in real income since
1970 as did AFDC mothers and their children.[42]

Second, black joblessness is not a result of young black men
making a rational choice not to work. Rather, deindustrialization had
a greater impact on black workers because they were concentrated in
inner-city areas.

Between 1947 and 1972, the central cities of the thirty three most
populous metropolitan areas . . . lost 880,000 manufacturing jobs,
while manufacturing employment in their suburbs grew by 2.5 million.
The same cities lost 867,000 jobs in retail and wholesale trade at the
same time that their suburbs gained millions of such positions, while
the black population of these central cities lost more than 9 million
whites and added 5 million blacks.[43]

Third, the geographic deindustrialization of urban and suburban
areas became national from the mid-1970s through the 1980s. These
employment changes had a major impact on family life that Wilson
conceptualizes in terms of what he calls the "male marriageable pool
index": the men who are available to marry and support a family.
Because of increased black joblessness caused by urban deindustrialization, "combined with high black mortality and incarceration
rates, . . . there has been a decrease in black men who are able to support families. This has resulted in the increase in black female-
headed families." Again, it is not welfare that has caused this situation.[44]

His solution to these problems is to remedy black joblessness.
His "hidden agenda" is that race-specific programs increase the stig-
matization of the target group. He prefers universal programs for
increasing employment, operating on the key assumption that "im-
proving the job prospects of men will strengthen low-income black
families."[45]

Central to Wilson's solution is a mixture of public and private
programs to increase economic opportunity. The truly disadvantaged

"would also benefit disproportionately from a program of balanced economic growth and tight labor market policies because of their great vulnerability to swings in the business cycle and changes in economic organization, including the relocation of plants and use of labor-saving technology."[46]

Though Wilson disagrees with Murray's contention that work is available to all who are morally willing to work, though he contends that deindustrialization has greatly reduced the number of jobs available to inner-city blacks, he shares with the conservative Murray a job solution to the problems of American poverty.

This job solution is further developed in *When Work Disappears.* "The jobless ghetto"[47] is the result of the social and economic dislocations caused by the global economy. All the problems of deindustrialization have been exacerbated by the new global competition. Globalization has increased the educational and training requirements for workers; along with new technological labor processes that eliminate jobs and displace workers and the tendency of new companies to locate in the suburbs, it has taken an immense toll on the inner city. "As the disappearance of work has become characteristic of the inner-city ghetto," Wilson continues, "so has the disappearance of the traditional married-couple family. Only one-quarter of the black families whose children live with them in inner-city neighborhoods in Chicago are husband-wife families, today."[48]

For Wilson, the impact of deindustrialization on the opportunity structure and changing societal norms on marriage must be viewed together: both "negative outlooks towards marriage" and "an environment plagued by persistent joblessness. This combination of factors has increased out-of-wedlock births, weakened the family structure, expanded the welfare rolls and as a result caused poor inner-city blacks to be even more disconnected from the job market and discouraged about their role in the labor force."[49]

Wilson is aware that myths about welfare are widespread: he knows that blacks were not the majority of AFDC recipients, nor were most recipients long-term. He also disparages the belief that government intervention and welfare itself are the greatest problems for the poor. Yet he seems to have reversed the causal nexus, and now the behavior of the black male in relation to marriage and the family has become crucial. The social and economic structure, still important, is no longer central, and Wilson has come closer to Murray's position. This is not surprising, since Murray's position on poverty has become common sense for American society. Thus, Wilson increasingly stresses the socialization process of the black inner-city family, warning that "weak families do not prepare youngsters for the labor market."[50] Though he understands the limits of Murray's arguments, he still emphasizes the same points: first, the need to rear black children to "avoid street culture,"[51] and, second, the need to get inner-city black men jobs at all costs. The belief that the extremely poor have a degraded culture of poverty is complicitous with Murray, as is the idea that hard work will automatically remedy the culture of the underclass. Wilson's analysis of the second point deserves closer examination.

The global economy has increased wage and skill inequality and strained the welfare state.[52] The diminished welfare state has taken a toll on the inner city, and homeless shelters, soup kitchens, and abandoned buildings attest to this decline. Wilson's solution—jobs at all costs—is an attempt to remedy the increasing immiseration of the poor. He first tries to develop a policy to meet the skill demands of the new global economy. In a society that has decreased its commitment to the inner-city public school, Wilson backs a conservative education policy. Instead of advocating better modes of curriculum, he comes out in favor of national performance standards, better teachers, and vouchers (public monies for private schools).[53] The problem of the jobless ghetto can be solved through the panacea of education and training. He provides scant evidence for this position, which, put simply, states that if you train the inner-city poor, the jobs will come. But education and training isn't Wilson's real solution; in fact, his solution is antithetical to the call for education and training. His real remedy is "WPA-style jobs of the kind created during the Franklin D. Roosevelt administration."[54]

These jobs would be provided by the government at minimum and subminimum wages, with the addition of wage supplements through an expanded Earned Income Tax Credit (EITC). "By 1996, the expanded EITC will increase the earnings from a minimum wage job to $7 an hour."[55] But $280 per week only sustains misery and poverty. Wilson is influenced here by the work of Sheldon Danziger and Peter Gottschalk,[56] whose "proposal offers a subminimum-wage public service job to any applicant. They would set compensation at 10 to 15 percent below the minimum wage to encourage movement into private sector jobs as they become available.... These wages would be supplemented with the earned income tax credit and other wage supplements."[57]

Wilson prefers Mickey Kaus's WPA-like plan, however. Kaus's program would be universal, not just for those on welfare. (Older workers would be excluded because retraining would be too costly.) These jobs would also be at minimum and subminimum wages. As Wilson states, "None of my immediate solutions offers a remedy for the growing inequality in the United States.... The jobs created would not be high wage jobs, but with universal health insurance, a child care program, and earned income tax credits attached, they would enable workers and their families to live at least decently and avoid joblessness and the problems associated with it."[58]

Would these poor families live "decently"? Wilson's scenario addresses education and health care but leaves out food, clothing, and housing. In America in the 1990s and 2000s, a family cannot afford a decent life at minimum or subminimum wages. Wilson's uncritical embrace of Kaus's WPA proposals is a key link to the conservative analysis that Kaus himself has embraced. Murray, Kaus, and Wilson all agree that the solution to poverty is hard work and low wages. None of them interrogate the nature of the available jobs or the likelihood that the global economy will create the jobs needed to end the problem of the jobless ghetto.

To put it simply, only above-poverty-wage jobs can end poverty. There isn't any evidence that those jobs are being produced. Low unemployment and a tight labor market have not resolved the problems of the inner city. The current boom has barely raised middle-class wages and has completely missed the urban poor. The job solutions of the conservatives and liberals have failed. The misery of the poor endures.

POVERTY AND THE LABOR QUESTION

Good Friday, April 2, 1999. The Association of Community Organizations for Reform Now (ACORN) is having "an action" at a sanitation work site at 126th Street and Amsterdam Avenue in Harlem. Work Experience Program (WEP) workers report to this site daily for their workfare assignments. This action calls for these workers to get the day off because it is a religious holiday. WEP workers, the WEP Workers Organizing Committee/ACORN activists, clergy, and concerned citizens all show up. The action is swift; the sanitation officers do not want any trouble. Officers Smiley and Simkowitz concede the day to the WEP workers and the ACORN activists. Officer Simkowitz shouts, "Everyone at this site will get the day off." Rosemary, an ACORN organizer, tells me that last year it took much longer to get Good Friday off. The rally continues, and one WEP worker shouts, "We demand that if we work a holiday we should get double time." Another man begins to chant, "No more workfare, no more slavery." Another man launches into a speech: "All poor people are being oppressed by this policy. Workers must have a decent wage and decent benefits." These are not degraded underclass black and Latino poor people; now they are underpaid and unemployed workers. They have redefined themselves, and now they have something to struggle for, real jobs with real benefits. In the process of defining themselves as workers, they are becoming autonomous. They want a union; they want to bargain for themselves. They do not want WEP.

One WEP worker tells me that she works 32 hours a week, soon to be changed to 35 hours. She is paid $49.50 every two weeks and gets $123 in food stamps and $117 toward rent every month. She works at Morningside Park: "I mostly clean bathrooms. The parks wouldn't be clean if it wasn't for us. You know we're supposed to get a job after six months. I've been here three years and still no job. You know you have to do something so you can live—but there's still no job."

Poor people questioning workfare and welfare bureaucracy. Poor people organizing poor people in terms of the labor question. Poor people taking class and work seriously, intertwined with the issues of wages, benefits, hours, and working conditions. The first step is to organize these WEP workers and then struggle for the right to grieve and strike. WEP workers are aware that workfare cannot be the "jobs-for-all solution" to poverty in the United States. The struggle has to be against subminimum wages and for at least a real living wage. In this struggle these poor workers are learning the language of possibility. They are learning to think beyond the reformist vocabulary of advocates and experts like Charles Murray and William Julius Wilson. Here in germ form is the possibility to struggle outside the parameters of the new welfare reform. If they don't, it means poverty is permanent, and the bleak picture of the WEP worker quoted above is permanent as well.

It is the central contention of this book that job solutions have to be examined through the lens of the social relations of labor. Thus poverty has to be understood in terms of exploitation, alienation, and class. It must be understood in terms of the labor question and the place of the poor in the new high-tech, global labor process. Poverty must not be seen just in terms of a growing wage and skill inequality but as part of class relations. It must be studied in relation to an industrial and postindustrial labor process. These class relations of poverty must be understood in terms of the everyday lived experience of women and men who are poor.

This book assumes that poverty has become routinized as an ordinary aspect of American society and that it is increasing. We should neither romanticize poverty nor treat it as pathology. I use the 13 years that I've worked in St. John's Bread and Life soup kitchen in Bedford-Stuyvesant as a basis for understanding the lives of the poor, but this is not another book that just documents their oppression or offers social policy as a remedy for a societal condition. This book shows hard lives becoming harder because of the ending of entitlements, the creation of workfare, and the channeling of poor people into low-wage jobs. In the face of this, poor people neither form a movement nor riot as they did in the 1930s and 1960s.

In Bedford-Stuyvesant over one thousand poor people eat breakfast and lunch at St. John's Bread and Life soup kitchen from Monday through Friday. During my time there the war against the poor has escalated,[59] abolishing entitlements and requiring time limits for benefits and welfare-to-work programs in all states. So welfare rolls were reduced, but poverty itself was not. This book views that war through the eyes of the poor people in the soup kitchen and on workfare, where the impact of these policies is directly felt as a component of everyday life (see Chapters 2 and 3). Their failure to form social movements is also embedded in the repetition and banality of everyday life. The poor, like the rest of us, try to ignore or forget what is painful in everyday life, instead of using it as the basis for critique or even change. The misery of the quotidian overwhelms the poor, and change is feared, but it is in the quotidian that possibility still exists. It is this possibility, in the time and space of everyday life, that explains how ordinary people sometimes get involved in the simple struggles that can lay the groundwork for larger social movements.[60]

In this context we are talking about a real that doesn't just exist as "a collection of dead facts,"[61] but that always embodies the possibilities of the rhythms of change, of the future. Thus in Chapter 2 I interrogate the notion of the real presented by two biographers of the poor—Frank McCourt and Alex Kotlowitz—in terms of the German debate over expressionism and surrealism between the 1930s and the 1950s.[62] My purpose is to demonstrate that the real is not only about the present, because then change itself would never be possible. My descriptions of the poor are like a montage of their lives in the spaces of New York City and in the time of the ending of entitlements—which, I argue, was really based on Daniel Patrick Moynihan's *Negro Family* study.[63] In Chapter 3 I describe life in the soup kitchen in terms of Thanksgiving, a holiday that seems to be the only time of the year when people in the United States care about the poor and hungry. I also try to show the possibility of the poor in the desperate times after welfare reform as they struggle for higher wages at an ACORN action in Brooklyn.

In the transformation from the modern to the postmodern, a poverty-based social movement becomes increasingly less likely. I use *modern* and *postmodern* not as cultural theorists use the terms, but as descriptions of social and political conditions. For me the postmodern and postmodernity collapse into each other, and culture constructs political economy just as it is constructed by political economy. They are reciprocally determining, not "either/or," as they are for economists or cultural theorists. Thus in the transition to a postmodern, global, computer-aided capitalism, the industrial base is decentered and the state is hollowed out. For poor people this means that programs are cut, entitlements are ended, and they are forced into the increased competition for lower- and lower-waged jobs. In this scenario it isn't just media that are hyperreal; just as important, so are the free market, competition, and the meritocracy that is attached to this postmodern, computer-aided capitalism.

As poverty increases and the iron cage of modernism is transformed into the cybernetic cage of postmodernism, there seems to be no way out. How do you build a movement when modernist and postmodernist social movements are not the answer? Is there a third alternative that is both a combination and a transcendence of the past and the new? Advocacy organizations? These tend to be underfunded, bureaucratic, and too moderate in their policies. At best they can make small struggles to slow the continual loss of assistance for the poor. They are not the basis for a new social movement to end poverty. To build a movement, we need advocates to become activists. They must learn a new language of possibility, and they must make the simple struggles needed to build the base for a social movement that exists in the multiplicity of race, class, and gender.

In Chapters 4 and 5 I argue that three conditions work against a social movement of the poor that could create an alternative to the current conservative political hegemony. First I explain the problem of advocacy in terms of "The Dialectic of Sister Bernadette." The daily difficulties of running a large poverty program make it almost impossible to create alternatives and engage in the political struggle to end poverty. Advocates and administrators know that they must make this fight but are doomed to fail because of bureaucratic obligations and the fundraising that occupies almost all of their time.

Here I argue that the dialectic of Sister Bernadette is an expression of Georg Lukacs' crisis in capitalist rationality.[64] This, simply put, is the rationality of details and the irrationality in terms of the whole of society. The professionalization and bureaucratization of activists as advocates prevents the development of social movements that could move social policy in the direction of the major changes required to end poverty.

Second, more than forty years after Michael Harrington wrote *The Other America*, his description of the poor as invisible continues to be used.[65] I begin Chapter 5 by contesting this notion and by arguing that the term *invisibility* is too passive. Instead, I argue that the poor cannot be seen because many Americans are not motivated to see them and willfully and purposely forget that they have seen them. The poor cause discomfort because they are indicators of the failure of capitalism. Most social scientists and journalists who investigate poverty in the United States also forget that poverty must be understood both theoretically and globally.

Third, the postmodern condition is expressed politically in terms of advocates struggling for piecemeal reform and against the last grand narrative of the postmodern, computer-aided capitalism. Foucault declared that only micro-politics is possible at this postmodern moment.[66] He is right, and that is the problem. The modernist grand narratives offer no alternatives, and micro-politics is a reformist alternative. Thus, we live in an endless present in which there is no possibility of reinventing the world. To end poverty, the world must be reinvented. This is not to deny that the voices of marginalized groups have emerged: women's voices, lesbian and gay voices, African American voices, postcolonial voices. This multiplicity of voices is now heard, but rarely does it move beyond the act of speaking. In a world in which the emancipatory project of modernism is exhausted, its voice is reduced to the language of domination and oppression. At the same time, new postmodernist social movements rarely move beyond deconstructing possible emancipatory alternatives. The political representation of the postmodern is piecemeal reform in the age of Empire.[67] The economic expression of the postmodern is computer-aided capitalism, which, in the guise of the multiplicities of flexible, fluid, personal, and decentered individual entrepreneurialism, is global and multicultural in the sense of a truly hegemonic domination. Computer-aided capitalism knows no space, such as the nation-state. It knows only virtual space, and its allegiance is to excessive profits. The state has been made hollow, and privatization fulfills everyone's expectations and satisfies all needs. In the age of Empire, the free market in a hyper form no longer needs to legitimate itself, and the "safety net" is reduced to a bare minimum. The free market in its computer-aided form will solve all problems. To ensure this, the poor and the lower classes are simply excluded from the discourse.

In the Conclusion (Chapter 6), I argue that the new, globally organized computer and robotics technologies have reduced both wages and jobs internationally, heralding the jobless future.[68] In the age of computer-aided capitalism, the United States has maintained low unemployment but with an increase of low-wage and contingent jobs. The future of the working poor people of Bedford-Stuyvesant is minimum-wage jobs or workfare that guarantees endless poverty. As noted above, if poverty is to be eradicated, workers must be paid above-poverty-level wages. If the layers of poverty are to be removed, they need a social movement that forces policy toward a 30-hour week, a guaranteed annual middle-class income, and a democratic and critical practice. In short, the examination of poverty must be concerned with the labor question and in continuum with the middle class and working class. If this is forgotten, the middle class and working class, without protection, will rush to the bottom as well.

Moving out of the cybernetic cage of computer-aided capitalism will be very difficult. We have all been witnesses to the failure of economic growth, social policy, and advocacy to reduce poverty in the United States. Entitlements have been almost eliminated, and the misery of the poor has been substantially increased, yet social movement building has not occurred.

Here I argue for focused simple struggles. These are prior to social movements. The poor can make simple struggles because such struggles come out of their own life experiences. These struggles breathe within the rhythms of their lives. Struggles for a guaranteed annual income, a shorter working day, and comparable worth, though limited and focused, call into question the relations of power and put the needs of ordinary people first. The same is true of simple struggles for housing, health care, and education as well. These struggles must be seen as forms of life, ongoing processes that continue over a lifetime and always have the intention of building powerful social movements. "Life, liberty and the pursuit of happiness" demands the end of poverty. This is the movement for the new millennium.

2   Soup Kitchen Blues
1988–1993

PROFESSOR E'S LAST LESSON, **April 19, 1990**   "There's continuous frustration. People are hungry. There's people here today who have not eaten for a day or two. I know you don't believe me, but for a day or two. And the politicians do they hide their faces. They know, if they don't do something, you're not going to go overseas for revolutions, they're going to have one right here. The poor people have to eat, they have to have a place to live. Instead, what do they do with their money? The poor have to get their fair share. Instead they get frustration."

Professor E has worked hard all of his life. Currently, he is having a hard time making payments on his house and is in danger of losing it.

"See all this crime. See all this violence. This is because of the frustration. If people have enough to eat, jobs, if they were employed, if they still had their housing, there wouldn't be all of this crime. People would be content; instead they are frustrated. You work your whole life, you raise your kids, you pay for your house, and then this happens and you're on the streets. The politicians better open their eyes, or there's going to be a revolution. Right here. People are that angry."

This is Professor E's last lesson. I never see him again after this day. This is very typical in the soup kitchen. Many people have come daily for all of the 13 years that I have worked at Bread and Life, but most people use it for only a short period of time. Sometimes it is months, sometimes years, but most people come only when they are in need. Needs change, and some people stop using the soup kitchen while others begin.

BIOGRAPHIES OF POVERTY

I'm in the playground with Malachy. I'm four, he's three. He lets me push him on the swing because he's no good at swinging himself and Freddie Liebowitz is in school. We have to stay in the playground because the twins are sleeping and my mother says she's worn out. . . . Dad is out looking for a job again and sometimes he comes home with the smell of whiskey, singing all the songs about suffering Ireland. Mam gets angry and says Ireland can kiss her arse. He says that's nice language to be using in front of the children and she says never mind the language, food on the table is what she wants, not suffering Ireland. She says it was a sad day Prohibition ended because Dad gets the drink going around to saloons offering to sweep out bars and lift barrels for a whiskey or a beer. Sometimes he brings home bits of free lunch, rye bread, corned beef, pickles. He puts the food on the table and drinks tea himself. He says food is a shock to the system and he doesn't know where we get our appetites. Mam says, They get their appetites because they're starving half the time.[1]

[A] young Disciple [a member of a gang at war with the Vice Lords for control of the Henry Horner Houses] nicknamed Baby Al, who was shot with a .357 Magnum not far from the Rivers' building. Wounded he ran into the high-rise, where, while trying to climb the stairs, he fell backwards and lost consciousness. Lafayette came running out of his apartment to see what all the commotion was about. He watched as Baby Al bled to death. Two years later, his blood still stained the stairwell.

A couple of weeks later, as Lafayette and Pharoah played on the jungle gym in midafternoon, shooting broke out. A young girl jumping rope crumpled to the ground. Lafayette ran into his building, dragging behind him one of the triplets. Pharoah, then seven, panicked. He ran blindly until he bumped into one of the huge green trash containers that dot the landscape. He pulled himself up and over, landing in a foot of garbage. Porkchop followed. For half an hour the two huddled in the foul smelling meat scraps and empty pizza boxes, waiting for the shooting to stop. . . . Finally, the shooting subsided and they climbed out, smelling like dirty dishes. They watched as the paramedics attended to the girl, who luckily had been shot only in the leg. Her frightened mother, who fainted, was being revived. It was at that point that Pharoah first told his mother, "I didn't wanna know what was happening."[2]

In these two passages from best-selling books we are told in great detail the realistic drama and adventure of being poor, the heroic struggle of three boys to survive the degrading misery of poverty and hopefully to become middle-class. These are two biographies of poverty. Frank McCourt tells his own story of coming of age in the poverty of Depression-era Brooklyn and Limerick, Ireland. Alex Kotlowitz tells the story of Lafayette and Pharoah Rivers, who come of age in the poverty of the Henry Horner Houses in Chicago in the 1980s. Their experiences, though they occur in different times and places, are very similar: they have weak fathers, one an alcoholic, the other a heroin addict, and longsuffering mothers; they are often on public assistance; and they are surrounded by hunger, terrible living conditions, and death. Pharoah and Lafayette learn to make the necessary adaptations to their lives of poverty. McCourt triumphantly leaves the poverty of Ireland for the opportunities of the United States. These are stories of individuals and their families struggling against poverty and transcending hunger, homelessness, violence, and death. These are not stories of poor people becoming politically conscious and organizing themselves into a social movement to end poverty.

Siegfried Kracauer tells us that biography became a widespread literary form after the first world war. For him it is a bourgeois form: "The motif of escape, to which the majority of biographies owe their existence, is eclipsed by the motif of redemption. If there is a confirmation of the end of individualism, it can be glimpsed in the museum of great individuals that today's literature puts on a pedestal."[3]

In our biographers' subjects we have both redemption and escape. Their heroic hopes of becoming bourgeois are the hopes of particular individuals, and not of poor people in general. The story is about individual success—maybe not "rags to riches," but individual achievement, because capitalism works if its rules are followed. There is no reason for the disenfranchised to organize and fight for justice; there is no need for an alternative to the system, because these biographies of success show that "the best of all possible worlds" already exists. In these biographies there is never Professor E's hope for a social movement to end poverty.

These two biographies tell a different story than the one I tell after 13 years of field work in Bedford-Stuyvesant. Kotlowitz and McCourt tell the actual, heroic stories of individuals overcoming their poverty. The stories are dramatic and end with the resolution of the conflicts faced by their heroes. They aren't ordinary like the stories I tell. The stories I tell are about the people whose impoverishment has no resolution. They are fragments, a montage of poverty. People pass through, like Professor E, and disappear, or they get low-wage or workfare jobs and can no longer come to Bread and Life. Or they die. The participant observation that I do in Bedford-Stuyvesant and the biographies are two different ways of making an account of social reality. There are many ways of describing social reality. The biographers tell individual stories of individuals transcending poverty. In the biographies, what becomes of most poor people is never told. I tell the stories of the poor people who have been left out of the biographies and left out of the possibility of overcoming poverty. Here we have a debate over the nature of social reality.

Loic Wacquant describes the power of ethnographic descriptions of poverty: "[T]here exists significant if fine-grained cultural and moral distinctions inside the ghetto, inscribed in both institutions and minds, that help explain the diversity of strategies and trajectories followed by their residents that only long-term ethnography can detect and dissect."[4]

But it is not enough to describe poverty ethnographically and statistically. Good descriptions are not enough; knowledge alone will not set us free. Both qualitative and quantitative studies of poverty present only parts of the social reality. Missing from these studies of poverty are both theoretical analysis and a discussion of possible actions for ending poverty. After all, within the limits of an objective science, we can study only what is verifiable or falsifiable. Stuck in the details of science, we seem to have forgotten that people are a moving target, always changing. It doesn't seem to matter that our data is already old by the time the study or the book is printed, so that only our concepts and our arguments are actually resonant. We have forgotten the truth in Foucault's statement that sociology is not a science but a form of knowledge—not only in the sense that it is not positivist and mathematical, with the finitude of the natural sciences, but in the sense that, in the human sciences, man in history is the object of study, and history is not finished.[5] So we study only what we can demonstrate scientifically, and, armed with limited statistical facts, we continue to study the poor and believe in the reality of our results. Social scientists never take seriously Quine's argument in "The Two Dogmas of Empiricism" that all-scientific studies are underdetermined. As he states, "Total science, mathematical and natural and human, is similarly but more extremely underdetermined by experience."[6]

Our ethnographic descriptions suffer from the same problems. Ultimately we study the social reality in too limited a manner: with a social science that says very limited things about very limited topics. A social science worth caring about needs to do more, and this chapter is an attempt to do more than what the data provides. Social reality is also a moving target. Beyond statistical descriptions, it must be understood in terms of change. To understand the reality of poverty, we must understand what it would take to end poverty in the United States. In the biographical accounts, we have the extraordinary adventures of individuals. The McCourts and the Riverses face extreme hardships that make the successful denouement even more impressive. But ending poverty requires much more than individual heroes: it will take a social movement of the poor. Stories of personal success do not help us to understand the social reality that it is necessary for the poor to produce a social movement to end poverty. If the poor fail to make this movement, are the stories of personal success all we can have?

The Question of Social Reality

Both the nature of reality and the possibility of change were issues in the debate over expressionism that began in Germany in the 1930s. On the surface Georg Lukacs, Ernst Bloch, Bertolt Brecht, and Theodor W. Adorno were debating about fine art and literature. Under the surface, however, the argument was about the power of these forms of representation to influence real social change. Far from being a worn-out modernist debate with little applicability to the poor, their discussion is helpful in understanding the different accounts of reality portrayed by the biographers on one hand and by my fragmented and incomplete account on the other. These two chapters about life in the soup kitchen were written with a belief in the continuous relevance of that debate over realism. I am not concerned with resolving it or doing an immanent critique; I am interested only in what we can learn about the nature of reality in relation to my accounts and those of McCourt and Kotlowitz.

For Lukacs both expressionism and surrealism are significant attacks on realism. He argued that the expressionist and surrealist assault is embedded in their embrace of fashion and immediacy, and that it undermines the totality of analysis that is required for class-consciousness.

> What has this all to do with literature?
>
> Nothing at all for any theory like Expressionism or Surrealism—which denies that literature has any reference to objective reality. It means a great deal, however, for a Marxist theory of literature. If literature is a particular form by means of which objective reality is reflected, then it becomes of crucial importance for it to grasp that reality as it truly is, and not merely confine itself to reproducing whatever manifests itself immediately and on the surface.[7]

The great realist writers such as Balzac, Tolstoy, and Mann present for Lukacs a representation of reality where the totality of contradictions is in opposition to the discontinuous and fragmented representations of the expressionist montage. Lukacs tells us that

> the realist must seek out the lasting features in people in their relations with each other and in the situations in which they have to act; he must focus on these elements which endure over long periods and which constitute human tendencies on society and indeed of mankind as a whole....
>
> Great realism, therefore, does not portray an immediately obvious aspect of reality but one which is permanent and objectively more significant, namely man in the whole range of his relations to the real world, above all those which outlast mere fashion.[8]

Bloch, in his critique of Lukacs, presents an alternative picture of reality. His notion of totality includes incompleteness and

nonsynchrony and the not-yet-conscious—that is, the preconscious
level of future possibilities.

> The not-yet-conscious is thus solely the preconscious of what is to
> come, the psychological birthplace of the new. And it keeps itself
> preconscious above all because in fact there is within it a content of
> consciousness which has not become wholly manifest, and is still
> dawning from the future.[9]

Bloch includes in reality the possibility of an anticipated tomorrow. Though Lukacs is concerned with the possibility of collective
revolutionary change and McCourt and Kotlowitz are concerned
only with individual achievement, they both tell a linear story in a
world of inevitable fixedness. Certainly, this is Bloch's view of Lukacs' critique of German expressionism.

> What if authentic reality is also discontinuity? Since Lukacs operates
> with a closed, objectivistic conception of reality, when he comes to
> examine Expressionism he resolutely rejects any attempt on the part
> of artists to shatter any image of the world, even that of capitalism.
> Any art which strives to exploit the *real* fissures in surface inter-
> relations and to discover the new in the crevices, appears in his eyes
> merely as a willful act of destruction. He thereby equates experiment in
> demolition with a condition of decadence.[10]

Adorno's critique of Lukacs is expressed in terms of nonidentity:

> Lukacs over-simplifies the dialectical unity of art and science reducing
> it to bare identity, just as if works of art did nothing but apply
> perspective in such a way as to anticipate some of the insights that the
> social sciences subsequently confirm. . . . the novels of the early 19th
> century, e.g. those of Dickens and Balzac that he holds in such high
> esteem, and which he does not scruple to hold up as paradigms of the
> novelist's art, are by no means as realistic as all that.[11]

It is in terms of the nonidentity of his concept of realism with
the object of the realist novel that Adorno makes his most basic critique of Lukacs. This contradiction in realism is basic to my critique
of the biographers. It is the identity in the biographers' accounts
between the individual achievement of their heroes as a recipe for
escaping poverty and the overwhelming impossibility of the great

majority of the poor to use the same recipe. In fact, both *Angela's Ashes* and *There Are No Children Here* became bestsellers because they tell extraordinary stories that distort the lives of most poor people if they are applied to the poor in general. It is as Adorno tells us: "There is a gap between words and the things they conjure."[12] Identity is the unity of the concept with its object, and this is a distortion.

> Identity is the primal form of ideology. We relish it as the adequacy of the thing it suppresses; adequacy has always been subjection to dominant purposes and in that sense its own contradiction. . . . The ideological side of thinking shows in its permanent failure to make good on the claim that the non-I is finally the I: the more the I thinks the more perfectly will it find itself debased into an object.[13]

In the two biographies of poverty, the authors tell the story that overcoming poverty is identical with becoming middle-class. In the fragmented and incomplete accounts of many poor people in this chapter, becoming middle-class through the achievement of particular individuals is not only a nonidentity but prevents the possibility of overcoming poverty as well. It is not the overcoming of poverty in a few special cases, but overcoming poverty in general that must occur.

My hope is that in these accounts are the not-yet-conscious foundations for ending poverty—that in my retelling of these stories of poverty and oppression, of alienation and exploitation, in the gap between concepts and reality, the possibility exists of producing a space for ending these conditions.

THE SOUP KITCHEN

February 16, 1988 This is my first visit to St. John's Bread and Life soup kitchen. I am the faculty moderator of the Sociology Club, whose student-members volunteer every year to serve food in the kitchen. I get there early. About thirty men and a few women are seated in the dining area. In about fifteen minutes, after Sister Bernadette says grace, they begin serving the meals. My job today is to give out napkins, utensils, and milk. From 11:00 A.M. to 1:00 P.M., meals of macaroni, meatballs, toaster-cakes, bread, peanut butter, milk, and tea are provided: 725 meals served under the direction of Sister Bernadette.

At first I see a lot of angry people fighting over meatballs. I seem to have missed that the majority of poor people are passive and gracious about the food they receive. I'm supposed to give out containers of milk, three at every table. The people at the kitchen know that I am new and that they can take advantage of me. I give milk to everyone who asks for it—seconds, thirds. I am not good at refusing food to hungry people. I make a good patsy and some people exploit it, though most don't. A little girl with three containers asks for another to take home to drink later; an adult asks for a container for her invalid mother. I give and give, not realizing the consequences. Sister Bernadette and some of the other volunteers explain that I cannot give out the milk so freely. It is already too late, and about a hundred people get no milk because of my generosity. Pat, another volunteer, tells me that I should open up each container before I give it out to prevent hoarding. On my first day, I am learning the zero-sum game of scarcity. At the soup kitchen we barely have enough food to feed the people who come for a meal, and so we are forced to police the giving out of food. One man with swollen hands gets angry because there isn't any milk and he sees a volunteer drinking some. Another person, looking discouraged, tells me, "God doesn't like us here; we're just going down."

Sister Kathleen explains that the soup kitchen was started nine years earlier as a temporary facility but that the clientele has continued to grow over the years. She tells me that the number of people in Bedford-Stuyvesant who are a paycheck away from homelessness is staggering. "The mission of St. John's is the mission of St. Vincent DePaul—it is to the poor and that all human beings deserve respect."

April 28, 1988   I have become a regular volunteer at the soup kitchen. I work with Bea, Ozzie, Sasha, May, and Gloria. They are also teaching me about the realities of Bedford-Stuyvesant. Today, people are lining up early; more and more people are using the soup kitchen. Bea tells me that there will only be seconds on the soup today. Before Sister Bernadette says grace, she tells our "guests" that everybody will be allowed only three slices of bread. There are grumbles and complaints, but Sister responds, "If you can find the money to run the program, tell me where to get it." Her statement reflects the continuous challenge of paying for the increasing population of hungry people using Bread and Life's services.

Sister Bernadette says the opening prayer. Ozzie brings the first batch of soup in a large aluminum pot. It's vegetable beef soup with a lot of pasta. It's very thick; Sister asserts that the guests like it thick. They're using small bowls today, to keep the portions down. I start dishing out, in a rush to serve the large crowd. As a result, sometimes I skim the top of the pot and people get a bowl of watery soup. One guest tells me, "Scoop way down and get all those good veggies." Vegetables are a luxury in the kitchen; everyone gets a little meat and lots of starch. It is often difficult to feed people a healthy and balanced meal. Another person tells me, "Dig down deep and get those veggies." When I do, she says, "That's real good, thanks."

In general people are polite in the soup kitchen, but periodically there are fights as hungry people wait to be fed. Yesterday Sister Bernadette banned from the kitchen a woman who threw her soup at one of the volunteers because she thought the portion was too small. The kitchen is packed and the line stops because the 17 tables are full and all 125 seats are taken. People are complaining about the wait, about the lack of bread, about the small bowls. Wherever there is a shortage, the people who come to the kitchen will complain about it. Their lives are about scarcity, shortages of most of the things they depend on. The soup kitchen is their place; they come to eat, chat with their friends, and feel safe. Shortages here are threatening. As the line begins to move again, the guests start to complain that I'm not serving fast enough. The soup splashes over the bowl and scalds my hand. I shout, "Damn these small bowls." Sister gives me a dirty look. I apologize.

People with empty trays are coming faster and faster. The line seems endless. As people come for seconds, Sister says, "No more seconds. We are running out of food, and there will be no seconds tomorrow."

One of the guests says, "Every day you're running out earlier and earlier."

We have served 724 meals, and we are not adequately servicing the needs of our guests.

A year later, in the spring of 1989, we are serving lunch to between 1,200 and 1,300 hungry men and women (guests) from Monday to Friday. Guests are served in an efficient, friendly, and courteous manner. Crack and heroin are sold openly in the streets or in the abandoned buildings in the neighborhood. Crack vials, with their multicolored plastic tops, litter the streets and sometimes find their way into the kitchen. Periodically a guest may smoke some crack inside the kitchen, but this is extremely rare. The majority of the guests aren't heavy drug users. They are almost all very poor, either working or on public assistance. Most live in public housing projects or tenement buildings. Some live in shelters, in welfare hotels, on the streets, or in subway stations: 1989 is a hard year in the largest African American neighborhood in Brooklyn.

The Bread and Life Program is run by its director, Hossein Saadat, but Sister Bernadette Szymcak is in charge of the daily operations of the soup kitchen. This is the largest part of the program, though job counseling, fundraising, medical care, drug counseling, and housing and welfare assistance are included, carried out by doctors, social workers, medical assistants, secretaries, and volunteers. Independent of the Bread and Life program, Father Thomas Hynes, pastor of St. John the Baptist Church, directs a housing assistance program, a food pantry, and a school, which also provides computer training. These are excellent voluntary facilities, successfully providing services to a community in great need. At the same time, they serve only a small proportion of the community. They cannot do enough.

October 11, 1989   We are averaging 1,200 guests for lunch. From 1982 through 1983, 50 guests a day were served; by April 1989, it was 1,026. (In 1991, we will be serving 700 to 800 guests a day—not because of a decline in need, but because St. John's Bread and Life and Catholic Charities, then our major funding agency, will decide that they can neither finance nor safely serve over a thousand guests per day.)

I am late today, and instead of serving the soup, Sister Bernadette assigns me to serve juice with Sasha. Kate walks up for some water and says hello. She is a white woman in her thirties, with sores on her face. When she first started to come to the soup kitchen, she weighed

30 pounds more than she does now. All of the drug addicts assume they have AIDS. I assume she has AIDS.

"Bill, can I have seconds on the Kool-Aid?" I give her more Kool-Aid and ask if she has a sore throat. "I have a bad throat. I can't get rid of it. Living on the streets, it's cold and you can't get warm. Now I'm living on the subway platform [Myrtle Avenue and Broadway]. Sometimes I ride the trains, but they chase you.

"My counselor wants me to go to the shelter in South Harlem. I tell her that if she's so hot on the shelter, why don't you go there? It's not safe. Everyone is always fighting. They fight over the sheets, over beds, over food; everyone has a bad attitude. I hate the shelters; everyone is always fighting."

She is coughing harder. Not knowing what to say, I tell her that she has to find a way to keep warm.

"I won't go to the shelter. The subway's bad but not as bad as the shelter. The other day some kids attacked me on the subway. One of them whacked me with a two-by-four. I thought he broke my back. It's still killing me. They didn't try to rob me or anything. The fucking bastards thought it was funny to whack me with a two-by-four." A male friend walks over and says they have to go. She says goodbye and leaves.

December 1, 1989   The soup kitchen is crowded even though it's check day. It's cold, and people are huddling together on the line that winds down Willoughby Street. Everyone is waiting for the soup kitchen to open. As I wait with them, a man goes through the line asking, "You want good dope, good dope?" No one is buying.

John, who works the door, allows some people to wait inside where it's warm. People are irritable. They begin to yell at John to let them in. Nicholas, a soup kitchen volunteer, is standing next to him. Seeing Nicholas, a woman starts to yell, "No wonder the line is moving so slowly— they have the dwarf at the door." This woman has two broad scars on her face, a quarter-inch wide and three inches long, the worst I have ever seen at the soup kitchen. But it is not uncommon for these poor black women to be bruised or scarred. Women at the soup kitchen have told me that these injuries are the result of the brutality of their boyfriends or husbands. Recently an African American women in the kitchen told me: "These women say, 'Look at how much he loves me,' and they come in with a broken nose or scars that make their faces look like a road map. That's love? That's not love. A man beats you up is a disgrace. . . . These men are good for nothing."

Most of the conversation on line is everyday talk about the ordinary trivialities of their lives. In this way their lives are like everyone else's. They trade information or anecdotes about social services, or they exchange neighborhood gossip, or they engage in good-natured fooling around, or they complain about the weather. They are used to waiting in line at welfare offices, shelters, emergency rooms, supermarkets, and even here at the soup kitchen. The man standing next to me tells me he's feeling sick. "I changed my methadone program because I'm working part-time now. I'm sick but I want to eat. If I don't eat now, when am I going to eat? Oh, I just went in yesterday, but my hours are different. I'm all screwed up." He's on a take-home program. He uses one bottle of methadone a day, but he gets three bottles at a time, reducing his visits to the clinic. "Do you have your bottle?" I ask. He answers, "Yeah, yeah, I got to go." He leaves. If he doesn't have his bottle, the nurse doesn't have to medicate him. He'll return to the clinic and give her his bottle, demonstrating that he hasn't sold it. She'll make him drink a bottle in front of her and supply him with enough bottles to last until Monday. The nurse's surveillance function seems to be more important than her pain-relieving function for her patient.

Another man standing next to me is also on methadone. "I haven't worked in years. I could never be on a take-home program. I've got dirty urine. I take Valium; it relieves the pressure, especially since I'm detox now. I hate it. I'm going back on methadone. Since I detoxed, I have no energy. I functioned better. When I took methadone, I never cheated. I never took other drugs, except Valium. I was an intravenous drug user for 25 years. I can't function without it. I'm too old. The methadone saved my life. I plan to be on methadone for the rest of my life."

We finally get into the kitchen. John asks me what I'm doing on line: "Too lazy to work today?" He laughs; I tell him that I'll work later. I sit down with Jose. I know that he's a single man on public assistance, and I would like to ask him some questions about welfare. He also jokes with me about working today. I laugh and ask him to explain check day.

"Well. Today is SSI [Supplemental Security Income] check day. You get SSI on the first of the month. That's why there are fewer people here than usually. On Tuesday, it's emergency food stamps. On Thursday, a lot of people will be getting welfare checks and regular food stamps. But it's all different; even the days are different. But SSI always comes on the first of the month."

"What are your benefits?" I ask.

"I get $100 every two weeks—that's welfare. I don't get SSI. I get $90 once a month, food stamps. I get a housing check, a rent check. I endorse it and give it to the superintendent; he deposits it. I can't cash it. Only the landlord can cash it. I think the maximum rent that they'll give for a single man is $215, not much. But different people get different amounts. My buddy here gets $111 in food stamps but no welfare. Everyone is different.

"I try to eat here as much as possible and then save $30 a month of my food stamps. All the bodegas around here will buy them. They give you $7 cash for $10 of food stamps. It gives me some freedom. Yeah, some buy drugs and alcohol, but you don't really make enough and you need necessities. A shirt, cigarettes, go to a movie. I also use them to go to restaurants. Get bacon and eggs for breakfast. I love that. And then I save them so that at the end of the month—I always save at least $30—I can go to the A&P and pig out. Cake and chocolate milk, some luxuries."

Unfinished Business: Report on the Interagency Task Force on Food and Hunger tells us that "13.5 percent of all people living in the United States were poor as compared to 23.2 percent of those living in New York City. The city's poverty rate for children was 37.9 percent as compared to the national average of 20.6 percent. . . . The effectiveness of federal food stamp programs decreased dramatically between 1980 and 1987. Food stamp participation rates dropped nationally by almost one million people; during the same period, the number of people in poverty rose by two million. In this same period, the number of soup kitchens and food pantries rose from 30 in 1981 to 603 in 1987. These six hundred programs feed approximately 570,000 people per month."[14]

Here we see the inverse relationship between aid and the number of poor people. That is, as poverty and hunger increased in the 1980s, there was less help from the federal, state, and local governments. Too many go hungry, and many people are forced to cheat and sell their food stamps to buy other "luxuries."

I sit down with Nellie. She lives in the Roosevelt Houses across the street from the soup kitchen. She has lived there all of her life. Even though there's crime and it's dangerous at night, she says, "Everyone knows me and I feel safe there." In general, the "projects" are the best housing the area offers. There are some well-kept and more expensive homes where middle-class and working-class people live, but the projects are better than most of the housing in the neighborhood.

Nellie says: "We have a five-and-a-half-room apartment in the projects. There are four of us—my sister and her son and my son. I get $48.50 in public assistance every two weeks. My son gets SSI because he's disabled—he's blind. The rent is $217 per month, and we get $196 food stamps per month. That's hard; things are expensive. I baby-sit and I clean house and I make about $75 more a week [this is not allowed—technically, her work makes her a welfare cheat]. That helps, but what we really live on is really nothing."

I ask about selling food stamps. She answers: "I don't think the system is fair. They don't give you enough to live on. But I think it's wrong to trade them in and not buy food. That's unfair. Food stamps is how I survive. They're like gold to me. I may have no money, but I always have food. Like now it's the first of the month. I'm going to buy my meat. I buy a case of chicken, a loin of pork chops, big shell steak, chopped meat, rice, and noodles. We'll have enough food for a month, and I'll eat my lunches here at least a few days a week. And I get to see my friends and talk. And Sister Bernadette is just beautiful. But again, I think it's wrong to sell food stamps to buy cigarettes, clothes, crack, or OTB [Off Track Betting]. Even though it's not much money and we don't have much, it's wrong."

Nellie is typical of the women who come to the soup kitchen and of the poor women who raise children without the aid of men. Female-headed families did not cause poverty but were caused by poverty and by race and gender discrimination. Life is hard for everyone, but poverty makes the ordinary hardships of life worse. The poor do not have the economic resources to dull life's misery, and every misfortune is amplified. Still, the poor, in general, conform to society's rules and regulations. The soup kitchen is most of the time a peaceful and safe place. We don't have social change here; we have a lot of people trying to survive as best they can. Poverty is not the result of overgenerous welfare programs, as the conservatives claim. Most poor people do not receive welfare, and the programs are not generous; they maintain people at a level close to subsistence. Further, the number of female-headed families kept increasing after the budget cuts in social welfare programs in the 1970s and 1980s. As Ruth Sidel describes the picture:

> Of poor people in the United States today, the vast majority are women and their children. According to the Census Bureau . . . in 1984, 14.4 percent of all Americans—33.7 million people—lived below the poverty line. From 1980 to 1984, the number of poor people increased by 4 ½ million. For female headed households in 1984, the poverty rate was 34.5 percent, a rate five times that for married couple families. The poverty rate for white female-headed families was 27.1 percent, for black female-headed families, 51.7 percent, and for Hispanic families headed by women, 53.4 percent. The poverty rate for the elderly, most of whom are women, was 12.4 percent in 1984. Two out of every three poor adults are women, and the economic status of families headed by women is declining.[15]

It's already 12:15 P.M. when I finally start to serve food. I find an apron and relieve Mary, who has been serving the tomato, rice, and vegetable soup. Because it's check day, there is plenty of soup left. I can give out seconds. Bill, who works the door, tells me that yesterday we had 984 guests. Sister Bernadette shares some good news: United Parcel Service is donating $50,000 to remodel the soup kitchen. The new kitchen will be in another part of the church's parish center, and it will seat 105, not 125. Even though there is increased need in the neighborhood, we will feed fewer guests.

January 8, 1990   Serving food like a machine and trying to be courteous and friendly. John counts the people coming to the soup kitchen and lets them in the Willoughby Street entrance. The guests are 70 percent black, 25 percent Hispanic, and 5 percent white. They pick up their trays, and then they pick up their food: the hot food first, followed by bread, dessert, and juice. They sit and eat at tables with eight other people. Most people socialize at the tables while they eat. I hear some talk directed at John. "Food's good here. At the shelter all you get is a little food and cold storage. Sleeping at the shelter is cold storage."

Even though the homeless are just a fraction of the poor, they have become the signifier of poverty. They are the visible poor, and homelessness has become the measure of the political failure of U.S. society to deal with the poor. At the same time, the emphasis on homelessness has mystified the issue of poverty and reduced it, wrongly, to a question of personal pathology. Poverty in the United States is in fact a question of society's failure to provide for all of its citizens.

John and a young, blond, blue-eyed man are rating the shelters—refugee centers for the homeless poor in Reagan-Bush America. These refugees of market capitalism are just two men among the 1.7 million people living in poverty[16] and the 60,000 to 250,000 who are homeless in New York City. The extent of the housing crisis was summarized in *City Limits*:

> As the 1990's approach, New York City remains mired in a housing and homeless crisis of unprecedented proportions. More than 250,000 people are homeless and living on the streets, in shelters, doubled or tripled-up in over crowded apartments or in substandard housing. The wait for an apartment in public housing hovers near twenty years. These facts bear witness to the city's mammoth shortage of affordable housing.[17]

The young man comments, "Port Washington is the worst, though I heard that Harlem 1 and 2 are not bad." I ask which shelter he's living at. "Atlantic and Bedford, the Armory. A thousand beds lined up, that's the worst. Gangs of guys go around beating up people, mostly the old and the sickly. They never beat up anyone who can defend themselves."

"Have you ever been beaten up?"

"No, I know how to take care of myself. You never show weakness. They stare at you, you stare right back at them. You give them the look. Tells them that you'll get them if they try to do something to you."

The homeless problem is the dramatic edge of a nationwide housing crisis for low-income families. This crisis is clearly stated in *New York Ascendant* by the Commission on the Year 2000:

> According to the 1984 Housing and Vacancy Survey, the poorest fifth of New York households earned 4 percent of the city's income, or $4300 annually. Median annual income of the city's 1.9 million households in rental apartments was $12800. Such incomes cannot usually command good housing. As it is, over one-fifth of the city's households pay more than 50 percent of their income for rent, and one-third pay more than 40 percent. Having to spend an excessive proportion of income on rent is most prevalent among those who are poorest and whose numbers will be growing in the future, including blacks, Hispanics, female headed households, and the elderly.[18]

Shelters for the homeless are terrible places, with violence, drugs, AIDS, and tuberculosis often running rampant; still, they are home for thousands of people. When David Dinkins was elected mayor, there was hope that conditions for the homeless and hungry would improve. In fact, conditions got worse. During this period, more and more homeless people were turned away from city shelters. In *100 Days of Neglect: Mayor Dinkins and the Homeless*, the Coalition for the Homeless reported:

> On February 1, 1990, Mayor Dinkins released a financial plan that proposed deep cuts in shelter services, drug treatment, supportive services to families, AIDS case management, information and referral, and permanent housing for the homeless. Since then, the Mayor has announced an additional $75 million in cuts for the homeless, and $500 million in service cuts. But if preliminary cuts are any indication, we can be sure that New York's neediest will bear undue burden.[19]

January 31, 1990   The kitchen is jumping, crowded and noisy. Bea, one of the volunteers, is serving the soup, thick with noodles, vegetables, and meat. Most of our volunteers are like Bea, poor black women on public assistance, living in a housing project. Bea is a single mother; her adult son has been bedridden since he was a teenager because he was seriously burned in a fire. As I enter the soup kitchen, many people greet me. I start to serve the soup. The line is continuous, seemingly endless, and I work like a machine. John tells me that last week they had over 1,600 guests.

Sister Bernadette is both saintly and competent. She wants to feed everyone who is hungry, even though she knows the constraints of the soup kitchen's resources. People are coming for second, third, fourth servings, and we use up seven pots of soup in the first hour. We have four pots for the second hour. John comes over to tell me that Sister is allowing seconds too early. The management of scarcity is always a problem at Bread and Life. The poor never have enough, and this constant deprivation creates a sense of hopelessness and desperation. But the soup is thick and the people are hungry, and Sister wants to solve this problem for at least this one meal. Hopeless and desperate, she starts to criticize President Bush: "He says this [voluntarism] works, but this doesn't work. He's a jerk and he says this works."

March 7, 1990   An ordinary day at the soup kitchen. Gloria wants to give out the soup, allowing me more time to hang out with the guests. I join in a conversation with John and Jerry. Jerry also works at the kitchen; he plays guitar, wears a big cowboy hat, and loves the Grateful Dead. "Bill, did you see that they arrested that Dr. Joseph (he has started a needle exchange program, where sterile needles are given to heroin addicts to protect them from AIDS). I hope they lock him up and throw away the key. He's a fuckin' asshole. I'm an addict— I know this shit. He doesn't know anything. Giving needles to addicts— you might as well give them 10 dollars for a bag of dope. You give out free needles and they'll sell five needles and they can buy a bag of dope. At the shelter, right now you can buy needles for two dollars a needle. What they should do is make it easier to get on methadone maintenance, especially for addicts who are hurting. A guy comes in needing help, and they send him back on the streets, and this guy goes right back into the drug world. Instead of helping him, they're going to give him free needles."

Jerry is concerned with the continuous pattern of bureaucratic, piecemeal programs where symptoms are treated, usually by incompetent aides. This is the world where following procedures is more important than helping. Jerry and others like him are dependent on this inadequate aid, and any "screw-up" is going to be used to take it away. His life is one of permanent scarcity. Thus he is worried about his welfare check because he hasn't followed all of the rules. "When I moved back in with my wife, they closed my welfare account at the Greenpoint Shelter, and they haven't opened it at my new address. I'm just making out now. I just got by this week by the skin of my teeth."

Many of the men who come to eat at the kitchen stay at the Greenpoint Shelter, which once was a hospital. Most of the men at this shelter are being phased out. John is worried about losing his room. Last week he told me: "They want the homeless off the street, and you saw in yesterday's *Daily News* that the TA [Transit Authority] is getting them out of the trains. People who are working cannot be put up close to the homeless. I wish these people had to live just one day on the streets in winter to see how cold it gets, just one day. If you have a full-time job, you can stay in the shelter; if not, you go. They're getting rid of people slowly. I'd say that they've gotten rid of 150 people already."

Jerry says: "Something, isn't it? I'd say 90 percent of the people in the shelter don't have jobs, any jobs."

John continues: "It is happening everywhere. A lot of guys who left Greenpoint and went to Sumner [another shelter] said it was great there; they left you alone. They didn't chase you during the day; you could watch television all day. Well, one of the social workers from Sumner told me that they're doing it there as well. They're getting rid of them there too. Slowly but surely, they're getting rid of all the people at the shelter that don't have jobs."

Today, John tells me: "I'm getting on the work program so that maybe they keep me at the shelter. It's not great, but it's a lot better than most shelters.... This work program is typical, they take your money until you have enough to have an apartment. They save your money, and it's not that the social workers take your money—they have, some just run off with the money—but even if you do it the way it's supposed to be done, they save money for you because you're a junkie and you can't save money for yourself. And then when you've worked long enough and you have a thousand or so, they give the money to the junkie who couldn't save it himself. They give the guy more than a thousand dollars, and they are surprised that he fucks it away. Are they that dumb? It doesn't work with their own logic. Can they really be that dumb?"

April 19, 1990   Froggy is explaining the crime problem. "That's it—$100 for a pair of sneakers. Can you believe that? It used to be $60, or $100, for a week's pay was good; now $100 for sneakers. That's crazy. You know, that's where all your crime comes from. You have regular old sneakers and no one would be selling crack on the streets. You stop having such fancy, expensive clothes and this crime would drop. I'm telling you. The crime would drop real low, you better believe it."

I'm serving soup in the new kitchen on the Hart Street side of the parish center. The walls are newly painted, and we have a stereo system playing Lite FM. There are two fewer tables than the old kitchen had, but everything is bright and new. Poor people are rarely exposed to new conditions, so the new kitchen is extra special for them. The directors have made a decision to slow the line down and feed 750 guests at lunch—not the thousand or more we had been serving. Sister Bernadette is angry at this new policy, but it is all that our resources can sustain.

On Sunday night muggers shot Father Charley Plock through the legs. Father Charley, an activist street priest who lives in the parish center, was returning home from helping a drug addict in rehabilitation. Crime by the poor is typically directed against their own, but people in the kitchen said that it couldn't be anyone from the neighborhood, because everyone knows and likes Father Charley.

July 17, 1991   A beautiful, sunny, 90-degree day, perfect for the St. John's Bread and Life Health Fair. A cooling breeze blows down

Willoughby Street, ruffling the pamphlets and fliers full of helpful information on diabetes, high blood pressure, and heart disease. Balloons and streamers hang from the tables set up by the various organizations that provide health information to the poor. Children are getting free balloons, rap music is blasting, and people are dancing in the streets. Ann comes over and takes my picture, documenting today's event. I go down to the kitchen and start to serve franks. I'm relatively slow today, and people complain. Franks are a favorite, and the people are both hungry and in a rush to get to the health fair. Bea helps me pick up the slack, and the line begins to move at its normal pace. She says that she almost had a heart attack and will no longer argue with anyone at the soup kitchen over seconds. "I'm trying to take it easy," she says.

I ask about Sergio, one of the men who did maintenance work for the soup kitchen. "Where's Sergio? I haven't seen him for a while."

Bea answers, "He's not here anymore. They say he robbed a lot of stuff. They caught this kid with the keys, robbing, and he said Sergio gave him the keys and that he was working with Sergio. Sergio denied it. He said the kid stole the keys. I don't know what to think. But it's pitiful to see Sergio. They took his apartment away, and they say that he was paid in advance so he had no pay coming to him. He has nothing; he's on the streets, riding the subway."

"They say he was using crack, heavily using crack?" I ask.

"That's what they say. He was using, but I don't know how heavy. But he has nothing. Everyone was taking. I know Cy takes stuff. And John—he's always selling whatever he can on the streets. Some people accuse me of taking stuff, but I never do. I only take what I'm given and what I ask for."

"They know more people are taking than Sergio. They seem to be committed to cracking down?"

Bea says: "It seems like they are. But Sergio wasn't the only one taking. I told him it wasn't worth it. But he didn't listen, and now he has nothing. Not even a place to live. He's pitiful; my sister took him home one day to feed him. I've taken him home to feed him. I brought him a steak and gave him a place to rest. It's really sad to see him."

I say, "They could have locked him up; he stole a lot of stuff."

Bea replies: "I know—television, phones. I know they could have; it's good that they didn't lock him up. But they did take away his apartment. He has no place to live. And it's really sad that they won't let him eat here. He must get into a drug program, and when he's in the program they'll let him eat here. . . . He should get into a program."

I serve franks with Bea for a while longer, and then I go outside and participate in the fair. I go from booth to booth, talking to the neighborhood people who are taking advantage of all the health information that is being provided and also to the health care providers. Vilma has organized the entertainment, including a young gospel group from Bedford-Stuyvesant, teenage actors performing a skit about a young girl who goes for an AIDS test, rappers, break dancers, singers, and another acting group.

Later I eat with Larry, who is in Narcotics Anonymous. Larry is proud of his ethnic identity, boasting that he is half Irish and half Italian but usually identifies himself as Italian. "I love this place; this place is a godsend for me. I started to come here to eat. I've been in the streets for five months. It's cold in the streets. And I'm a Teamster from Masbeth. But I can't get work—I load trucks, but I love drugs more. I had a house and a wife, and I lost both. Crack, cocaine, and when I was young even acid." Poor whites at the soup kitchen almost always tell the story of how drugs ruined their lives. African Americans and Hispanics tell this story also, but they more often tell the story of being born poor and of never having opportunities either in school or in the workplace. African American and Hispanic addicts often saw dealing drugs as a way out of poverty. For most, it just led to a drug-addicted disaster.

I ask Larry, "Do you have AIDS?"

"Nah," he answers, "I'm a coke head. I never liked needles. I only snorted heroin. I never liked it. I like ups, cocaine and crack. For 20 years I was high; now I'm straight for three months. I have a room; I'm not on the streets. I love NA; I go to meetings 11, 12 times a week. I go to meetings in Maspeth, I go to meetings here. I've got to go every day. I don't even drink beer now. My friends say, 'Larry, this isn't like you.' But it's me. I even go to church now. My friends really can't believe that. I love NA. If I don't go to meetings, I'd be dangerous again."

"Do your parents help you?"

"Nah, my parents are fed up with me. I'm their little good-for-nothing junkie son. My mother won't have anything to do with me. I don't have a family now. I'd like to see my mother. I don't know if you are aware of the 12-point program, but that's part of the program—making amends to all the people you hurt when you were doing drugs. I have to make amends to my mother. I'd like to see her.

"Do you get high?" he asks me.

I answer, "No."

In disbelief, "Not even a little?"

"No."

He continues: "That's what's good about NA. It's addicts taking care of addicts. You're not an addict, how can you help me? You don't know where I'm coming from. You don't know what it's like to live for drugs. Fuck up your life for drugs. I had it made. I had a good job, a wife, my own home. I had it made. I lost it all because of drugs. You don't know what it's like to be an addict, to lose everything because you're an addict. But other addicts—they know, they've been there. I come to NA meetings and people care about me; they want me to come back; they hug me. That's what NA is: addicts taking care of addicts. Shit, my mother doesn't care about me, but these addicts care about me. I don't know what I'd do without NA. I even go to AA meetings. I think God is watching over me. These NA meetings have saved my life. And that's what I do at the soup kitchen [working at the health fair and attending NA meetings]. I'm giving a little back for all that I've taken. Instead of being a junkie, always looking for drugs, always looking for a way to get over on someone else, now I'm giving. . . . Hey, I get depressed, I'm separated from my wife, I had a house, I was on top of the world. But NA gives me hope. I'll get back there."

"You sound good," I say. I know this may be all talk, he may start using drugs again, but right now NA is working for him.

I go back outside to the health fair. I never see Larry again. I don't know what happened to him. People are always coming and going at the soup kitchen. For years I saved the ends of the bread for a tall man who was always dressed in an overcoat. He never said anything to me; he would just nod when he took the plastic bag full of the ends.

One day he stopped coming, and no one knew what had become of him. Joan and Jerry, who were always friendly and quiet, also stopped coming one day. The rumor in the soup kitchen was that they had died from AIDS. John Robles, the drug counselor, said they were never tested; he didn't know what happened to them either.

As the fair is ending, Marisol, who seems always to be pregnant, tells me, "This is great. I can't wait for the next one. I hope they have this every year." We chat for a while, and then I walk over to Hossein. He is noticeably tired. "Next year this will be bigger and better," he says. "This was very cheap to run—everything was donated. I was worried that Woodhull Hospital didn't see enough people. But they came over to me and said that they gave 93 people check-ups, took blood pressure. They saw more people than they thought they would. They were very happy."

November 27, 1991   It's Thanksgiving Day and we are serving Kraft Premier Instant Potatoes with vitamin C, Bea's delicious stuffing, chicken cutlets, greens, walnut cake, and, for the children, bubble-gum jawbreakers. I eat bowl after bowl of stuffing covered in gravy while I photograph the festivities for the soup kitchen. Students from St. John's University are serving the meal. Volunteers are always available on holidays. The regular volunteers are basically watching as Sister Bernadette directs the novices. Holidays are good days at the kitchen—there is always plenty of food, and everyone seems happy about the bountiful servings.

But this is a soup kitchen full of people who ordinarily do not have enough, and even on the good days the bad news is bountiful as well. Though the kitchen is usually a peaceful place, the desperation of people who are always worried about their own survival often infects it. Today, Hossein tells me that 200 guests were tested for HIV, and 28 percent were positive. A lot of people also tested positive for tuberculosis and hepatitis.

Sister Bernadette is nervous today and has been short-tempered with everyone. John is one of her favorites and is not used to being treated this way.

He says, "Y'know, the Sister is really bugging me."

"She gets this way when Sister Kathleen is here," I say. "She's always afraid that Kathleen will find some reason to cut the program, and she always wants to impress Kathleen."

"Nah, that's not it. She saw me taking Valium almost a year ago, and my eyes were glassy, and now she thinks I'm some big drug user. She doesn't even know who the big drug users are. Cy, he's slick and he steals from the kitchen and buys crack, and she is only nicer and nicer to him."

Though most of the people at the soup kitchen are law-abiding, some people will do anything to make their lives better. Some will steal food, televisions, and computers and sell them on the streets. The quick pleasures of drugs are also a temptation. As a result soup kitchens and food pantries often have a problem with robbery. A minority of the people who come to the soup kitchen—people like Cy and Sergio—steal to pay for drugs.

Thus, I ask, even though I know the answer, "Has anyone seen Sergio?"

"He's in bad shape," John answers. "He's on the streets begging for money. Y'know that Cy was Sergio's partner—he sold that stuff and bought the crack. He sold televisions right on Broadway. Sister sends him with the truck to pick up food, meat, canned goods, and he sells a portion of it before he comes back. Buys some crack and sells that too. He's very smart. He knows I know, so he tries to make me his friend. He comes over to me and says he has a present for me and tries to palm crack to me. I tell him I don't want this shit. But he wants me to be dependent on him. He's not that smart. I don't want to owe him anything. He works high on crack. I told the Sister that he's doing the stealing, but she doesn't pay attention to me. I'm the bad one; she saw me take the Valium, just Valium, and I'm now the big junkie. He steals and works high and he's all right. I'm sick of this."

Freddy, one of the guests, comes over and says, "Well, the white boys are sticking together, envious of our black skin."

"I'm half black," John jokes.

Freddy says: "I knew there was something I liked about you." A few other guests join in the fun, all of us trying to top each other in this bout of interracial humor, until Freddy, slightly worried, says,

"John, you know I was just fooling around? All the people are the same to me. I have nothing against white people."

Toward the end of the day, I talk to Hossein. I put in a good word for John, knowing that, even though he's pissed off, he still needs this job. I also ask about Sister, who is looking tired these days. "Oh, she's all right," Hossein says. "She goes to the doctor regularly. She did have that ulcer, but it's better."

"The stress in the soup kitchen doesn't allow ulcers to get better," I respond.

January 20, 1992   An ordinary day at the soup kitchen. I serve soup to about 800 people. Hossein and I disagree about the proportion of homeless people among our guests: I say that it's about 30 percent; he says 60. He tells me that I'm undercounting because I'm leaving out all the people who are doubled up with friends and relatives.

Later I ask Ellen, a kitchen volunteer, what she thinks. "About 30 percent are homeless, another 30 percent live in the projects, and another 30 percent live in the tenement buildings that surround the soup kitchen," she says.

Vilma comes over and tells me that I have to have a tuberculin test because Sasha's tuberculosis has become very serious and I often worked next to Sasha. I have the test and, like everyone else, hope that TB doesn't spread throughout the kitchen.

July 27, 1992   Pink, blue, and yellow caps from crack vials litter the streets of Bedford-Stuyvesant as I walk to the soup kitchen. In the early 1990s, television and newspaper reports on poverty are all about homelessness and crack, even though homeless people and crack users represent just a fraction of the poor. The media focus fits in with the taken-for-granted notion of the poor as a degraded form of humanity, of poverty as a pathology and not a socioeconomic formation. If the media shifted its focus, it would have to recognize that poverty isn't a pathology of the poor but a symptom of American capitalism.

Still, homelessness is a dramatic and visible demonstration of poverty. That people live in the streets in urban areas of the United States today is shocking. Writing about the dispute over the 1984

Housing and Urban Development (HUD) report that estimated that 250,000 to 350,000 people were homeless in the United States, Joel Blau addresses the politics of definition and how definitions shape the parameters of social problems. HUD's definition of the homeless— "where, in addition to other arrangements, temporary vouchers are provided by public or private agencies"[20] —reduced the number of homeless people in the United States by excluding the long-term homeless, who often live in welfare hotels, and "the street people," who do not seek out shelter but live on the streets, in abandoned buildings, and in subway tunnels. For Blau all definitions of homelessness are politically informed: "In keeping with the definer's political agenda they can be used to decrease or increase the reported size of the population."[21]

Homelessness is, of course, an important part of being poor in the United States, but only a fraction of the poor—one percent or less— are homeless. The homeless and the drug-addicted are the "visible poor," overrepresented in media accounts of poverty.

More typical of the experience of poverty in the United States is today's crowded soup kitchen. When I walked by St. Stephen's on Myrtle Avenue, which also has a soup kitchen, the line was longer than usual, maybe because most soup kitchens and pantries are closed over the weekend. This Monday at Bread and Life we serve over 1,100 people. Bea says it's because it's Monday and we didn't make enough food for our guests. I know that we are running out of food too fast when Sister tells me first to give the women half bowls because they are throwing it out and then to use the smaller ladle. With 20 minutes to go, we run out of soup, even though I've been giving out such small portions that some people yell at me. Bea says that tomorrow we will have to make more food—at least nine pots of soup and 11 trays of chicken. We start giving out cheese. Sister takes over because the people will not yell at her.

I begin to talk to John and Jerry, who are part of Blau's "visible poor," both homeless and drug abusers. John inherited over $40,000 from his mother and shot 20 bags of heroin and five bags of cocaine a day until he found himself homeless and maintaining a $250-a-day habit.

I once interviewed him about his first day at the Greenpoint Shelter.

"First of all, don't forget it was the summer, so the first three nights I slept in Washington Park under the Williamsburg Bridge. Which is a very bad neighborhood. But I had that wild abandon attitude, like who the fuck cares—if I die, I die. I had no one to answer to. No one was going to see me in my troubled state. I didn't have to worry about that. I was already evicted; everything in the apartment I got rid of. I had nothing. So I had nothing else to lose. I started thinking of death as a great liberator. . . . If I die, put me in Potters Field. I really don't care. . . . I've been through burying my family. I'm not concerned what happens to my body after I pass away. My faith in God and what's going to happen to my soul and all that . . . I've never sold my soul to drugs. I've sold everything else. Like I've said, I have no problem with my theology or my faith."

I ask him what a normal day is like at the shelter.

"When I first came in, they thought I was the man or an HRA [Human Resources Administrator]. But that stopped fast when they saw that I did have tracks, I did have a methadone card, and I did get high.

"Six o'clock in the morning with a military whistle. It's six o'clock, breakfast is ready, shredded wheat."

"Do you have shredded wheat every morning?"

"Not every morning, but most of the time. Even when they don't, when they have Rice Krispies, it's two little, small boxes.

"There's one thing I learned in the shelter: don't fuck around with a hungry man, OK. This is serious shit. You don't tell somebody that they're giving out free hamburgers in Building 4, and when you get there, it's not there. Men will stab you to death for that type of joke. And I'll be the first guy to stab you . . .

"So my normal day is wake up at 6:00 with the whistle. You have to be at the building at 6:30. You have to be in the breakfast room by 7:00. If you get there by 7:30, all the breakfast is gone. The only things that's left would be a box of shredded wheat, two sugars, and eight ounces of milk. The fruit juice will be gone, bananas will be gone, the bread will be gone. So some guy who works for Burns Security who jokes about stretching your muscles for bacon and eggs—I don't like it, OK."

"There's never bacon and eggs for breakfast?" I ask.

He yells at me, "Of course not. *Never!* BACON AND EGGS—MY GOD!

"We wait for our tokens. People who are on methadone programs, or who have to go to places get tokens, OK. Or who need tokens to get to welfare. Anyone who knows welfare—you've got to be there early in the morning. They don't give out tokens until after nine o'clock. All your appointments are shot to hell while you wait from nine to ten for them to call out your name for tokens. And your name doesn't come up, you question them. They say your counselor didn't write out your ticket because she just didn't feel like it or she wanted to get home early. So even if they write you out a slip, then they tell you there's no tokens left, they're all gone. So even if you get your two tokens to go to the program—I haven't paid the fare on the subway since I've been at the shelter, it's one year. I have enough summonses to put me on Rikers for at least a week. My tokens are spent on my breakfast, $1.25 special. OK, that's what my tokens are spent on. . . . I'll buy a bacon, well, bacon's too expensive. So I'll buy regular eggs and toast for $1.25 let's say, spend 50 cents on a quart of fruit punch and a quarter on two Lucies [cake]. That's my $2.00. Then I'll jump the turnstile to go to the program."

These men who live at the shelter, who experience permanent scarcity, see their free tokens not as a means of transportation but as currency. That they will wait for hours for two tokens worth $3.00 attests to their desperation. Technically they are ripping off the system, but politicians who see only the formal and petty illegal act miss the greater immorality of homeless poverty in the richest country in the world.

John continues, "I try to get back here [the soup kitchen] to help out. I'm guaranteed a meal here. That's my first incentive to come here. Look at this container of juice I have with ice cubes, ice cold. Must be 98 degrees outside, and this is refreshing as hell. That's my incentive.

"So after you get your tokens at the shelter, we all split up into different groups to go to our programs. And we all do the day's business. I went scrapping several times. I'm not a scrapper. These guys in the shelter are metallurgists; they know metal by looking at it.

They trade in copper, and they know the prices of aluminum and copper daily. They see aluminum on any type of wall, they'll take it off. And a lot of these guys live that way. And you can tell them because their arms and hands are all cut up and a lot of them get infected. And the most important drugs in the shelter are Kalex, penicillin, antibiotics. And people sell that kind of stuff. There's a doctor at the shelter. I've never went to him, and I shouldn't say this, but I have no respect for him. I don't have any respect for any of the caseworkers at the shelter. I resent the doctors at Woodhull [Hospital] who are medical doctors, and they'll make you sit for eight hours. . . . I know its overcrowded and I know how the system works, EMS and all this bullshit. But to me emergency medicine—it's an emergency. You take care of emergencies. When I went for my seizure, I sat in a chair like this for 13 hours before I got an IV in my arm. . . .

"I don't even know if the city requires these counselors to have degrees. Some of them, all they do is give out tokens. You can spend hours waiting for one. Your mail gets lost for months. If you miss a letter from welfare, your case is closed. Twice my case got closed because they never give you mail—lackadaisical attitudes."

I ask, "How big is the Greenpoint Shelter?"

"Greenpoint is one of the biggest shelters in the system. There's five buildings. One is the biggest, with the biggest population. I think there are 1,800 men in the shelter. Building 2 is one of the most dangerous buildings because they're all the young black gladiators who think they are tough, and they all want to be mobsters. Building 3 is for working people that have steady jobs."

"A lot of people would say that if you have a steady job, why would you be in a shelter?" I observe.

"The reason is these guys in Building 3 give half your paycheck. They take half and let you keep half, and after a three-month period they hook you up with a room and start you out on a new life. But all the guys screw up. Because, first of all, they resent giving half their paycheck that they worked so hard for. The half of the paycheck they do get is going right for drugs. There's a few of them who are making a sincere effort. There are a few of them who marshal their energies in an honest attempt to get the fuck out of there. Some of them do, and they disappear, and you never see them again, OK. Some of them go back to their families that you thought they didn't have, guys who have wives and children.

"I'm in Building 4, a very nice building. Each building has its own flavor. Building 1 is extreme abuse of narcotics, specifically needles. You'd better watch going into the showers—there's needles on the floor. Some of the guards will say, 'You're not allowed to use a needle in my building unless you give me four dollars.' . . . And tuberculosis is running rampant. Tuberculosis is really a strong factor in that shelter . . . .

"I'd say 85 percent of the crime in Greenpoint, Brooklyn, is due to that shelter [Greenpoint is a low-crime neighborhood]. Everything circling the Greenpoint Shelter is due to the clients that live there. Everything, the subway alone—the token room in the morning, maybe 300 guys, all on programs, six days a week. They get two tokens a day. Nobody pays the fare. So figure 300 guys a day, six days a week, 52 weeks, how much the Transit Authority is losing at that one station, Graham Avenue station . . .

"The people who wind up in the shelter are there because they got no other place."

I ask, "How many whites in the shelter?"

"Not too many, 10, 20 percent.

"Latinos?"

"The same. More than 75 percent are black."

"How do you feel about living there?"

"The worst part is waiting every morning for the tokens. Sitting there, you have to wait for two tokens. All my life I worked, and now I have to wait. . . . Just to see your caseworker you need a referral from the doctor. You'd have to wait an hour just to talk to the guard to ask permission to talk to the caseworker. One morning I had my X-rays in my hand. "Mr. Saunders, I have to go to Kings County Hospital to be admitted for neurosurgery. Here are my X-rays." [The guard says,] 'Not now, not now.' And I never saw her; she wouldn't speak to me the whole day."

John is typical of these men without families, homeless and living in shelters in New York City. They depend on two tokens a day for their steady income, soup kitchens for steady meals. By sneaking into subway stations and cashing in the tokens, they can buy a meal or cigarettes. It's their extra daily stipend. John makes $25 a week by working at the soup kitchen. These men do not have much, and they cheat whenever they can to extend the less than bare minimum that they live on. In a world in which owning property is the most important value, they do not even own their beds. At a time when welfare benefits are being cut and aid for the poor is disappearing, what would happen to them if they didn't cheat? How would they live if they were honest and followed all the rules? When John urgently needs to go to the hospital, the caseworker ignores his request. (His condition is serious, and he will die from a seizure in August 1999.) They are continually subjected to a system that increases their degradation, to a bureaucracy that serves itself. John is also in a methadone program, and his needs are always secondary to the program's rules. His life is bounded on all sides by institutions that control his daily life and that subject him to continuing control.

November 3, 1992   I ask, "Do you want some sauce?" The guest answers, "Yeah, give me all you got. I'm hungry, really hungry. What d'ya got? I want it. I haven't eaten since yesterday. I'm really hungry."

I hear a commotion and loud threats. "I'll kill you!" The large Latino guy everyone calls the Kid is threatening a smaller black man. The Kid has him by the collar, saying, "You got my soup; they gave you my soup." Sister always saves extra soup for Kid, who has a number of congenital illnesses. The Kid takes the soup home to his mother on his bike, which is his most valuable piece of property. The two men begin to grab each other, but Kid is just too big for the other man. John tries to separate them, and Sister, right in the middle of the brawl, is yelling at them to stop.

They are finally separated. The small guy sits down, but Kid just picks him up out of his seat. The yelling and screaming continue. Now John is screaming, "Take it out of the kitchen, take it out of the kitchen." The Kid raises his hand to hit the small guy. Just as he throws his punch, I grab him, making him miss. But now I have this bull of a man in my arms. He flicks me across the room like a flea. Bully, who is Ellen's boyfriend, joins the peacemakers, along with John, who is still saying, "Take it out of here." The Kid is moving on the small guy; luckily, though strong, he is very slow.

Sister yells, "Bully, stop this." Kid comes at Bully, and Bully hits him low and pins him to the ground. The Kid can't move. Sister tells him to leave, but he won't. A woman walks over and starts to calm him down. Finally he leaves, threatening to wait outside for the small guy.

Bully comes over to me and says, "It was like playing football, but I'm usually the quarterback. I'm not used to blocking. That guy is strong; it took everything I had to stop him." People are congratulating Bully. Wendy says, "We knew he was crazier today than usual. . . . They almost had a fight earlier. He didn't like that guy even before today."

Later, Kid comes over to me and asks me to fill his container with soup. "After one o'clock," I tell him, "when we finish serving, if there's any left." He moves away, still angry.

The same woman is still trying to calm him down. The sauce runs out with 30 minutes left to go. Sister starts serving cold cuts. I walk over to the door and talk with a bunch of men about the fight. One says, "They're going to ban him from the soup kitchen. He won't be able to come back." He looks at me, "Do you know what it's like to live on the streets without being able to come here?" Another man says, "If he keeps this up, he was trying to start with the guy yesterday. Sister says, they'll close the kitchen, and then where will we all be."

The Kid comes back with the wise woman who has been trying to soothe him. She says, "You can't let everything affect you like that. There's lots of people out there; everybody out there will try to get you down. They'll do anything to get you down on yourself. You can't pay attention to it; you can't let them bring you down, like they just did."

Another man says to him, "You know there's an old saying, you don't shit where you eat. Y'know that one?"

The wise woman, agreeing, says, "Hello!" The Kid shakes his head and apologizes to me. He starts to walk up the ramp with his bike. The small guy comes out of the kitchen and throws a beer bottle at him. It misses him but smashes against the metal fence above the ramp and shatters over two men and a little girl. They are covered in glass but unhurt. I help them clean the glass fragments off. John tells me that Kid is chasing the small guy through the projects, but he can't catch him.

November 4, 1992   People at the soup kitchen tell me that so far there haven't been any repercussions from the fight. They were impressed that I got involved, even though I didn't stop it. Getting involved in the fight made me look a little less clean and a little less like an outsider. Many people at the kitchen still think that I'm a priest. Even after volunteering at Bread and Life for more than four years, I'm still viewed as a stranger by the kitchen's regulars. After yesterday I'm a little less strange.

I work with Bully and Ellen, serving the juice. Bully says, "Bill, when you grabbed that guy high, around the shoulders like that, there was no way you could hold him. I couldn't have stopped him if I grabbed him around the shoulders. That's why I hit him low. I was trying to get the other guy out of the kitchen. I heard Sister yelling, 'John, stop him.' But when you grabbed him around the shoulders, I knew you needed help. I'm 38, I'm a running back. I still play football. I'm not used to hitting guys, but I know how to do it. And this kitchen is my place—you act right in here, and if you don't, I'll take care of you."

We continue to talk about the fight. Bully and Ellen seem to think that the guests are particularly rude today. Ellen says, "Sister is too generous—that's the problem."

More important, it's the day after the presidential election, and everyone is excited that the Democrat, Bill Clinton, won. With a Democrat in the White House, they hope, poor people will get a fairer share of America's wealth. The Reagan and Bush years have been hard on the people who come to the soup kitchen. Most people there, both guests and administrators, believe that Reagan's and Bush's welfare policies made the soup kitchen necessary. It isn't surprising that Bernard, Jerry, and Sergio, who is working in the kitchen again, are happy about the election results. Sister had been worried that Bush was going to win again. Bernard says, "I'm happy that it was a blowout." They know that everything will not get better, but they believe that Bush didn't care about them and that Clinton does.

February 2, 1993   Twelve degrees outside when I left my apartment in Greenpoint at 10:30 to go to the soup kitchen. The wind chill is below zero, and the sky is that cloudless, cold blue of winter as I walk down Myrtle Avenue. At Bread and Life I serve soup with vegetables and spaghetti. I'm a sloppy server today, and I splash soup and spaghetti all over the counter. Sister eventually tells me to be careful because I'm wasting soup. The soup is thick and tasty but burnt at the bottom of the pot. I try to avoid scraping the bottom, but no mater how careful I am, some burnt soup gets into the bowls, making the whole pot of soup taste burnt and bitter.

Sister comes over to check out the soup because the guests have been complaining. They expect the usual level of quality and will not eat food that is not up to their standards. She takes the large spoon and scoops some of the burnt portion out of the pot. "Cookie didn't stir the soup enough," she says angrily. Bea says, after Sister leaves, "Cookie never stirs the soup enough."

Some of the guests will come back and ask for a new serving without the burnt parts, slowing down the line and keeping other people waiting. But these are hungry people who deserve a thick and tasty bowl of soup, so I am apologetic and try to give them bowls without burnt soup. This scene continues until, just a little before closing time, the last pot of soup is finished, and then the remaining guests on line get cold cuts or cheese instead.

Poor people, like most people, talk about their everyday lives. They often believe that there is very little that they can do about their social and biological conditions. They take action when they can but rarely expect relief. They are used to struggling to maintain their lives at this minimal level, but most of the time they are unable even to imagine any change for the better. Still, pleasure and special times find a place in their lives along with the misery.

Bea, in her early fifties, lives in the Kingsborough Houses. "I've been living there since a month after I was born. I feel safe there even though you have to run. I still feel safe. But it's bad, it's bad all over."

Our conversation is typical of the kind of talk people have at the soup kitchen, except that as a sociologist I know less about what goes on in the neighborhood than most people there, and I am recording this conversation. Thus she tells me that it's hard for most of the people who come to the soup kitchen to get decent-paying jobs because they aren't educated. She tells me how difficult it is to make ends meet. "Some things are very expensive, but you just have to shop around. I go to about four different stores to do my shopping, one store for meat, one store for vegetables, one store for dry goods and other things. So you can get the best things." Shopping is important to her. "Because there are six of us in our house, my sister and her children," and because she has to make their public assistance check and food stamps last all month. As a result, she rationally calculates her use of her limited resources, and the loss of any money is a small disaster.

I ask what she does when she comes to the kitchen in the morning. "When I come here, I get all the pots out. I come here at seven o'clock in the morning. . . . I put oil in each pot. I put two pots of water on the stove, and when Kevin opens up the cans, I put all the meat and vegetables and everything in it. Cookie seasons, and if there's any spaghetti, I dig it out and put it in each pot. . . . When we open up, the people who are sleeping in the street are just grabbing, just grabbing at the food because they're so hungry."

We don't talk only about problems; we also talk about her social life and what she does for fun. To survive in this hard world you must have fun, or all of the struggling doesn't make any sense. For the poor, as for the middle and upper classes, pleasure is a basic human need. The history of the African American ghetto is also a history of music and dance, from jazz to Motown to hip-hop. The pleasure principle of this music that also provides a world of meaning and movement is central to the experience of poor people.[22] Bea loves to dance, but complications from diabetes have cut her dancing years short. But dance and music are important to her. Some people would say that because Bea is on public assistance, she shouldn't use her scarce resources for pleasure. Yet Bea often goes to Harlem to socialize. "That's because I'm Eastern Star. Y'know about the Masons? Eastern Star is on the same order . . . they're the men and we're the women. When I first joined, someone has to take you in. And they have to investigate you, and then they select you in, they initiate you in. And so my sister was in it for four years, and then she brought me in. We're all in the same temple; we pray together. It's more like a club. We have bus rides, dances. Y'know we have a Queen. In April we have from East Chapter, we have a dance, it's called the Queen dance. The more raffles you sell, the more ads you sell, and the more money you bring in, you win.

"I like spirituals, most of the time I listen to a lot of spirituals. I like Aretha Franklin. . . .

"I watch TV but not during the day. I leave here at a quarter after one. Then I go home, cook dinner. I go shopping to get a little something to take home. I clean sometimes. Sometimes I go to bed around seven or seven-thirty because I'm tired."

I tell her that she looks tired. She says, "No, it's because of the lasers in my eyes yesterday. It's bleeding behind my eyes from the pressure, and I had the laser, and the doctor did it too rough, yesterday. He pressed too hard, and he irritated the eye. But otherwise just a little tired. I didn't sleep good last night."

I ask about the stipend that she gets from the soup kitchen.

"Yes, 10 dollars a day. They say they're going to give us an extra five dollars a day, they say it's just for travel, lunch and coffee. . . . When I was home I had a headache, a foot ache, I was sick every day. So my sister said, 'Why don't you come and work with me?' So she had me come down and meet everyone. Because we had to, over there to our lodge, y'know, I came and I worked that day. And she asked me to work the next day, and she kept telling me to come, and finally I came every day. You work so many times, volunteering—you come in for a couple of weeks and you don't get no pay. And then after a while if you're going to stay, then she [Sister] will give you out of her own pocket, which I thought was very nice. And I told her, 'I wish you didn't do that.' This behavior of giving money to people who either was helping out or to whom she believed need extra money was typical of her. As a result, she never wanted birthday or Christmas presents for herself. If you wanted to give her a gift, she would tell you to give her money so that she could give it to those people who came to the kitchen who she thought were particularly needy."

Bea continues, "Then after a while they put me on payroll, and they give me a little stipend. Y'know a lot of people say, 'Well, that's not a lot of money,' but it gives me something to do every day, and not only that, but you don't have to take it home with you. And then she gives you things; you say, 'Sister, can I have such and such?' Sometimes she'll come out with anything and just give it to you. So actually you are not losing anything. But a lot of people feel like, 'Oh, that little 10 dollars you make a day, and I wouldn't run down there.' But like then she'll give you a little rice or macaroni and that keeps you from having to go to the store. Even the can goods . . . and I like to help people that want help. She's a beautiful person."

May 5, 1992   "I don't want to die in the streets. Hossein, don't let me die in the streets," says an 18-year-old black teenager who is no longer a kid. His life is only hard times. His parents threw him out two years ago. His mother's boyfriend didn't like him. He has been on the streets ever since. His hands are red and swollen. His face is leathery. Two years on the streets, and he looks old and sick.

Hossein says, "I won't let you die. You shouldn't be on the streets. You should be in school. You should have a life." I listen to this. Hossein knows that I know that all the resources of the Bread and Life program, St. John the Baptist Church, and public assistance might not be enough. Hossein may not be able to prevent this youth's death on the streets.

I go to work, serving food on the line. I see Beverly and I ask how Sasha is. "Oh, she's better. Yeah, she's finally over the tuberculosis. She even came in to eat last week. But the doctors want her to have more bed rest because she has a cold in her lungs. Bill, if you saw her you wouldn't know her." (Sasha never fully regains her health and eventually dies.)

It's only a few days after the Rodney King verdict and the Los Angeles riots. As a sociologist, I am ready for the dramatic and angry responses of these poor people. Dramatic responses do not come. Instead, I get quiet resignation. "Sure, people over Bed-Stuy were outraged that the police, they weren't found guilty, but what did you expect? This is nothing new for us." People tell me about incidents in downtown Brooklyn; at the A & S department store, they say, a woman was killed, but it was hushed up. Whether true or not, this becomes a part of the story for these people who live too close to police brutality. "Yeah, it was terrible in my neighborhood; my neighborhood is always terrible," a woman laughs. "That's normal in my neighborhood."

As a sociologist, I was ready to study the tragedy of poverty and thus unintentionally romanticize it. But poverty is neither tragic nor romantic; it is ordinary. It is part of the everyday life of millions of Americans, and it is as a part of everyday life that it must be understood. It should not just be studied when the extraordinary occurs, like a riot.

Cornel West wrote, "What happened in Los Angeles was neither a race riot nor a class rebellion."[23] He's right. Why are there no new vocabulary shifts in opposition to the language of limitations that dominates poverty policy? Where is the new movement to end poverty? There are myriad programs and thousand of poverty advocates and professionals, but they all compete for a shrinking poverty pie. Many do good work, like Sister Bernadette and Hossein at St. John's Bread and Life. But good works and even a few innovative programs do not make a social movement. A movement would posit an alternative to the current immiseration and mobilize the population to work for the elimination of poverty.

As we have seen in this chapter, the poor are worn out by the hard work of surviving. Making a social movement would be very difficult for them. Most poor people aren't like Lafayette and Pharoah Rivers and Frank McCourt. Most poor people are quietly resigned to their condition. The poor did not benefit from the Wall Street boom during the Clinton years. In fact, from 1993 to 1999 their alienation and oppression only increased. As Henri Lefebvre tells us:

> For people who have been unable to overcome alienation, the alienated world—social appearances, the theories and abstractions which express these appearances—seems the only reality. . . .

Moreover this illusion has a real solid basis, for it is not a theoretical illusion; it is a practical illusion with its basis in everyday life and in the way everyday life is organized.[24]

Domination is normal in the everyday life of poor people. Whether they are at the soup kitchen, the workplace, the welfare office, or the methadone clinic, authority over their lives is externally imposed. They have very little say in their lives, and there seems to be no alternative. This is their fate. The real brutality of their lives is this seemingly permanent institutional control over them. As their lives get worse, they are silent. The drama of the struggle to build an antipoverty movement is not a part of their ordinary lives.

3 Beggars Can't Be Choosers

1993–2000

Miss liberty, I never met her
For you choose to keep me fettered
You lied to me Brooklyn
I thought things were getting better
　　　　　　—from Kayo (Kraal Y. Charles), "Brooklyn (you lied to me)"

"I AIN'T GOT NO BOOM," she responds when I ask how the eight-year economic surge has benefited her. This is a typical answer from the pregnant women and new mothers in Bread and Life's MOM's program. When I refer to the current low unemployment rate in the United States, they disagree with me because they know that low unemployment is not true in their world. They are unaware of both the current prosperity and the tight job market because the poor have been excluded from the new high-tech economy. However, they are aware of the cuts in welfare and food stamps, of time limits, sanctions, workfare, and forced job searches. For them this isn't a good economy. It's almost impossible to find a good job—that is, a job that pays a truly living wage and offers good benefits as well. These moms realize that somehow in this economic upturn, they are having an economic downturn. The supposedly endless growth of the "new economy" has bypassed the ghetto.

These are the Clinton years, 1993–2000, and the world of the people who come to St. John's Bread and Life has been made more miserable by the success of welfare reform. The Clinton presidency and Representative Newt Gingrich's *Contract With America* defined a new welfare policy, ending AFDC and introducing TANF (Temporary Assistance for Needy Families), time limits for benefits, and, most important, workfare. The era of the high-tech economy, with its new billionaires and its seemingly endless growth, is "not for everyone," and two-thirds of America's workforce still earn the same wages they were getting in 1973.[1] As for the unemployed and poor, their benefits have been cut despite the general fiscal prosperity. There are budget surpluses, but spending increases bypass the poor, as when New York City's Mayor Giuliani increases spending by $4.7 billion after 1997, but decreases spending on public assistance by 40.7 percent.[2] It has become increasingly difficult for the poor to get welfare, and even when they qualify they receive lower benefits and are forced to work for them. As New York City prospers, austerity is maintained for the poor.

The stage was set for the maintenance of austerity and reduced benefits by the redefinition of welfare policy in Newt Gingrich and Richard Armey's *Contract With America*, though Clinton participated in the conservative reinvention of poverty when he signed the welfare reform act. The logic of these new policies is "personal responsibility" and "welfare to work," not an end to poverty. The poor are treated as an aberration, both morally and biologically—after all, the opportunities of industrial and postindustrial capitalism are available to all. I argue that the poor are continuously punished because in a global world where American capitalism is dominant, the poor are the indicators of the limits of the free market. It is a pernicious reversal of blame: the poor are blamed for the failures of both local and international capitalism. There is more than enough for everyone, but for the free market to maintain its universal economic and political power, it must maintain the scientific and economic myth of scarcity. "Objective" social scientist policy makers take for granted the inevitability of scarcity and, as a result, see poverty as permanent. Thus the poor have been put into a pathological bind, reinforced by welfare dependency.

Welfare dependency is a form of systematic control and surveillance, offering the possibility of escape only to the few and only through "self-help." It is in these terms that the new assault on the poor—embodied in the *Contract With America* and President Clinton's signing of the Personal Responsibility and Work Opportunity Reconciliation Act (PRWORA)—has been actualized into law.

Most citizens view workfare as the basis for upward mobility for the poor and therefore view welfare reform as an unmitigated success. In the midst of the celebration of the new economy, only the poor and their advocates seem to notice that this celebration excludes the poor. Thus President Clinton in his final State of the Union address declares:

> My fellow Americans, the state of our union it is the strongest it has ever been. . . .
>
> We ended welfare as we know it—requiring work while protecting health care and nutrition for children and investing more in child care, transportation and housing to help their parents go to work. . . .
>
> Every family will be able to succeed at home and at work—and no child will be raised in poverty.[3]

But the president should know that welfare reduction without poverty reduction merely increases the immiseration of the poor. Thus the report "Hunger Is No Accident" documents widespread hunger in the richest country in the world. "According to the USDA [United States Department of Agriculture], 10 million people in the United States live in households that suffer from hunger, 400,000 live in New York City alone. Such hunger exists because the Food Stamp Program is underfunded and underutilized . . . and the federal government excludes entire classes of people such as immigrants, depending on the political climate of the day and without regard to human need."[4] Other indicators of the harshness of the new poverty policy abound: the failure of workfare to find above-poverty-wage jobs for its clients, the lack of adequate and affordable housing for the poor and near poor, and the mere fact that there was no significant reduction in the number of poor people during the economic prosperity of the nineties. These failures are ignored and misconstrued by a public that sees the reduction in welfare rolls as a success.

This conservative success in managing public perceptions was embodied in the 104th Congress, which was sworn in on January 1995. Conservative Republicans organized around the *Contract* dominated this elected body, and they were mobilized to change the liberal policies of the last three decades. From their point of view, these were "a bad set of ideas" and they had to be changed. These conservative members of the House of Representatives blamed President Lyndon Baines Johnson for the current problems, seeing "welfare dependency" as an unintended consequence of Johnson's "war on poverty." The *Contract* would reverse the failures of the past, and they would introduce the Personal Responsibility Act (PRA) on their first day in office and begin the process of "ending welfare as we know it," as President Clinton had promised:

> Government programs designed to give a helping hand to the neediest of Americans have instead bred illegitimacy, crime, illiteracy, and more poverty. Our *Contract With America* will change this destructive social behavior by requiring welfare recipients to take personal responsibility for the decisions they make. Our *Contract* will achieve what some thirty years of massive welfare spending has not been able to accomplish: reduce illegitimacy, require work, and save taxpayers money.[5]

For Gingrich and his allies, the PRA would end the three decades of counter-culture welfare policy that led to dependency for the poor, reestablishing the work ethic and demolishing the culture of poverty in the name of the "opportunity society." Gingrich writes, "The people who have the most to gain from eliminating the culture of poverty and re-placing it with a culture of productivity are the people currently trapped in a nightmare . . . and living in a community where taxes and red tape and regulation destroy their hope of creating new entrepreneurial small business and doing what every other generation of poor Americans have done, which is to leave poverty behind by acquiring productivity."[6]

Somehow, the PRA's reduced welfare benefits, time limits, block grants, and workfare requirements were supposed to accomplish all this for poor people. It clearly didn't work: in a time of prosperity the income gap between the poor and the wealthy has increased,[7] and workfare has not led to real jobs or decent wages for three-quarters of its participants. Yet this failure is continuously ignored, and welfare reform is actually celebrated as a success. More important, the *Contract* inspired both parties to continue these austere welfare policies even in a time of budget surpluses. Surpluses would be translated into tax benefits for the upper classes while the suffering of the poor would just increase. Thus AFDC is ended and food stamps and public assistance greatly reduced.

The *Contract* has a surprising pedigree: it can actually be traced back to Daniel Patrick Moynihan's work on poverty in the 1960s. Though Moynihan was a committed Democrat in the Senate and was in fact critical of *The Contract*, the subtext of Gingrich's arguments corresponds to Moynihan's argument in *The Negro Family: The Case for National Action* that Negro poverty is the result of a pathological family structure and that continuously high African American unemployment is a secondary feature, indirectly caused and reproduced by the "cycle of dependency" and a "tangle of pathology."[8] Moynihan was responding to an increase in welfare enrollments, sometimes referred to as the "welfare explosion of the 1960s." Though he never used the phrase "culture of poverty," his description of the deterioration of the black family closely resembles a conservative use of Oscar Lewis' "culture of poverty" theory.[9] The power of the report was legitimated when President Johnson gave a speech at Howard University on June 4, 1965. Family deterioration and the special nature of African American poverty were a major focus: "When the family collapses it is the children that are usually damaged. When it happens on a massive scale the community itself is crippled."[10]

The Moynihan report has been controversial since it was first published in 1965. Without reviewing years of debate over the meaning of the report and Moynihan's intentions, I want to stress here the impact it continues to have on poverty policy. The report legitimated the replacement of a class argument with a racial family-pathology model in poverty policy. Its influence was based in part on Moynihan's stature as a Harvard professor and, at the time of the report, an assistant secretary in the Department of Labor and in part on the fact that it was written for the Johnson administration. Over the years other social scientists had proposed the same analysis, but now it had a federal mandate—and from a liberal administration.

The Negro Family offered a solution to racial discrimination and poverty that ignored the impact of class differences. Moynihan's solution is neither political nor economic but ultimately therapeutic: only a new governmental therapy can make the black family healthy again. If we ignore the history of slavery and discrimination and identify the problem as internal to the black family, political struggle is unnecessary and so is building a social movement to transform the society politically and economically. In fact, Moynihan disparages political and community struggles and implies that minorities cannot struggle for self-determination because they are a part of this self-perpetuating tangle of pathology. Thus he sets the stage for solving poverty and racism one family at a time. The possibility of a collective solution, a class solution, to poverty is not taken seriously. Moynihan follows the lead of Martin Deutch and Bert Brown in discounting class and arguing that the key variables are to be found in "the consistently higher frequency of broken homes and resulting family organization in the Negro group."[11] Moynihan pays tribute to the accomplishments of African Americans and acknowledges the racism in American society and "the disaster levels for 35 years" of African American unemployment,[12] but for him it isn't necessary to change American society or a racist labor market. If the ultimate problem is the internal pathology of the black family—that is, families headed by mothers, with absent fathers who supply neither income nor emotional support—the new solution is for the government to help the black family one mother, one father, at a time. The black family must be held together so that the proper socialization can be achieved and "the discipline and habits which are necessary for personality development"[13] can be provided to black children. In the language of the *Contract*, this is a model that provides the appropriate family values for the black family. Moynihan's is a self-help solution with governmental assistance. *The Contract With America* offers a self-help solution with severely time-limited government assistance.

President Clinton, who believed in welfare-to-work programs and agreed with many aspects of the *Contract*, nevertheless worked against it, believing that the Republican legislation wasn't protective enough of the poor.[14] This was a political strategy to appease African Americans and liberals, but in the end he signed the resulting welfare legislation. Moynihan had sown the seeds for the 1996 law in 1965, and Clinton and Gingrich are part of a continuous policy line that was started during the war on poverty. Even though Moynihan understood the relationship of unemployment and low wages to poverty, his focus on the "cycle of poverty" and the deterioration of the black family set the stage for over forty years of focusing on out-of-wedlock births, juvenile delinquency, narcotic addiction, psychological alienation, and isolation from the white majority. His policies failed to resolve the problem, but the fault was not his: blame the unstoppable deterioration of the black family. Moynihan concluded his analysis: "In a word: the tangle of pathology is tightening."[15]

Contrast Frances Fox Piven and Richard Cloward's *Regulating the Poor* (published originally in 1971 and updated in 1993), which stresses welfare as a social-control mechanism.[16] Welfare spending increases when the poor cause political and social turmoil and decreases when they become more passive, at which point work norms are enforced and the poor are forced back into the workforce. This seems to describe the current situation. Piven and Cloward do not deny that the black family has suffered, but this is a result of poverty and discrimination: poor blacks, in order to survive, have had to create a culture of adjusting and coping with being poor. This resembles Robert Merton's notion of anomie—a situation where norms fail to regulate human behavior—more than it resembles a pathological family structure.[17] Faced with the impossibility of economic success, the great majority of the poor try to adjust to high unemployment and terrible wages. Some do not conform, and their anomie leads to pathological forms; they become criminals, heroin addicts, and rebels.

Though Moynihan cites the unlivable $1.25-per-hour minimum wage of 1965, he emphasizes the pathological aspects of Merton's anomie theory. For Piven and Cloward, Moynihan's family deterioration thesis doesn't explain the welfare explosion of the 1960s. Moynihan saw the rising AFDC rolls as the result of an increase in the number of eligible families, most crucially the increase in female-headed families. But Piven and Cloward observe that his argument is insufficient: "even if all of the new female headed families in the period between 1959 and 1966 had received AFDC assistance, only about 10 per cent of the AFDC increases would have been accounted for. It is clear, then, that the rise in the number of families receiving AFDC cannot be explained by the rise in the number of poor families headed by females."[18]

Piven and Cloward see the origins of the welfare explosion not in the supposedly self-perpetuating tangle of pathology of the black female-headed family, but as "a response to civil disorder caused by rapid economic change—in this case the modernization of southern agriculture."[19] This resulted in a massive immigration to northern cities, where there were jobs and less discrimination and, as a result, it was easier to get public assistance. This powerful new urban black population responded politically to the inadequacies of both wages and public assistance, and, in time, the welfare bureaucracy responded by increasing public relief. Welfare is a mechanism of control in times of civil disorder and protest by the poor, a form of labor regulation when market incentives fail. It functions to discipline the workforce and to degrade and punish those who are unemployed for long periods of time. Thus, in the current setting of forced work for benefits—workfare—even an unlivable minimum wage of $5.15 an hour is preferable because welfare is so degrading. As Piven and Cloward argue: "To demean and punish those who do not work is to exalt by contrast even the meanest labor at the meanest wages. These regulative functions of relief, and their periodic expansion and contraction, are made necessary by several strains towards instability inherent in capitalist economies."[20]

Moynihan's theory exonerates capitalism, placing the problems of black poverty and the welfare explosion of the 1960s on the shoulders of the weakened black family. Such problems had to be internal to American blacks because, after all, American society was beyond reproach—a surging economy with low unemployment and high wages. Even the unionized blue-collar worker could have a middle-class life in the suburbs, proof that the American dream was open to all. If people were poor in this booming economy, it was their own fault. It became clear to Moynihan that the culture of poverty was not limited to the urban ghetto and Appalachia; the difference for the urban poor was that they were poor in the midst of abundance. What he called the "cycle of dependency" explained poverty as an internal pathology that would be difficult to cure. This was the context for Edward Banfield's claim that poverty could end only if the chronically poor died out.[21]

This tradition continues up to the present in the work of George Gilder and Lawrence Mead and, in its most pernicious form, in Richard J. Herrnstein and Charles Murray's *Bell Curve*, which attributes the position of blacks in U.S. society to their genetic structure.[22] None of these thinkers offer Moynihan's poor urban Negroes a way out. Piven and Cloward, in contrast, show a way out of Moynihan's "iron cage" of poverty: through political struggle. They have understood the problem of poverty in terms of the labor question. For them welfare is both a form of control and appeasement and a form of punishment and discipline. Welfare as a means of control and labor discipline is a social and political construct and thus can be redefined and changed through political struggle. They help us to understand the work requirement of welfare reform as a form of labor discipline and as a mechanism for maintaining low-wage jobs.

In *Poor People's Movements*, Piven and Cloward go beyond the analysis of poor people on relief to talk seriously about the self-organization of the poor into a movement to end poverty.[23] They offer an alternative to Moynihan's cycle of dependency and tangle of pathology theory and his nonpolitical, therapeutic solution to poverty.

The background to this account is the civil unrest that tore up U.S. cities from 1964 to 1968: "there were twenty-one major riots and civil disorders in 1966 and eighty-three major disturbances in 1967." In part this happened because the poor had stopped blaming themselves for their poverty and had begun to blame a society that didn't provide them with jobs. They understood that the problem was unemployment and underemployment. There was no longer any need to be ashamed of their situation; instead, they were angry at the system. The system that "denied them jobs and adequate wages did at least owe them a survival income."[24] Unlike Moynihan, urban blacks attributed their hardships to the welfare system that controlled them and supplied insufficient aid and to an American economy that reinforced their plight during the economic boom of the 1960s by offering too few jobs at decent wages. It had become obvious to both the poor and the welfare activists that more access to more money would solve many of the problems of the urban ghetto. A poor people's movement was a way to get access to living wages and to end welfare by ending poverty. Even though urban unrest in the 1960s had led to significantly better antipoverty programs incorporating education and training as well as direct relief, these programs were still insufficient and living-wage jobs were not abundant. As a result of the political struggles and the increased rights of the poor, they flocked to welfare. "In 1968, the year that rioting reached a crescendo, applications had doubled over 1960 to 1,088,000—and they exceeded one million in every year thereafter. A relief movement involving millions of participants had unmistakably emerged."[25]

Piven and Cloward give us another model for ending poverty: a political mobilization of the poor around the issues of welfare rights and adequate income, the kind of self-organization represented by the creation of the National Welfare Rights Organization (NWRO). *Poor People's Movements* presents a complex description of NWRO's successes and failures; what is important here is that its authors provide an alternative to Moynihan's model. Thus, we have one model that assumes poor people who are passive and pathological, and one that offers the possibility of building poor people's movements to end poverty. In short, Moynihan provides a model in which there are other causal variables, but ultimately the behavioral pathology of the poor is the main cause. The poor are to blame for their own poverty, not the system, and thus capitalism is never part of the causal matrix. In fact, as I have argued above, the reason for the exclusion of the poor in this society, and for the therapeutic approach to poverty, is that poverty is an indicator of the limits of capitalism. It is the "dirty little secret" of capitalism's failures, evidence that capitalism really serves the few, while the majority struggle for a decent life and the poor live between subsistence and misery. In opposition to piecemeal programs that assume the pathology of the poor, Piven and Cloward argue for continued political mobilizations to force government policy to respond to their needs. For them, the self-organization of the poor in a mass social movement is the requirement for ending poverty.

These two models frame the rest of this chapter and the two questions that are explored here. First, how did poor people live the ending of entitlements that began with "welfare reform" in 1996? More specifically, how did these drastic changes in welfare affect the everyday lives of poor people in Bedford-Stuyvesant? Second, why did most of the people who complained about these changes still accept them passively? Even people who spoke in a radical and impassioned way about them rarely got involved in political struggle to rectify the ending of their entitlements. Yet a small active fraction did respond to the new immiseration and became politically active: the WEP Workers Organizing Committee (WWOC) of ACORN, which is trying to create a union of WEP workers.

LIVING THE ENDING OF ENTITLEMENTS

Alexis de Tocqueville never walked the streets of Bedford-Stuyvesant. He never saw the concentration of poverty and racism that characterizes this neighborhood and places like it all over the United States. In 1835 in *Democracy in America* he observed inequality but stressed the enterprise of hardworking Americans as central to this new democratic society.[26] In this age of unfettered free enterprise, Tocqueville is often quoted by conservative scholars and journalists, but it is obvious that they never walked down the streets of America's ghettos either. Tocqueville, in this conservative reading of his work, never completely understood that American class and race discrimination was intractable and limited the possibility of democracy or that hard work would not always be rewarded. The neoliberalism that dominates the current economic discourse argues that the free market will solve all problems. As the poor are thrown off welfare or find welfare-to-work jobs, they will finally have the opportunity to become self-sufficient. The fact that this isn't happening seems to bother only the poor.

Soup Kitchen Thanksgiving, 1996   Thanksgiving at St. John's Bread and Life soup kitchen in Bedford-Stuyvesant is a moment of celebration every year. Turkey and all the trimmings are served.

Those who have been excluded from the economic boom have a special day and get the traditional feast.

There are 141,532 people in 1997 in City Council District 36, where St. John's Bread and Life program is located. Of these, 80 percent (112,544 people) are African American non-Hispanic; 14 percent (19,236) are Hispanic; 5 percent (7,646) are white non-Hispanic; and 1 percent (2,106 people) are Asian non-Hispanic. Between 1992 and 1996, 7,220 immigrants arrived in the 36th District. In 1998, 15 percent of 36th District residents (20,904 people) are receiving TANF; 3 percent (4,220) are receiving other safety net payments; and 8 percent (10,820) are receiving SSI.

In 1998 the AIDS epidemic continues and there are 2,613 AIDS cases, including 61 children. There is a 13.9 percent infant mortality rate, making this district the third-worst in New York City in 1997; 12 percent of all new babies are classified as low-birth-weight.

In 1997 there were 67 cases of child lead poisoning, 37 deaths due to alcohol and drug dependence, and 25 homicides. These are some of the demographics of this neighborhood, where poverty is as ordinary as apple pie, and where the median income, $27,664 in 1997, is only two-thirds of the city's median income of $43,380.[27]

The line of soup kitchen guests stretches down Hart Street and around Lewis Avenue. Both television and newspapers are here to cover the country's greatest feast day at Brooklyn's largest soup kitchen. The poor are not used to so much attention, but it is the Wednesday before Thanksgiving and soup kitchen stories have become a normal part of holiday news coverage. Some of the people do not like the exposure, while others flock to the camera. Hossein Saadat, the executive director, introduces me to a reporter from the *Daily News* who wants me to explain the kitchen's daily activities. This interview serves two purposes for us. First, it makes the soup kitchen more visible in New York City and may lead to more monetary donations. Even though our volunteer board of directors works hard to raise money and we are relatively successful at fundraising compared with other hunger programs, we are never more than a few months ahead on the rent, the utility bill, the small staff stipends, and the food we serve. Second, media attention helps us make the point that the needs of poor and hungry people are enormous, and that we help only a small fraction of them. The article comes out on Thanksgiving Day, and Lisa Sandberg concludes with: "Feeding the hungry is old hat for the St. John's Bread and Life staff; in 1996, the soup kitchen served a total of 300,000 meals to the needy."[28]

Sister Bernadette Szymcak, of the Daughters of Charity, continues to add a spiritual component to the soup kitchen, but she is ill and only comes down for brief appearances. The guests ask about her health every day. When she pays a visit, they flock to her and tell her that they love her. She will die of cancer in January 1998. Last year she was still strong enough to run the kitchen, manage the volunteer workers, make the decisions about the Thanksgiving meal, and begin it with a prayer. Now Bishop Thomas V. Daily, head of the Brooklyn and Queens diocese, says the opening prayer and serves the turkey, while the coaches, administrators, and staff members from the athletic department at St. John's University hand out utensils and napkins and serve the stuffing, cranberry sauce, vegetables, dessert, and juice. Though the university doesn't have a formal relationship with the soup kitchen, it helps with fundraising and provides faculty, staff, and student volunteers.

The soup kitchen is packed, and 1,500 people are served. This is a prosperous day for people who have been excluded from the current prosperity in American society. Poor people come with their spouses, their pre-school-age children, and their friends, or they come alone. It is rare in Bedford-Stuyvesant to see so many people having fun together. Poor people have fun, too, although they have to cope with the hardships of living in America with inadequate resources. The soup kitchen functions as a safe house for them. They get a hot meal, a place to take a nap, and most of all a place to talk with friends or even just the people they happen to be sitting next to. Most people eat their meals in seven to 10 minutes, but others sit around and talk in a leisurely way to the people eating next to them. They gossip about people, local politics, and the changes in the welfare system; they talk about the Mets or the Jets, an exciting event on *The Guiding Light* or the latest riot on the *Jerry Springer Show*, and, of course, the weather. The people in the kitchen are smiling and laughing more than usual as they stuff another spoonful of stuffing into their mouths. This is a special day at St. John's Bread and Life.

The press gets to view the kitchen on one of our best days of the year, and we will be on television and in the papers tomorrow. Some graduate students from Germany are visiting—we have had visitors from all over the United States and the world. The Germans are astonished by the magnitude of the problem. "But haven't welfare recipients been reduced in this country?" one asks. I respond, "Yes, welfare rolls have been reduced, but that just means that people no longer receive benefits. It doesn't mean that there are fewer poor people." I repeat what one poor man recently told me: "There are just more poor people on the streets trying to survive."

On a typical day at the soup kitchen in 1996, we served breakfast and lunch to 1,100 people. When workfare was introduced in New York City in 1995, our daily numbers decreased to 700–800. An improvement? Were people leaving our program for the training and good jobs promised by the Work Experience Program (WEP)? No: WEP only meant indentured service, working hard for inadequate benefits with little hope of getting out of poverty. As entitlements ended and food stamps were reduced and cut, the families who came to the soup kitchen were barely surviving and terrified about their futures. In 1998 the numbers started to increase. In January 1998 we were up to 950 people per day, and by April 1,087. In the last two weeks in April, we were up to 1,267 per day, and 1,411 people came to eat on April 28, 1998. When people in WEP are punished for a violation of the program's rules, they are sanctioned off workfare and lose all of their benefits. As WEP workers become discouraged with working just for their benefits and realize that WEP will not lead to real jobs that pay above-poverty-level wages and have benefits and job security, they leave workfare.

Though there are always fluctuations, by April 1999 the number of people coming to the kitchen begins to decrease again. By October 2000 we are averaging 611 guests per day because so many are participating in the WEP. As Kathy tells me at the soup kitchen during the Christmas 1999 meal: "Yeah, it's good to see you. I never get here anymore since I'm working in the park in Williamsburg. I have a good supervisor, and I just had to get here for this meal, and then I'll get right back to work. I miss this place. It's not the same without Sister Bernadette, but it's still a good place." She's right: the soup kitchen is not the same place. Workfare has significantly reduced the number of people who use the kitchen, though our food pantry and More Than a Meal program have expanded. We are now serving more than 500 families and individuals a week at our pantries, mostly women with children. It is already clear in 1996 that WEP isn't benefiting the poor. Who does benefit? The Community Food Resource Center (CFRC) study *Workfare: The Real Deal II* provides an answer:

> Workfare is beneficial to primarily one group—employers. Employers in the public and private, non-profit and for profit sectors are the only people that reap the benefits of a sub-minimum wage labor force with mandatory assignments and stiff sanctions for failed performance. Absent in the debate about workfare is how the vast majority of the community is adversely affected by workfare policies. The negative effects of workfare on those in the labor market far outweigh the perceived benefits to taxpayers.[29]

Workfare as a full-employment plan is supported by Mayor Giuliani at the local level and by a conservative Congress and a Democratic president at the federal level in order to ensure more workers at lower wages. Kathy, one of these WEP workers, not only has to work for her benefits but cannot extend them by taking advantage of what St. John's Bread and Life offers. Workfare has changed the needs of many of our guests, and as a result we are working at extending our pantries to over one thousand families and individuals.

Over the years Sister Bernadette has created a caring atmosphere, and people feel welcome. Sister Nora Sweeny took over the kitchen when Sister Bernadette became ill and has continued the practice. On an ordinary day Sister Bernadette or a volunteer would serve the soup and other volunteers would serve meatballs or tuna fish, salad, vegetables, dessert, and juice. On special occasions like Thanksgiving and Christmas and on ordinary days as well, the kitchen is a momentary respite from a life with few moments of peace and grace.

Jimmy waves and I walk to his table. He is an African American man in his fifties, chronically ill. He lost his benefits recently because the welfare administration said—incorrectly—that he didn't show up for training. After he received a fair hearing, his benefits were reinstated. During his 45 days without benefits, he walked around Bedford-Stuyvesant with a loaded gun. "I knew where the money is, and I'm going to get it. I thought about shooting someone, but I couldn't because I'm a good Christian."

A Hispanic women in her thirties is happy to be getting on workfare but worried about who's going to watch her children (this is a major concern for women with children). She is still receiving benefits, and yet she tells me: "Life is getting harder. I eat here at the soup kitchen because I have no money left."

The staff and the volunteers do good work at St. John's Bread and Life, but it is not enough. We serve only a small fraction of the hungry people in the neighborhood. Even on Thanksgiving too many are poor and hungry in the United States of America.

Thanksgiving is the most important holiday for emergency food providers. It is a totally American holiday that celebrates devotion to God, hard work, sharing, tolerance, and renewal, and it is linked to a feast. Soup kitchens and food pantries have special meals, give turkeys to families, and attract plenty of volunteers and media attention. By 2000 there would seem to be a lot to celebrate: the eighth year of an economic boom, unemployment rates at a 30-year low (3.9 percent). But we should remember that the Thanksgiving story is a myth and that the Native Americans who shared that first Thanksgiving meal with the pilgrims were in general the objects of scorn and violence. Here in the "Other America" of the poor, who are also the object of America's scorn and violence (given that hunger is a form of violence to the body), there isn't a lot to be thankful for. An increasing client base is overwhelming soup kitchens and food pantries.

New York City Coalition Against Hunger is about to release its annual study of emergency food programs, *Poor in the Land of Dollars*, a week before Thanksgiving 2000. In last year's survey, soup kitchens and pantries were turning away on average 2,300 people per day. This year, that has been reduced to 1,500 needy New Yorkers per day. Demand is actually up 36 percent, but pantries and soup kitchens have become more efficient in serving their clientele. The good news of this study is that the rate of increasing need is decreasing after eight years of economic growth, low unemployment, and low inflation. The bad new is that this means that the poor and the hungry have missed the prosperity of the 1990s. Half a million poor people, mostly children, have lost their food stamps in the last three years.[30]

Unemployment may be below 4 percent and more people have moved from welfare to work, cutting the rolls by 50 percent, but these jobs are low-paid, temporary, contingent, and part-time. In general, these jobs pay 70 percent of what a family received on public assistance, and the official poverty line is far below what it actually costs to survive in New York City.[31] As the 31,000 people who are in WEP move on to the inadequate training offered by Job Search or to a low-paying job, their lives aren't improved. The cost of rent, food, and childcare increases, and their wages are not equal to the paltry benefits that they received when they were on welfare. *Poor in the Land of Dollars* shows that the reduction in the welfare rolls is not the end of hunger and poverty in New York City, but an increase in misery and despair for people who can barely maintain themselves.[32] Clients are forced to make escalating demands on emergency food providers. Since more hungry clients are working, there has been a 44 percent increase in people with jobs using emergency food services. Working people cannot often make it to soup kitchens and become more dependent on food pantries on weekends. The need for pantries has grown even though there are 1,150 emergency food programs in New York City. Food providers now often speak about opening on weekends, but this will be difficult for most overworked kitchens and pantries. The increasing need for emergency food programs to provide more services has caused them to spend more time raising money for these services as the safety net has been hollowed out by federal, state, and local government cutbacks.

Of course, in all of this women and children continue to be the worst victims of poverty and hunger. Thus *Poor in the Land of Dollars* found that children count for 57 percent of the total who were turned away. As emergency food programs increase their client populations, 73 percent are families and children. In this time of economic boom, 500,000 to 600,000 people rely on pantries and soup kitchens for their meals.[33] Overwhelmed food providers try to stretch their funds by curtailing services, offering smaller portions, and turning away clients. Spending more time fundraising means that providers spend less time helping their clients. It should also be remembered that as government budgets have been cut for the poor, even during a time of budget surpluses, the emergency food network that was originally supposed to be an adjunct to food stamps has become a central component of an inadequate safety net. *Poor in the Land of Dollars* defines the limits of Thanksgiving at St. John's Bread and Life and for the poor in New York City.

HOW THE POOR WERE EXCLUDED FROM THE ECONOMIC BOOM OF THE NINETIES

From October 1996 to May 1997, aided by my graduate student, David VanArsdale, I conducted intensive, open-ended interviews with 50 guests from St. John's Bread and Life soup kitchen. During this period between 800 and 1,000 persons per day had breakfast and lunch there. Of those interviewed, almost two-thirds (62 percent) were men, and 38 percent were women. The great majority (80 percent) were African American; 12 percent were Hispanic; 4 percent were Caucasian (not Hispanic); and 4 percent were "other." Almost three-quarters (74 percent) were 30 to 49 years old; no one was under 20 or over 65. This is approximately representative of the ordinary population that regularly attends the soup kitchen. Our interviews focused on coping with scarcity, welfare reform, and workfare.

Making Ends Meet

Every informant reported that it is always hard to "make ends meet"—paying rent, having enough food to eat, and buying toiletries; 64 percent reported that it is getting harder. Seventy percent of those who receive benefits of any kind (public assistance, SSI, food stamps, unemployment compensation, etc.) responded that it is getting harder to make ends meet, as did 30 percent of those who didn't receive any benefits. As one African American man tells me: "I'm homeless, I live anyplace, all shelters, anywhere, good ones, bad ones, drop-ins. I don't support myself. I used to do odds and ends jobs, . . . before I used to live in the streets for three years." Another African American man who doesn't receive benefits and works odd jobs says: "I used to be ashamed. Now when I'm hungry I eat. I wish I had money to shop and a place to cook. I'm not bragging but I'm a good cook." He's relatively well dressed, and I ask him about his clothing. He replies: "I have what I had before I was homeless. I buy hot clothing—that's where I got this leather jacket. I sew. I had money in the past, so good clothes last." He continues: "I came here to eat. When I leave here, I'm going to another soup kitchen to eat. It's hard. I'm lucky to get odds and ends jobs. It's tough but I won't commit crimes. It's hard for me to stay right. It makes me stronger. A lady dropped a 10 dollar bill. I was tempted, but I told her she dropped it. Yeah, it's getting harder, but I don't give up—I'm an Aries."

Of those who received benefits, 14 percent reported that they worked off the books as well and still had trouble making ends meet. A 40-year-old African American man who has seven children tells me: "I get $68.50 every two weeks, $106 in food stamps, and a $153 rent subsidy. I do odd jobs on the side like contracting and painting—it varies. I do it freelance. I make just enough to put food on the table. I give what I can to my children." I ask him if it's getting harder to make ends meet. He responds, "Yes. Things are going up. If there's a job, they only pay minimum wage. I make it, odd jobs, food stamps. I go to the supermarket every day. I come here about three times a week." It is obvious to him and almost everyone at the soup kitchen that the minimum wage isn't sufficient to survive on. Thus between his off-the-book jobs and his benefits, he can just about make it. He is cheating the system, but there isn't any "Welfare Cadillac" here, just basic survival at the poverty level. The "welfare queen" who cheats by collecting more than one check is rare.[34] Working off the books is a much more typical way of cheating.

My findings are in line with Kathryn Edin and Laura Lein's study of single mothers on welfare and working at low-wage jobs. "On average," they found, "cash welfare, food stamps and SSI covered only about three-fifths of welfare reliant mothers' expenses. A small amount also came from the earned income tax credit (EITC) for wages earned in the prior year. From our conversations with mothers, we learned that they made up the remaining gap by generating extra cash, garnering in-kind contributions, and by purchasing stolen goods at below market value."[35]

The 14 percent of soup kitchen guests who didn't receive any benefits also worked odd jobs and still had great difficulty in making ends meet. A middle-aged African American man with a wife, a grown child, and an eight-month-old baby tells me: "I deliver liquor. It's currently slow. I make $300." I ask if he receives any benefits. He responds, "None." How does he make ends meet? "I find ways to keep my money coming. I do odds and ends work. I'm a jack of all trades: mechanics, painting, cooking, any kind of work."

Interviewees consistently reported that it has always been hard for poor people in Bedford-Stuyvesant to survive and that for most people it is getting harder. Soup kitchen guests are angry, miserable, and desperate despite a Wall Street boom that sent the Dow Jones average over 9,000 in 1997. A Hispanic woman tells me, "Of course, it's getting harder. I'm here at the soup kitchen 'cause I have no money left." A 40-year-old Puerto Rican woman says, "I have three children, two boys and a girl. I get $309 food stamps. I get $187 PA [Public Assistance] every two weeks. I get $156 rent subsidy, but my apartment is $500. I get WIC vouchers, I don't know how much. I would like to get a part-time job. But I can't find one, and then someone has to take care of my daughter. That's a problem." Her expenses are more than her assets, and she would like an off-the-books job so that she can keep her benefits. It's obvious to her and most people in the kitchen that to survive they need both a job and benefits. They must cheat because neither welfare nor a low-wage job is enough to support a family in New York City. This is the commonsense reality of survival for them and their families.

Welfare Reform

The Personal Responsibility and Work Opportunity Reconciliation Act (PRWORA) of 1996 ended entitlements and introduced time limits, block grants, and workfare. Not one of the soup kitchen informants believed that ending entitlements and introducing time limits are good for poor people.

People who receive benefits are worried about them and report that the headaches of the welfare bureaucracy have increased. Clients tell of being sent "here and there," of increasing frustration and confusion, and of a resultant rise in mistakes and lost benefits. They say that caseworkers are looking for excuses to terminate benefits, and rumors abound about bonuses for caseworkers who do so. "More oppression and depression," one man reports. "It's all about a New World order; the government and its people want complete control."

Many people express their fear of welfare reform by threatening to commit crimes. Thus one respondent says, "If they cut my food stamps, then I'll have to hold somebody hostage." Another warns: "Welfare reform is full of shit. I'll do anything not to starve. Cutting benefits is going to create crimes." An African American woman states: "They don't give me enough to shake a stick at. If they gonna cut it," she yells, "*cut it!* People are gonna rob and steal."

Cutting benefits is a frightening idea, and that is what welfare reform has meant for most of the guests. It is obvious to everyone at the soup kitchen, both guests and staff, that the criteria for the economic costs of daily survival are insufficient; no one can live on current benefit levels; and instead of increasing allocations, they are cutting them. And this is occurring during a time of economic prosperity. As one woman told me about her own lack of prosperity, "If food stamps were enough, do you think I would be here?"

Workfare

Workfare is a complex issue for the people I interviewed, so I deal with it separately. Half (50 percent) say that workfare is bad; 10 percent say that it is good; 26 percent didn't know or were not eligible for the program; and another 14 percent have mixed feelings. People in the last group typically say that it's fair to have people work for their benefits but that real training and skills have to be offered that will lead to a real job, with living wages and childcare for those who need it. The wage question is vital: one man who works "odds and ends jobs" is typical: "I feel that they're not getting paid properly. They're putting city people out of work. They should be paid at least a minimum wage. I would never work for that kind of money. I worked for that kind of money when I was 17 years old."

Of those interviewed, 16 percent had actual experience in the WEP, and almost all of them criticize it. A rare positive comment about the program is: "I think it's good to get people back on their feet. You get $36 extra for carfare. You be working for your benefits—it's good." Another African American man states: "You work for your benefits, it's fair. You are getting something for nothing, it's fair that you work for it. But they should get you real jobs with real pay that you can live on. But it's fair."

More often, people with WEP experience say that they are not paid enough, that city workers doing the same work are paid more money and have more benefits, that the work is hard, and that workfare doesn't lead to future jobs. These informants complain that you can be sanctioned and terminated too easily. A 52-year-old man tells his story: "I'm not allowed to work because I have arthritis and high blood pressure. I'm under care right now.... It's been hard; they cut me off... that was the hardest part. Because they say that I didn't show up for the OES [Office of Employment Services]. It's something new, but I showed up. They're giving me a fair hearing. I got a diploma from there, proof that I showed up."

Thus I ask the off-the-books painter about workfare: "They're trying to put more people to work. I'm already involved in that [WEP]. They're trying to send me to sanitation, but I'm trying to get out of that. I have a bad knee because of my accident. I think it's unfair to a certain extent because some people are unable to work and then they cut them off. I'm a painter; there's no stress or heavy lifting. So I should be assigned a job without heavy lifting.

"I think the city is getting over on this program. I'll give you an example. They want me to work sanitation six days a week from 7 A.M. to 3 P.M. for $68.50 every two weeks. Now would you say the city's getting over?" This is also commonsense knowledge in the soup kitchen: that the city is profiting from the WEP at the expense of the people who are working in the program. They have a common-sense notion of exploitation.

As workfare was introduced in New York City, the number of guests in the kitchen decreased but the number of working people and families who rely on our food pantry has increased. The WEP's unintended consequence is that people who begin to work for their benefits become aware of how "the city is getting over on them." They realize, just as if they were "practical Marxists," that they are being exploited; that is, that in terms of their own "commonsense knowledge" they are being underpaid for the value of their work and that the city is profiting from this reduction in costs. They also realize that workfare will not lead to real jobs with good wages, benefits, and job security, and they become angry. When they realize that workfare is a temporary program that doesn't benefit them in any way, most continue to conform, but some get angry enough to quit, and a few actually become political.

Some get so political that they have joined the WEP Workers Organizing Committee (WWOC), which won the right to grieve and is still fighting to become a union of WEP workers. Thus, on May 9, 2000, with Reverend Al Sharpton, Jr., in the lead, I'm marching down Third Avenue in Brooklyn next to Susanna and Bruce, two organizers for the WWOC. I fall behind because I have a broken foot, but I finally reach the Atlantic Mall by the Brooklyn Academy of Music. It is a large-box mall developed by Bruce Ratner of Forrest City Ratner. The businesses in these malls typically pay wages that are barely above the minimum ($5.15) with few to no benefits. For the WWOC, these poverty-level wages mean that people will be out of the welfare system but still poor. This is the best of all possible worlds for the Republican mayor: lower taxes because of severely reduced welfare rolls, plus the maintenance of a large pool of cheap labor.

I sit down in front of the mall as the speeches begin. The media are present: Channel One and Joyce Shelby from the *Daily News*. ACORN has a camera crew. I start to take photos as Sharpton begins to speak:

> There is probably no need to convince the people here that working people are getting the short end of the stick in New York City. We don't need economic research to tell us what we already know: Good jobs that pay living wages are hard to find. Too many working families have to choose: Will I pay the rent this month, or buy clothes

for my children, or pay the hospital bill? Families should not have to choose between shelter, health and clothing. Wall Street is experiencing an unparalleled economic boom but where is the effect in our neighborhoods? We keep hearing about a raging Bull Market that all of America is riding—well, that Bull isn't being ridden in our neighborhoods—in our neighborhoods that Bull is riding us. That Bull is using our backyard as a stomping ground.

The data tell us what we already know: In New York City, the richest 20 percent of the city's families saw their average income increase by $23,373 in the past ten years. But, the poorest 20 percent of families saw their average income decrease by $1,164 to $7,774. Middle income families have also seen their incomes fall: the middle 60 percent of families saw their average income decrease by $5,084.

And the story gets grimmer. The jobs that are being created are in sectors that pay well below the average wage.... In child day care $16,543, in individual and family services $19,208 and in retail jobs, $13,000. This trend of increasingly more and more low-paying jobs, particularly in the retail sector, is exactly why we need a living wage campaign geared to the retail sector. The culprits here are the developers of these retail outlets who receive millions of dollars in tax subsidies and city grants but do not insure that those moneys will go towards creating sustainable jobs for working families in neighborhoods where these malls are built....

We are here today to denounce these practices and to tell Bruce Ratner: We will not allow you to enslave our communities. Mr. Ratner, you must meet with us—you must come to terms with the poverty you are creating using public dollars.[36]

Michele Demilly, a spokeswoman for Forrest City Ratner, would later respond to the charges as follows:

[T]he organization has a vigorous affirmative-action program and works with communities to ensure equal employment during the development of a project.

But we have no authority to mandate how tenants hire.... It's not within our power to do this. They [ACORN] need to contact the government or the tenants.[37]

Meanwhile, the demonstration continues, with other speeches and chants: "Who are we? Who are we? ACORN! ACORN!" and "No justice, no peace."

This has been a long struggle. On April 20 I gather with the WWOC on Livingston and Court Streets to protest against another Forrest City Ratner project: a Barnes & Noble–Regal Movie Theater complex. ACORN claims that Regal Cinemas pays only slightly above the minimum wage. The demonstration flyer says, "We stand for a FAIR DAY'S PAY FOR A FAIR DAY'S WORK—Something Regal Cinemas and Bruce Ratner have never heard of before." We picket on Court Street and plan an action for the Forrest City Ratner head-quarters. Then we march down the street to 1 Metro Tech Center, where the Forrest City Ratner offices are located. We pile in, de-manding to speak to Bruce Ratner. We are told that he is out of town. We still demand to talk to him. Metro Tech's security team threatens to press charges against us. Then the police come and mediate a resolution in which the office manager promises to make Ratner aware of our demands. We leave peacefully.

At the May 9 demonstration in front of the Atlantic Mall, WWOC's chair, Eliot "Skip" Roseboro, begins: "We are here today to denounce the practices of Forrest City Ratner and its owner Bruce Ratner":

> No one knows the need for real jobs better than I do. I am currently a participant in the city's welfare to work program known as WEP. Everyday we are told to go out and look for work—and this is what we find—dead end, poverty wage jobs that will not feed a family and will insure that I and other WEP workers will stay exactly where we are at the bottom. The City is giving Ratner the money to build these malls and then trying to get welfare workers to fill them. I hold in my hand referrals from a city sponsored program called Business Link that is supposed to link welfare workers with good jobs. It is interesting that some of these referrals are to companies located in this mall and other Ratner projects. Companies like Staples—who offer wages of $6.50 with no benefits . . . or Regal Cinema who will only offer part-time work at $6.00 an hour with, once again, no benefits. These are the jobs that the City and Mr. Ratner want us to take. How will we feed our families? How will we bring our children out of poverty? How can the City give out flyers and tax dollars for jobs that will benefit no one but the employer?
>
> I am a man who stands before you ready to work but what kind of work will change my situation? I'll tell you—living wage work. You

see what we are being offered—you see the cozy "hand in hand" relationship Bruce Ratner and the City have. We are here to say No More! No More publicly funded poverty. No more low wage jobs. No more publicly funded plantations.[38]

Skip Roseboro understands that it is impossible to move out of poverty by working for poverty-level wages. He understands that the WEP's function is to maintain a large supply of low-paid workers and that developers like Bruce Ratner and companies like Staples benefit from this low-paid workforce. For leaders like Skip Roseboro, it is obvious that WEP workers must be organized and must struggle against policies that use poor people working at low wages to increase corporate profits and the attractiveness of New York City to the business community. Skip Roseboro, Mayor Giuliani, and Bruce Ratner are central players in what WWOC members call the new "plantation economy." For the mayor and the developer, it is obvious that the new development in Brooklyn is creating jobs and economic opportunity for poor people, and this is good for everyone involved. For WWOC and community leaders like Reverend Al Sharpton, Jr., this isn't obvious. This new development is dependent on a low-wage, no-benefits workforce. It only benefits the developers and the business community.

The demonstrators form a picket line in front of the entrance to the Atlantic Mall, but they do not block anyone from entering. The demonstration gets good coverage in the press and on television. Weeks later Bruce Ratner meets with members of the WWOC. They negotiate a settlement.

The struggle for living wages is crucial to the possibility of ending poverty. There are real victories, such as winning the right for WEP workers to grieve when they are being treated unfairly. The move to unionize WEP workers continues: thousands have signed union authorization cards, and, more significantly, 18,000 voted for union representation.[39] Still, it's hard to get more than a hundred WEP workers to show up at meetings and actions. WWOC's plans to organize at welfare centers and at Job Search have not yet materialized. It is hard for poor working people to find the time to struggle for better wages and benefits and against the two-tier plantation system of the new global, computer-aided capitalism. Yet this is the struggle that has to be made if poverty is going to end. The condition of a real Thanksgiving is that everyone can sit at the table in freedom and equality, and there cannot be freedom without political, social, and economic equality.

The MOM's Program

The MOM's program began in 1997, developed by Hossein Saadat, Janet Popendieck, and me. It has two components: a support group consisting of about thirty women and a food pantry that feeds 500 mothers and their children. We developed the program for poor pregnant women and new mothers and their children up to the age of two. The support group is mainly concerned with providing access to experts on health issues and child rearing, a forum for women to discuss parenting, nutrition, budgeting, domestic violence, and other issues, and group activities for mothers with limited resources. The pantry supplies food, toiletries, diapers, vitamins, toothpaste, and clothing. Over half of the women in the program are single mothers.

The MOM's program is a reaction to the feminization and in-fantilization of poverty: the fact that women and children make up the majority of the poor. In her historical study of poor single mothers, *Pitied but Not Entitled*, Linda Gordon says: "Poverty has long been feminized, particularly because women alone with children have been exceptionally poor."[40] Poor women have been stigmatized, and the stigma is transferred to the children. They are defined by society as a problem and learn to see themselves that way.

As Valerie Polakow writes, these women are labeled: "Mothers without husbands are cheap; they deserve less and if deserted, divorced, or unmarried constitute a gray and dubious category of the undeserving poor." Part of this process of public humiliation "is the discourse of benefits—food stamps that brand her, visibly humiliate her, in the supermarket, welfare offices that regulate her sexual relationships and judge her mothering as at risk."[41]

Scarcity increases the degradation that poor women continually suffer. In the operation of the More Than a Meal program, I observe the way in which poor people are made to feel like beggars. St. John's Bread and Life provides basic products, from toiletries to clothes, for people who are registered in the program. A woman is angry because the program's administrator tells her that she cannot receive her package for four months. The woman argues that she didn't skip her prior appointment—she left because she was told that the administrator was too busy. When she came back later, it was still too crowded. The administrator repeats that the schedule is full until March 20. The woman angrily says that she shouldn't have to wait for four months and doesn't want the package anymore.

Another woman is waiting. She sits down immediately and asks if she can have shoelaces. She picks up her pants leg and shows the administrator that she is wearing shoes without laces. The administrator says that they don't stock laces. The woman then asks for a turtleneck shirt because it's so cold. She is told that she must wait until her scheduled appointment or try the church thrift store. The women replies, "But I don't have any money." The administrator tells her to see Sister Rosemary—maybe she can help.

The administrator is doing her job. The More Than a Meal program has limited resources, and it serves the MOM's program and men and women guests in the soup kitchen. "It would be chaos if we didn't have these bureaucratic procedures," the administrator tells me. "We don't provide emergency packages. If we did, everyone would want special treatment. I know it's unfair to that women who missed her appointment, but we have to follow the procedures." Still, dealing with welfare and soup kitchen bureaucracies is one of the hidden injuries of poverty. Even when they are right, the under-privileged are often denied what they have been told they are entitled to. Even when wronged, they still have to abide by the standards of middle-class civility. They are not allowed to be angry. In fact, anger only proves to the middle-class administrator that this lower-class black woman is wrong. The administrator is always civil, and her civility allows her to deny this client what she deserves without taking any responsibility. Here, civility doesn't allow for better communication; it merely facilitates bureaucratic procedures that control and deny the rights of lower-class people. Similarly, poor people applying for food stamps or benefits at the welfare center are forced to behave with middle-class civility while they are being degraded. Both the More Than a Meal and MOM's programs provide important aid within the limitations of the scarce resources of St. John's Bread and Life, and they try to provide services with kindness and dignity. Still, St. John's Bread and Life too often reproduces the class relations of this society, where the poor remain poor and are often civilly degraded, carrying on lives circumscribed and controlled by bureaucracies. Impersonal administrators and clerks following bureaucratic procedures decide whether they will receive the aid they need for bare survival. The experience of poverty is always the experience of scarcity, of living with less than you need. In a consumer society centered on buying and owning new products, the poor almost never have anything new. They have a second-rate life, and if they have something new, it is usually cheap and of inferior quality. Having something new that isn't cheap leads to suspicions of cheating and other irregularities, and fear of being unjustly investigated and sanctioned. The poor are faceless in these bureaucracies, and they know that they can be sanctioned—that is, excluded from receiving benefits—by welfare workers who have been given a mandate to reduce the rolls. Thus Mayor Giuliani gloated: "Over the past four years we've moved 410,000 people off the welfare rolls—more than the entire population of St. Louis."[42] (Giuliani exaggerated his success. In 1994, 18 percent of New Yorkers received AFDC, TANF, SSI, or other welfare benefits; by 1998, it was down to 16 percent—a 2 percent decline in four years.)[43] The mayor and his Human Resources Commissioner, Jason Turner, refused to give out food stamp applications and in general slowed down the bureaucratic process, keeping 800,000 eligible New Yorkers from receiving them. Judge William H. Pauley 3d of Federal District Court in lower Manhattan barred the Giuliani administration from continuing to deny applications for food stamps.[44] Still, this harassment of the poor is all too common in New York City and the country as a whole.

The woman who missed her appointment is expressing the anger of a human being who faces scarcity every day of her life. It's a life where dignity and kindness are also scarce. It's a life where she is forced to refuse the More Than A Meal package that she depends on to preserve her dignity. This is the life of most ordinary poor people—one where they are constantly reminded that beggars can't be choosers.

Valerie Polakow writes about the resilience of single mothers and their children.[45] Certainly many of the mothers in the MOM's program are resilient, but their diverse lives include quiet desperation and isolation, as well as anger. Sometimes there is optimism and even happiness. Thus, Daphne, a 25-year-old white woman who lives in Bushwick, tells me: "The MOM's food pantry, it's helped me a lot. It provides three to four days' supply of formula, regular food, and things that don't go bad, and it's not junk. It's things that you need. Other pantries give you things that you don't need. Here it's stuff that you actually use—diapers, baby wipes, baby food, everything. And that stuff runs into money. Diapers and formula are the most expensive because stores know you need it and you'll buy it."

Daphne's husband is in drug rehabilitation, and she has two girls, a two-year-old and a two-month-old baby. Her rent is $804, of which she gets $754 from Section 8 housing assistance. Her family also receives $226 in public assistance every two weeks and $391 per month in food stamps. She says, "It ain't easy, it's not. You figure everything—food, diapers, carfare—it's very difficult. My grandma helps me. More Than a Meal helps a lot because those are things I would have to pay cash for."

I ask if it's getting harder to make ends meet. She says, "Yeah, another baby. This one is making it harder. They only increased PA [public assistance] less than $50. Clothing, they grow so fast, it's harder."

I ask Daphne about feeding her family. "I'm OK foodwise. The food stamps at $391 a month ain't too bad. The food pantry helps a lot; you get a bag every two weeks, rice, potatoes, diapers, wipes." Feeding a family of four on $391 per month is unimaginable, but poor mothers become experts at extending the family food budget in many ways, including eating as much as possible at the soup kitchen and shopping carefully. "Edwards [supermarket]—they're the best, they're the cheapest, double coupons. It's a long walk and cabs cost $3 to get home, but it's worth it. I go once a month.

I spend about $299 to $225, and the rest of the stamps go for odds and ends, bread, butter, Chinese food. Chinese restaurants take food stamps. I go there once a month." Paying for food at the Chinese restaurant is technically cheating, but Daphne and her family want to eat at restaurants as ordinary American families do. Daphne continues, "I've got a restaurant card for the McDonald's on Myrtle and the Popeye's on 14th Street in Manhattan. When I was in the shelter system, I used the one at the Allerton Hotel. I buy a lot when I shop: the meat stays for three months in the freezer. I buy chopped meat, chicken, pork chops, milk, eggs, rice, potatoes, Rice-a-Roni, but mostly store brands, like Finast Rice."

I ask about her apartment, and she tells me the following story. "It took about 14 months to get this apartment. I was in the shelter system for 14 months. It was August of '96. . . . I had no lights, no gas, and the junkie downstairs broke the door down, and I was pregnant with my two-year-old. . . . It was summer and I just hung out. In December I got back into the shelter, and I was five months pregnant. My daughter was only three pounds, 14 ounces when she was born. She was born early with a hole in her stomach. She's OK now, just a little hyper. This one was six pounds—we knew about her."

Were her benefits ever cut off? "They were cut when I first started coming here. I wasn't getting anything; they totally shut my case down, March 1998. They said I failed to recertify, but they sent papers to the shelter and I wasn't there. I was living in my new apartment for six months." Just as she finally got a new apartment by continually struggling for it, her resiliency allowed her to fight for herself and get a fair hearing. As in most fair hearings, she won and got her benefits back. People on welfare who aren't resilient often just give up.

I ask Daphne what she does for entertainment. "I have no social life," she replies. "I sit on the stoop with friends. In January I went to the movies on my wedding anniversary to see the Jerry Springer movie. My two-year-old watches TV. I watch *Wheel of Fortune,* and *Jerry Springer.*" "I have no social life" sums up the experience of women in the MOM's program: poor people rarely go out. The most frequent answer I get from these mothers is that they spend a lot of time playing with their children. Thus another woman in the

MOM's program tells me: "We watch *Sesame Street* with the kids. We make a tent out of a sheet and play. We take them to the park. We play cards or dominoes. We took them [her toddler, twin girls, and stepdaughter] for their first restaurant meal at Burger King. We got two kids' meals and chicken nuggets. The burger didn't go over well. We plan to take them again. We were going to take them to Junior's, but my fiancé said, 'Boy, are you expensive.' We almost do very little, but I like to take the twins. We go on picnics, and someone put ketchup on the frank, and did they make a mess!"

These poor women spend lots of time with their children. In a culture where most women with children have to work, the joys of spending time with young children are too often missed. The value for the children of spending time with their parents is missed as well. As Arlie Russell Hochschild writes, "The idea of more time for family life seems to have died, gone to heaven and become an angel of an idea."[46] You would think, in a culture that stresses "family values," that people would have mobilized for shorter hours with higher wages and for daycare, but they haven't.

I ask Daphne about the support group. She tells me: "When I first started the support group in October [eight months ago], we just sat around and bullshitted. But now they have speakers and programs on children with asthma, daycare. They're having a zoo trip at Prospect Park. You're with a lot of people whose problems are a lot worse than yours. They talk about food stamps now for only five years and workfare. I've made friends. I brought my sister-in-law here; it's her second week. We have guest speakers and eat and talk amongst ourselves. Of course there are cliques, but it's great to talk. I get things off my chest. Otherwise I would be screaming at my husband and my neighbors.

"When I first started coming here I was real angry because my life was all screwed up. But no matter how angry I was, there was always someone here to listen and help me. This was Grandma's church when she was young. Believe it or not, I've told her I'm going to take her here."

Daphne found her dignity in the MOM's program. Liegia found friends there. She is 30 years old, African American, and lives in the

Eleanor Roosevelt Houses across the street from the soup kitchen. She has two daughters (ten and one and a half); she does not live with their father. Liegia praises the support group: "I think it's a wonderful program. It helps us women help ourselves. I learn a lot by sitting in the groups. The food helps . . . and people help me with my problems. They have a doctor here that I use. They talk about things that happen every day, and you get solutions to what you can do.

"The speakers are great. The speakers that come in teach us about diabetes, childcare. They give us insights into things you didn't know. There are some great moms in here. It's like an extended family in here. You talk to them, and they become your friends. It's good for me because I don't have many friends."

I ask how she supports herself. "I used to be on public assistance but I got cut off, so now I work. I was cut off because they said I wouldn't comply with the WEP program. But I have skills and I didn't want to work for nothing. I work at Urban Strategies: Runaway Assistance Program. It's a runaway and crisis center for youth. I am a counselor there. I make $5.15 per hour. That's better than WEP. You don't get benefits until after three months. I work 30 hours per week. My oldest daughter is in school, and my mom takes care of the youngest. I get no other assistance, no food stamps. I've been working there since April [almost three months]."

I ask about workfare. "I never went on WEP, but I was in their BEGIN program. BEGIN is where they teach you skills for workfare, but that didn't work. I learned more in this church than there.

"Before the WEP thing I received public assistance: $92.25 every two weeks, $180 in food stamps and they paid my $117 rent. . . . I was angry because they wanted me to comply to a program [WEP] that wouldn't help me. When I could get the same job and get paid for it. WEP is a very manipulative program, and you get nothing out of it. . . . I know several people who either lost their food stamps or who had them reduced because they were sanctioned by WEP. If you didn't comply with WEP, I thought they were to sanction just you, but they took my kids off too, and the way they're going it affects the whole family."

Liegia tells me how she makes ends meet: "By working I pay the rent, I buy food. The MOM's group gives me a bag of food every two weeks. I shop at Junior's supermarket on Myrtle. I shop there once a month. I buy meats from there, I buy juice, potatoes, because I get rice here, cans here, pasta, spaghetti here. I have to budget carefully."

"How do you pay your rent?"

Liegia replies, "I pay it every two weeks. I pay $58.50 at the beginning of the month and $58.50 at the end of the month. As long as it's consistent like that, it's easier. I don't have to pay the whole thing at the beginning of the month, so I'm not short at the end of the month."

I ask her where she shops for clothes. "I shop at the thrift store around the corner, and More Than a Meal gives clothes. I never go to big department stores. I can get three times as much outfits at the thrift store. They have decent things there."

In general Liegia keeps to herself: "I don't mess with too many people. I take my kids to the park and when they're finished we go home. . . . We watch TV, play games with kids, read books, and listen to music. We don't go to the movies—$7 a person—but we did receive passes from the Bread and Life program. I saw *Enemy of the State* with Will Smith."

I ask her how she has been affected by the country's economic boom. "It has an impact on everyone," she responds. "Since Wall Street is doing so well, I should be doing better than $5.15 an hour. They say there's jobs, but they want a degree, they want this and they want that. I've enrolled in school, but then you still have to take out loans. I didn't want to take out loans, so I left." Most mothers say that the national prosperity hasn't affected them in any way. Many of the mothers are shocked by the question: they are unaware of the boom and the low unemployment rate. Thus one mom answers, "No, I haven't heard that Wall Street is booming." Another mother says, "It ain't booming for me. I don't see it." Another answers: "I haven't benefited. Basically there's a lot of cutbacks on welfare. They're only giving me what I need to support my family. . . . Jobs are hard to find without a diploma or a GED." Responses like the following are rare: "Yes, because a lot of people are working and they don't need welfare. On the street there's no thieves or robbing and all that. Things are getting better." The great majority of mothers respond differently.

I ask Liegia how she will make her life better. "A college degree and a better-paying job. I'd like to go into business management. I'm planning to go back in the near future. I'm looking into Long Island University, but it's very expensive." This is a very typical answer: these women plan to get their GEDs, go to college, get better-paying jobs, and get off welfare. One very optimistic mother says: "I'm probably going to start college in September, New York City Tech in Hospitality and Hotel Management. I plan to get married soon. My fiancé is a kindergarten teacher. We plan to stay in New York City for now."

Also atypical are political answers: "Protest to make minimum wage higher. I always made more than minimum wage." Another mom answers: "Find a way to make some extra money. Just can't wait until Mayor What's-his name is out of office. I didn't think things were hard until he got in, and then he gives himself a raise."

The support group that Daphne and Liegia value so much is only a small part of the MOM's program. The great majority of the women come for the food pantry and More Than a Meal. For most of these women, childcare, finishing school, finding a job, or working in WEP creates many difficulties. Some are resilient, and some are not. Nona, a 28-year-old African American woman with two daughters and three sons, is in the nursing program at LaGuardia Community College. She tells me about her experience with WEP when I ask if she has been affected by welfare reform: "Yes, but I told them I wasn't working because I can't get a babysitter. Then they wanted me to go to their person and I'm not sending my kids to anyone, there's too much going on. So they sanctioned me, they took away my money. That's why we get so little PA and the food stamps too [$207 every two weeks]; it's only the kids' [benefits]. Thank God they still pay the rent [$157 for a five-room apartment in the Sumner Houses], and they left me my Medicaid. I put in for a fair hearing. They said they will find me a babysitter—it doesn't matter if I don't like them. They said, if I don't work, I don't get money. Well, I'll have my degree soon, and I will be able to do what I want.

"If I do what I'm supposed to do, get that degree and take care of the kids myself and not have to answer to anybody, then I'll get my relief. I mean, welfare, they stay on your back. They have to know everything. You get a dollar from your relative, they have to know. You win a fair hearing and they still send you down to the investigative unit and they check you for lies. They want to know everything. . . . It's like you always being punished for other people who have cheated. But everyone shouldn't be punished. They play a psychological game. I don't want it no more. They purposely get on your nerves until you say, 'Leave me alone, I don't need you.' "

Nona's experience of continual harassment by the welfare system is common. She is punished because she is concerned about the quality of childcare that her children will receive. In New York City, workfare was implemented with inadequate daycare. Women with children who become part of WEP have to make a decision between good daycare and keeping their benefits. Nona's college education gave her more options than most single mothers, but she was still made to suffer because she questioned the competence of the care her children were offered.

If this wasn't enough for poor mothers to cope with, many of them also have to deal with domestic violence and other familial disruptions. This is a problem across the country and for all class and racial categories. In the United States in 1997, 10 percent of all rapes and sexual assaults were committed by relatives and 38 percent occurred at home. The same is true about familial disruptions, such as divorce. There were 870,600 divorces in 1997. Actually the divorce rate went down in the United States during the economic boom of the 1990s, from 4.7 per thousand in the population to 3.3 per thousand.[47] Mark Robert Rank writes about the causes of familial disruptions:

> What does appear to be of the utmost importance is the condition of living and growing up in poverty and hardship. . . . To a large extent recipients follow in their parents' footsteps; however, this is not because children learn from their parents the easy life of welfare. . . . Rather, their educational and occupational opportunities have been severely limited as a result of parental financial constraints.[48]

The stories of women with children who are living at the Family Project domestic violence shelter give us a sense of the struggles such women have to overcome just to have a normal life. A 22-year-old Dominican woman with two girls gets $109 every two weeks from public assistance and $187 in food stamps per month. She comes to the food pantry and the support group. "I'm separated from their father.... The abuse was more mental than physical. He just didn't provide for the childs, still doesn't provide for the childs." She has completed two years of college and plans to become a lawyer. She cannot participate in WEP while she is at the domestic violence shelter. "I has to go to appointments and that takes money; I have to go to court and that's expensive, because of the father's abuse. The pampers, how much the kids eat and clothing, it's always more expensive.... It's not easy, but I'm getting through. The expense of the kids is not easy."

The second woman also lives at Family Project. She is a 20-year-old Puerto Rican with a two-year-old girl. She has a "new budget because I'm living at the shelter. I've been getting $234 every two weeks [for her and her baby]. It will probably be reduced to $140 because my rent will be taken out [of the calculation] at the shelter. Food stamps [$212] will probably be increased. It's not enough, y'know, because I used to live with my mother and I didn't pay rent." Even though she has an order of protection against her husband, she can't live with her mother because "he knows where she lives." She tells me: "I can't move back with my mother because he will be looking for me there. I don't want to go into the same situation. I want to live independent and get my own apartment. I don't want to get into the situation with my husband. He harasses me, yells, and even hits me."

These women need a lot of support and nurturing to make it. They have both economic and emotional problems, and Family Project and the MOM's program are helping as much as they can. The MOM's support group can accommodate only a limited number of women: it would be difficult economically even to extend it to 60 mothers. More help is required, and only the government can fulfill that need.

THANKSGIVING 2000

I take the B54 bus down Myrtle Avenue to Lewis. I get off the bus at Lewis Avenue and walk to Hart Street on this cold, clear November day. A line runs up the alley to the soup kitchen. It's covered by a scaffold, while St. John the Baptist Church undergoes renovation. The soup kitchen is already packed with people waiting for the meal to begin.

I have been taking the bus down Myrtle Avenue or walking to the soup kitchen for almost 13 years. Over the years St. John's Bread and Life has grown from a soup kitchen to a large multiservice organization. Though the soup kitchen still defines the program, the pantries already feed over 500 families per week and will continue to grow. Since Sister Bernadette passed away, Sister Nora Sweeny has done an excellent job of running the soup kitchen. Though Bea, Ozzie, and May no longer work there, Jim still does, and Sylvia and the rest of the paid staff are doing very good work. Eight members of the HIV Support Group have died.

John passed away on August 22, 1999. The chapel was packed, and there were many touching eulogies. John had overcome so many obstacles: a serious drug addiction, the loss of his family, severe health problems. Ultimately, a seizure brought on by a congenital brain disorder would kill him. John had gone back to school and worked at the soup kitchen as supervisor of the stock room. The continuing pressure of trying to straighten out his life overwhelmed him. As impressive as his personal transformation was, there was always something else that he had to work on. He could never relax. He eventually fell into a deep depression and, without the medical care that he required, he died. In the last few months of his life, he neither answered his phone nor returned messages. Hossein told me that there were 92 unanswered messages on John's answering machine.

Still, over the years John had helped many poor and homeless people with their problems. At the funeral mass, many of these people testified about how he had helped them and changed their lives. John liked to refer to himself as "just a street person," just another ordinary poor person. He was smart and very stubborn; it was hard for him to listen to advice, even his doctor's. Hossein said: "He would make up his mind about something and then even God couldn't change it. He just wouldn't listen to anyone. The pressure from work and school was just too much for him."

John was given a proper funeral, paid for by a board member. His story shows the limits to the individual resilience of the poor. More often than not they are overwhelmed by the hardships they face in their individual struggles for survival in a very wealthy United States that excludes the poor from its economic treasures and cultural life.

On this Thanksgiving, Bishop Thomas Daily walks up to the people who are seated and waiting for the meal to begin. Everyone is hungry and the wonderful smells of the turkey, stuffing, vegetables, and dessert have made them impatient. He silences the crowd, and this big man who is the bishop begins to speak: "Hello, everybody. We have to pray, and I can pray because I am the bishop of Brooklyn and Queens." In a big, boisterous voice he begins the prayer: "Dear God—and I can say dear God because we are in God's presence.... This is a happy place, so smile and be happy today."

The bishop and the St. John's University basketball team serve food to over 1,300 people. The press is here. NBC-Channel 4's sports reporter, Bruce Beck, does a segment on the basketball team helping out at the soup kitchen.

Sister Connie is helping to keep the long line orderly. "Everyone is so patient," she remarks to me. Just then a man yells out, "We got a line like a mother." Another guest says hello and asks me, "Why are Thanksgivings always so cold?" Another man says, "You don't know what the kitchen means to us in the community. I remember when you were over on Willoughby. I've been going here for a long time. You do a lot for this community, bringing the basketball team and all you do at Christmas, all the turkeys. You've helped a lot of people in this community. Happy Thanksgiving."

St. John's Bread and Life has done a lot for the community and plans to do more—possibly a weekend pantry. Yet all this help still isn't enough. Public assistance, food stamps, low-wage jobs, and all of the aid from St. John's Bread and Life is still not enough. All of the hard work and individual resiliency will barely be noticed, and the great majority of these poor people will remain poor. Though the neoliberal free market theorists emphasize individual solutions to poverty, these work only for the very few. Nor is the liberal strategy to save the safety net the solution. If poverty is to end, a poor people's movement is required: one that will struggle for a middle-class wage with middle-class benefits and a real education that would provide the skills and credentials needed for "new economy" jobs. This is the way to end poverty in the United States. If this occurred, we could finally have a real Thanksgiving.

However, this poor people's movement isn't happening, even though all the conditions for it exist. In the next two chapters I attempt to answer this most important question: why is there no poor people's movement to end poverty in the United States?

4   The Dialectic of Sister Bernadette

The Limits of Advocacy

If there are any who thought they joined this congregation only to preach the gospel to the poor but not to comfort them, only to support their spiritual needs but not their material ones, to them I say this. We should assist the poor in every way and do it both by ourselves and by enlisting the help of others.

> —Vincent de Paul, quoted in Thomas McKenna,
> *Praying with Vincent de Paul*

A sphere that does not stand partially opposed to the consequences, but totally opposed to the premises of the German political system; a sphere finally that cannot emancipate itself without emancipating itself from all other spheres of society, thereby emancipating them; a sphere in short, that is the complete loss of humanity and can only redeem itself through the total redemption of humanity. This dissolution of society existing as a particular class is the proletariat.

> —Karl Marx, *Critique of Hegel's 'Philosophy of Right'*

IN NOVEMBER 1988, the day before George H. W. Bush is elected president, the soup kitchen (still on Willoughby Street) is very crowded. At 12:30, we run out of food half an hour before closing, when people are still waiting on line. Sister Bernadette—knowing that we hadn't any food left and that we would be unable to feed the people waiting outside—loses it. This very competent woman who prepares food for over a thousand people a day starts to scream. She knows what a disaster Reaganomics has been for the poor. It is obvious to her that continuous cuts in spending have increased the everyday misery of the people in the soup kitchen. At one point she goes from table to table to tell people to vote for the Democratic candidate, Michael Dukakis. Now she screams: "Four more years of Reagan! Four more years! How will we survive?"

This is the dialectic of Sister Bernadette, and these are the contradictions of social welfare in a free market capitalist society. Sister Bernadette knew that the need in Bedford-Stuyvesant and the surrounding areas in Brooklyn was immense, and that the food and other services she provided were essential to reduce people's misery. She was also aware that the St. John's Bread and Life Program is a Band-Aid. All of the soup kitchens, food pantries, and other services run by the state or the nonprofits do not begin to meet the needs of the poor people of New York City.

Sister Bernadette and the rest of us deal with the consequences of poverty and only rarely with the premises of this condition. She knew that feeding more than a thousand people a day took all of her time and energy. Spending all her time providing food and services meant that she spent very little time helping to mobilize the poor politically. But if the poor do not become political, their condition only worsens. The soup kitchen doesn't provide political alternatives; it can do no more than feed people and help them to retain their benefits. Sister Bernadette's frustrated refrain of "four more years of Reagan" expressed her understanding of the limits of what can be accomplished through charity and entitlements. People lined up on Willoughby Street then; 10 years later, the lineup continues on Hart Street. She understood that poor people's failure to mobilize and construct an alternative has led to ever-worsening conditions. Since there is no movement of the poor to force political and social change, benefits continue to be reduced. Even the government deserted them: a Democratic president, William J. Clinton, who was supposed to be their friend, signed the Personal Responsibility and Work Opportunity Reconciliation Act (PRWORA), terminating entitlements, instituting block grants, term limits, and workfare, and removing immigrants from the system. Immiseration increases, and more people are forced to use the services of soup kitchens and food pantries.

As funding is cut for the poor, Hossein Saadat and the kitchen's board of directors must figure out creative ways to fund the programs and increase services. Even less time is spent on poverty politics. As more people come to the door who require more services because of the new requirements of welfare reform, St. John's Bread and Life has been trapped in an endless cycle of funding cutbacks, mounting demands for more diverse services, program expansions requiring more money, and yet another round of fundraising.

In her important work, *Tyranny of Kindness,* Theresa Funicello recognizes the contradiction but comes to the wrong conclusion. She understands that charities and social welfare agencies often serve to maintain the immiseration of the poor. Money that should be going directly to the poor through a guaranteed income instead spawns soup kitchens and shelters and also creates poverty bureaucracies. She contends that these agencies provide jobs for middle-class advocates who misuse and waste both government monies and private donations: "The charities old and new, food distributors, shelter providers and the rest are ill suited to care for poor people—especially families with children. They are driven by the logic of self perpetuation which almost without fail leads to a relentless pursuit of government contracts and donated dollars."[1]

Although Funicello blames the charities and the social welfare agencies, the problem is really the result of a much larger bureaucratic system. She sees corruption—specifically the behavior of individual advocates—as the problem. She overlooks the larger interests that benefit from the artificial reproduction of poverty and the part played by global capitalism and the new technologies that have destroyed decent jobs through automation and computerized displacement. She is willing to blame the state but fails to see how diminished it is. Her analysis highlights both the state and the nonprofit sector, but it ignores the role of both national and global capital.

Funicello uses a commonsense notion of bureaucracy as corrupt and inefficient. This is an insufficient critique. She doesn't take into consideration the fiscal pressures that force service providers and advocacy groups to adopt a corporate model. As she notes, scarce resources and the everyday requirements of running an agency under the conditions of dependency on large contributors, whether they are states or private foundations, restrict their flexibility. The real problem of agencies is that in adopting the corporate model, they function like any bureaucratic organization. Emergency food programs, created to meet what was seen as a temporary crisis caused by Reagan's budget cuts, have become permanent bureaucratic organizations. They developed boards of directors, executive directors, and professional staffs. They became formal hierarchical organizations that administered contracts, implemented programs, became sophisticated at fundraising, and even developed political initiatives. Increasingly crucial for the professional staff is its special knowledge of the emergency food network, housing regulations, welfare procedures and regulations, the writing of foundation grants, and networking with foundation administrators.

The emergency food network and antipoverty advocates evolved into a bureaucratic world where "the devil is in the details" because the maintenance of these agencies depends upon them. But this also resulted in a diminished political vision and a loss of the broader goal of ending poverty. The goals of these agencies became practical: the maintenance of the "safety net" and a reduction of the misery of the poor. In the world of antipoverty agencies, the broader vision became utopian and impractical, especially in the face of the successful conservative attack on the poor embodied in PRWORA. The organizational requirements make it politically difficult either to have an alternative vision to current poverty policy or to act. Thus when I participate in an advocacy group planning a demonstration at the Stock Exchange, we must do an informal cost-benefit analysis of the political outcomes. Will gaining a lot of publicity for our cause outweigh the possibility that some corporate funds will be lost because we offended a foundation or corporate donor who doesn't agree with our political strategy? When advocacy groups discuss political actions, they have to take into account the chances of a negative impact on fundraising. They depend on external funding for their survival, and political activism can seriously hurt their ability to raise money from the government and the private sector. Now that the state has been hollowed out, we are increasingly dependent on "the kindness of strangers."

Welfare reform has ended entitlement programs except for food stamps. Both Democrats and Republicans hope that the nonprofits will eventually replace government programs for poor people as the "new safety net"—a task that the nonprofits recognize as impossible. As Julian Wolpert has observed:

> The critical question is, will donations increase enough to fill the void left by federal cutbacks? The evidence strongly indicates that they will not. The real increase in donations was only 0.5% overall in 1993. . . . Other estimates range as low as 1 to 2%. Even if donation levels were to rise substantially, only a modest share of the gain would likely be channeled to assist the most disadvantaged groups. Higher giving rates typically benefit higher education, culture, and the arts more than social services.[2]

Many nonprofits have tax-exempt status under section 501(c)3 of the Internal Revenue Code. On one hand, the code provides favorable tax treatment for nonprofits; on the other, it prevents them from engaging in partisan politics: either endorsing political candidates or participating in political campaigns and electioneering. They are reduced to limited lobbying, nonpartisan voter registration, and education.[3] Movement building requires partisan politics, but section 501(c)3 has made this impossible.

How, in any case, can advocates find the time for politics when they are running the agency, providing services, maintaining the physical structure of the facility, raising funds, writing grants, dealing with clients, and handling board and neighborhood problems? These activities take up almost all of the time of (generally poorly paid) administrators, staff, and volunteers. In this situation political work is often carried on as a defensive action: it's what you are forced to do when the federal, state, or city budget is cut again. This defensive posture explains the narrow vision of antipoverty advocates. They are bogged down in the practicalities of what they believe to be possible and have only a short-term view of the world. Movement building and ending poverty and hunger are always put on the back burner, and saving the ever-dwindling safety net becomes the highest priority. The piecemeal politics of advocacy groups and their tiny victories obscure the possibility of real change—of reversing the sea change that produced "welfare reform" in 1996. Thus, advocacy groups will organize an action in New York City or Albany to lobby politicians about the misery that cuts in public assistance will cause the people of Bedford-Stuyvesant or Brownsville. Advocates and some poor people will go to public hearings, where they will wait for hours in order to testify for three minutes while the politicians walk in and out of the hearing room. This is piecemeal politics: trying to maintain an insufficient welfare system while the state gets hollowed out.[4]

When nonprofits replace the social services that were once provided by the government, this is not an equal tradeoff. Government programs do a better job. A better food stamp program would make emergency food programs unnecessary. Janet Poppendieck calls the process in which charity replaces government programs the "Wenceslas syndrome," after the old Christmas carol. This is

> the process by which the joys and demands of personal charity divert us from more fundamental solutions to the problems of deepening poverty and growing inequality, and the corresponding process by which the diversion of our efforts leaves the way wide open to those who want more inequality, not less. The Wenceslas syndrome is not just something that happens to individuals and groups that become deeply involved in charitable activity; it is a collective process that affects our entire society as charity replaces entitlements and charitable endeavor replaces politics.[5]

What Poppendieck describes is the endless cycle of a manufactured permanent crisis. Charity is less effective than the inadequate government programs that it replaces, and it reduces politics to charitable fundraising. She explains why advocates are in a permanent problem-solving mode as crisis after crisis must be confronted and resolved. On one hand the agency is trying to provide more services as the government provides fewer benefits. On the other, the nature of the services is constantly changing. Thus the workfare component of the PRWORA means that fewer poor people can stretch their food stamps by eating free lunches at soup kitchens, increasing the demand for food pantries and forcing nonprofit programs to expand them. St. John's Bread and Life has already expanded its pantry to serve over five hundred families and plans to accommodate a thousand families on a biweekly basis. Bread and Life is also investigating the possibility of serving dinner from Monday through Friday and of serving breakfast and lunch on Saturdays—an expensive undertaking that would require more food, more space, and a higher rent to St. John the Baptist Church.

At the same time, all institutions have internal problems. There are power struggles between board members for control over the organization. There are differences between the administrators over the size and the scope of the mission. Nor does the board of directors always agree on the need to get involved in poverty politics. For some, helping the poor is in the tradition of Christian charity and brings you closer to God, even if it does nothing to end poverty. Organizations often founder as a result of these internal strains.

Between the bureaucratic structure of advocacy institutions, the continuous problem-solving mode of operation, fundraising, and the maintenance of their tax-exempt status, political activity is minimized. The advocates' meager political vision does not encompass anything broader than going back to the old welfare state. They haven't forgotten that it was insufficient and oppressive to poor people, but it was better than "the end of welfare as we know it." At the same time, they do not have an alternative vision of how to end poverty because the bureaucratic mindset gets in the way.

THE BUREAUCRATIC MIND AND THE PRIMACY OF ORGANIZATIONAL GOALS

The bureaucratic mind limits the vision of advocates and their organizations. As Karl Marx tells us about the "mind of bureaucracy":

> The bureaucracy is a circle from which no one can escape. Its hierarchy is the hierarchy of knowledge. The highest point entrusts the understanding of particulars to the lower echelons, whereas these, on the other hand, credit the highest with an understanding in regard to the universal; thus they deceive one another.... Accordingly authority is the principle of its knowledge and its being and the deification of authority its mentality. But at the very heart of bureaucracy this spiritualism turns into crass materialism, the materialism of passive obedience, of trust in authority, the mechanism of an ossified and formalistic behavior, of fixed principles, conceptions, and traditions.[6]

Though Marx is explaining the state bureaucracy, as Max Weber tells us this description applies to all bureaucracies, including the corporate and, in the current context, the nonprofit ones as well. "The development of modern forms of organization in all fields is nothing less than identical with the continual spread of bureaucratic administration," Weber tells us. "This is true of church and state, of armies, political parties, economic enterprises, interest groups, endowments, clubs, and many others. . . . If bureaucratic administration is, other things being equal, always the most rational type, from a technical point of view, the needs of mass administration make it today completely indispensable. The choice is only that between bureaucracy and dilettantism in the field of administration."[7]

Thus the antipoverty advocate functions in much the same way as Karl Marx's state bureaucrat, but also in accordance with Weber's characterization of bureaucratic organization as highly rational, efficient, and promising a very "high degree of calculability of results."[8] The advocate's vision is always delimited, not by greed as Theresa Funicello would say, but by the requirements of institutional maintenance and organizational power. The organization takes on a life of its own and becomes more important than the poor who are its object. The bureaucrats are separated from their own supposed organizational goals of helping the poor, and the organization becomes its own subject and object. Its goals become neutrality and efficiency, and servicing the poor is subordinated to fulfilling these institutional perquisites. The bureaucracy becomes self-referential in that its real concern is the organization itself. The poor are only the means to the end of building a better bureaucratic organization. Far too often the main goal of the antipoverty organization is to solve the problem of continually increasing administrative costs. Because cost containment is crucial, the staff's limited vision is reduced to the "crass materialism" of the practical. They don't have the time and energy to create an alternative vision, and they keep reproducing their past failures, stuck on the endless treadmill of narrow practicality. A political vision to end poverty or build a social movement never makes it onto the agenda. In the current context, even Lyndon Johnson's "war on poverty" is unimaginable.

For antipoverty bureaucrats, their organization is "deified." Their authority is embedded in its health, and thus fundraising becomes their official mandate. They are dependent on poverty and the continuous depiction of it as a serious social problem—this is the basis of their fundraising. To sustain their antipoverty organization, they must get foundation grants and individual contributions. They provide help for the poor but never "rock the boat"; with few exceptions they maintain the status quo of a world where there will always be poverty. The problem isn't greed; most of the executive officers of antipoverty organizations could make more money in the private sector. No, their loyalty is to their organization and its continued growth; a political solution for ending poverty is paid lip service only.

Though antipoverty/antihunger organizations are not as bureaucratic as business firms or state agencies, their organizational vision is based on a perception of what is practical, and they emphasize efficiency and calculable results. This bureaucratic mindset leads to what Merton calls "the structural sources of overconformity."[9] The tendency of the bureaucratic mindset is to be too committed to conformity to rules. This overadherence to rules by officials within the organization becomes dysfunctional in terms of meeting organizational goals, a "trained incapacity." Merton states:

> Discipline readily interpreted as conformance with regulations whatever the situation is seen not as a measure designed for specific purposes but becomes an immediate value in the life organization of the bureaucrat. This emphasis, resulting from displacement of the organizational goals, develops into rigidities and an inability to adjust readily. This may be exaggerated to the point where the primary concern with conformity to rules interferes with the achievement of the purposes of the organization.[10]

This kind of conformity limits advocates and providers to a politics of the practical and makes significant social change almost impossible. It explains why so many providers and advocacy groups working so hard over so many years have barely helped the poor keep their heads above water. The problem of bureaucratic conformity is compounded by bureaucracy's tendency toward permanence and oligarchy. As Weber states, "where administration has become completely bureaucratized, the resulting system of domination is practically indestructible."[11] Robert Michels' important point about hierarchy in social movements and political parties applies to all organizations: "it is organization which gives birth to the dominion of the elected over the electors, of the mandataries over the mandaters, of the delegates over the delegators. Who says organization, says oligarchy."[12] Even well-meaning organizations that help the poor have a tendency toward oligarchy.

The failure of advocates and providers to overcome poverty, to provide more than a Band-Aid for the poor, is grounded in their conformity of vision based on their organizational inflexibility and tendency toward oligarchy.

This is not the place to review the extensive literature on bureaucracy and organization. My purpose is to demonstrate how organization itself is a problem for antipoverty and antihunger organizations. Consider W. Richard Scott's description of the "Three Pillars of Institutions," vital ingredients of institutional analysis. These are the regulative-economic, the normative-social, and the cultural-cognitive.[13] The normative pillar emphasizes values and norms, "it introduces a prescriptive, evaluative and obligatory dimension into social life."[14] The cognitive pillar "stresses the central role played by the socially mediated construction of a common framework of meaning."[15] The regulative pillar controls human behavior but has become primarily economic. Economists "are likely to focus attention on the behavior of individuals and firms in markets and other competitive situations, where contending interests are more common. . . . Economists view individuals and organizations that conform to rules as pursuing their self-interests, as behaving instrumentally and expediently."[16]

Unlike Scott, I am not concerned with a review of the institutional literature but with the institutional framework that structures antipoverty and antihunger organizations and the corporate logic that has become the dominant mindset of the current crop of bureaucrats. Thus, the economic-regulatory pillar has become the most powerful, regulating both the normative and the cognitive pillars and constraining human thought and behavior. The neoliberal, free market model currently regulates human behavior and is the basis for most institutional behavior, including that of the nonprofit sector. This one-dimensional corporate model governs both the daily work and the development of organizations. The free market rationality of the CEO of a transnational corporation has become the structural logic for all organizations, private, public, and nonprofit.

This new global free market rationality seems to have taken a Lukacsian turn, combining Weber's bureaucratization of the world with Marx's commodified capitalism. Lukacs' theory of reification in *History and Class Consciousness* is influenced by Weber's theory of bureaucracy and by Marx's theory of the commodity fetish. Lukacs posits that in capitalist society human relations become secondary to the needs of the marketplace, and that this is not just another economic problem but "the central structural problem of capitalist society in all of its aspects."[17] Lukacs recasts Weber's emphasis on formal rationality in capitalism, the endless calculation of means and ends, in terms of the fetishism of commodities, identifying this as the basis for the crisis in capitalist rationality.

For Lukacs, "reification requires that a society should learn to satisfy all of its needs in terms of commodity exchange. The separation of the producer from his means of production, the dissolution and destruction of all 'natural' production units, etc., and all the social and economic conditions necessary for the emergence of modern capitalism tend to replace 'natural' relations which exhibit human relations more plainly by rationally reified relations."[18]

Herein lies the crisis: capitalism is rational in the details of commodity production and accumulation but deeply irrational at the level of the whole of society. This is true not only at times of recession and depression, but in boom times as well, because capitalism must always reify human relations to create "endless profit." As Lukacs states, "it is evident that the whole structure of capitalist production rests on the interaction between a necessity subject to strict laws in all isolated phenomena and the relative irrationality of the total process."[19]

Thus, at the level of an ever-expanding free market, formal rationality has been reduced to gambling. "The capitalist process of rationalization based on private economic calculation requires that every manifestation of life shall exhibit this very interaction between details which are subject to laws and a totality ruled by chance."[20]

This is the essence of the crisis of capitalist rationality, but it is a crisis that is ordinary in capitalist society. It governs the society in "every aspect," objectively and subjectively. Everyone is subject to its "inner and outer logic"—that is, the rationality of details and the irrationality of the whole. The crisis is valid in society's hierarchical, bureaucratic modes and in its horizontal, postbureaucratic modes. This crisis is at the center of organizational theory, where reifications are treated as rational and subjective, human relations are viewed as distortions of rationality. At this current, postmodern moment, organizational theorists and practitioners tell us about flatter hierarchies and more innovative and diverse organization structures for the business firm that are decentralized, less bureaucratic, less rigid, flexible. As Walter W. Powell writes: "These radically decentralized corporations are remaking both the geography of production and the administration of large scale organization."[21] This reorganization has made the nature of jobs and work problematic and uncertain, and so is the way in which employees view themselves. Thus James Meadows, a vice-president of human resources, says: "People need to look at themselves as self-employed, as vendors who come to the company to sell their skills. In AT&T, we have to promote the concept of the whole work force being contingent (i.e. on short-term contract, no promises), though most of our contingent workers are inside our walls. Jobs are being replaced by projects and fields of work, giving rise to a society that is increasingly 'jobless but not workless.' "[22] This twenty-first-century business firm is the model for all other organization structures, just as Weber's bureaucracy was the model for the twentieth century.[23]

These new organizational developments have changed the nature of work and administration, but these changes are limited by the bottom line—by the ever-important profit margin and the need to control labor and limit wages. At this crucial point, the flexible, postmodern form of organization retains its hierarchy. These new forms of organization are not devoid of power and control; a flattening of hierarchies does not mean that they are without hierarchy.

In fact power is still wielded by CEOs, executive management, and key members of the board of directors. Thus, the mind of bureaucratic capitalism is still dominant, and the commodity fetish is still the governing principle of the higher irrationality of the system.

This is demonstrated not only in the recent spate of corporate scandals, but in the unprecedented concentration of global corporate power and, as Lukacs understood, its dominance over every aspect of society. The overwhelming irrationality of the dominant American model means that there are more winners than in the past, but that the multitudes of people in the world still lose. This means that the poor are made continually poorer and truly good jobs, though they exist for the few, are disappearing for the great majority of ordinary people. In terms of this logic, job programs and the like really mean more low-paid jobs and fewer benefits, even after education and training. In this context we can understand Jeffrey E. Garten's *The Mind of the C.E.O.*, which forecasts the globalization of the American way of doing business, and its consequences. "In developed countries like France, Germany and Japan, radical economic changes are occurring along the lines of the U.S. model: less regulation, more financial transparency, more accountability to shareholders, more mergers and acquisitions, more entrepreneurship, more flexible labor markets."[24]

For Garten the influence of the U.S. model on the world economy is "indisputable": "Although the United States accounts for about 25 percent of global production, in the last few years its stock market capitalization has hovered around 50 percent of the world total. And this is not the whole story. Markets everywhere are heavily influenced by what happens in Wall Street and Silicon Valley. They base their behavior on U.S. interest rates, on the patterns of security trading, and on the trends in venture capital."[25]

What are the consequences of this model in which venture capitalists are seen as innovators and not as commodity "fetishizers"? And what is its relationship to poverty? Garten quotes James Wolfensohn, president of the World Bank: "Something is wrong when the average income for the richest twenty countries is thirty-seven times the average for the poorest twenty—a gap that has more than doubled in the past forty years. Something is wrong when

1.2 billion people live on less than a dollar a day and 2.8 billion live on less than two dollars a day."[26] This model and its consequences are hegemonic, not just for the twenty-first-century business firm, but for all organizations, including nonprofits.

What happens when we translate the crisis in capitalist rationality and the commodity fetish that has displaced human relations into the realm of advocacy organizations? Fundraising and organizational maintenance become primary. Providing services for the poor becomes secondary. Political actions to end poverty are not on the advocacy agenda. Here, even the dialectic of Sister Bernadette loses its critical edge. Advocacy is the bureaucratization of activism, committed to maintaining the ever-shrinking safety net and to realistic electoral politics. This is now even further diminished by the professionalized nonprofit antipoverty organization, which is increasingly concerned with providing "world-class service." Even advocacy becomes a secondary activity as these professionalized nonprofits concern themselves with providing direct services in goods or social and administrative services (filling out forms for food stamps or EITC) to a permanent population of the poor. These services are very important for the people who receive them, but they do not actually change the situation of the poor or end poverty. Ending poverty is viewed as unrealistic and utopian, especially in light of the continual reduction of state services.

More and more state services for the poor and unemployed are privatized. Here privatization is understood as the commodification of formerly state functions—which become profitable enterprises for business and provide less service for people. This commodification can be seen in the continuous attempts to privatize education, prisons, and Social Security. The tremendous increase in nonprofits in the last 20 years is the result of hollowing out the state and commodifying services that were formerly more generously provided by the government.

This process applies to both types of antihunger and antipoverty organizations described in this book: providers and advocacy organizations. To compete in the funding marketplace of both individual charity and foundation grants, you must use the corporate model.

A good executive director has internalized the free market logic. He or she seeks not only corporate funds, but corporate expertise as well. The bureaucratization and corporatization of these organizations have an effect on their leadership. Thus in the midst of the fiscal crisis of New York City in 2002, when already austere health, education, and welfare programs were facing further cuts, the ED of an anti-poverty organization explained to me why he opposed increasing taxes in New York City: "It will chase away the corporations; it will make it impossible to redevelop the city after 9/11. We can't just look at the bad side of not taxing them, we have to look at the good side, about getting more jobs in New York City. Even President Bush has been good for the hungry. Even if he hasn't been good on poverty overall, and he's been bad on TANF, we have to see the good side. As progressives we have to see the benefits of business and the president at least for the hunger populations." This ED has internalized the free market model and cannot imagine that jobs can be produced by anything but that marketplace. He sees jobs—almost without reference to wages—as the solution to hunger and poverty. Never for a moment does he consider what wages and benefits are necessary to end poverty. Nor does he consider the role of the free market in causing poverty.

Of course, as Scott says, "organizational participants do not always conform to conventional patterns but respond variably, sometimes creating new ways of acting and organizing."[27] Some of these alternative ways of acting and organizing, such as the WEP Workers Organizing Committee, are essential to my analysis. For the most part, however, the imaginary of the organizational world is that "business does it better." This logic increases conformity and limits innovation, even for progressive organizations.

CONFORMITY OF VISION AND THE BUDGETING OF SOCIAL CHANGE

Without a vision of how to end poverty, the politics of advocacy is unable to mobilize a mass poor people's movement and is reduced to fighting battles over budgetary details. Advocates fight an important fight, but only for a better share of a shrinking pie, never for poor people's control over their own destiny, and never for a middle-class lifestyle for all people. These struggles are costly in terms of time and effort and have failed to decrease the immiseration of the poor. The conservatives have won, and they control the debate, defining welfare as the problem and ignoring poverty. Thus they can call the current reduction in the welfare rolls a success, even though the number of people living below the official poverty line has barely decreased. Their victory allows them to define poverty in a totally unrealistic way and to call the working poor "middle-class." It allows them to maintain their utopian vision of free market capitalism as providing for all of the people when it doesn't. They have made this neoliberal utopian vision seem practical, and, in the process, they have transformed the politics of welfare and ended entitlements in the United States while antipoverty advocates engage in piecemeal struggles and wage practical political battles within the narrow parameters of what they believe to be possible.

Ending poverty requires, first, that the poor must be mobilized—helped to organize themselves politically. Second, poor people and advocates must join together and take the time to democratically develop an alternative vision of a world without poverty. At a minimum, advocacy agencies must begin to be jointly run by advocates and the poor. This will require changes in both the poor and the advocates. Here I am in agreement with Theresa Funicello that a guaranteed annual income is worth fighting for because it would reduce the welfare bureaucracy and give poor people more independence. But it must be a real middle-class income, based on a living wage of $15 an hour with good benefits.

Right now, advocates are dependent on foundations for most of their revenues, and for the most part foundations do not want their grants used for advocacy. The executive director of an antipoverty advocacy group told me: "Foundations limit the kind of advocacy that you can do. Many of them make it plain that they don't want you to do advocacy at all but that they want you to develop new programs, always new programs to help educate the poor to the available programs. Since most advocacy organizations are always desperate for funds because their organizations are rarely in the black, they are forced to closely abide by the rules of the funders. Especially for welfare-to-work." In this context we can understand the poverty of antipoverty advocacy, as illustrated in the following encounter between the emergency food network and the Human Resources Administration of New York City.

On June 10, 1997, at 3:30 P.M., the New York City Coalition Against Hunger (NYCCAH) convenes a meeting with the new Human Resources Administration commissioner, Lilliam Barrios-Paoli, and her staff. Judith Walker, the executive director of NYCCAH, has arranged the meeting, and the emergency food network is well represented: Food For Survival (the city's food bank), Community Food Resource Center, Yorkville Common Pantry, St. John's Bread and Life, Neighbors Together, and many others.

New York City's soup kitchens and food pantries are serving more people, compensating for heightened demand by cutting portions, reducing hours, or eliminating categories of recipients. At the same time, voluntary food programs have experienced growth in the ranks: 200 new emergency food agencies opened last year in New York. These 1,000 programs serve 60 million meals a year to half a million New Yorkers, but they are sinking under the sheer volume of need.[28]

It is getting harder to raise money from private donations and from private foundations. Private funders often will fund only new programs and not the massive everyday costs of running pantries and soup kitchens. The federal government has reduced grants, and the state hasn't increased them in years. The city has added $1 million in Emergency Food Assistance Program (EFAP) money, but the anti-hunger advocates have asked for $10 million. We are here to ask the HRA commissioner for help.

Commissioner Barrios-Paoli is aware of the crisis. She understands that welfare reform means that 130,000 New Yorkers will lose their food stamps in August. (Mayor Giuliani eventually signs the waiver that allows them to receive food stamps for another year.) Commissioner Barrios-Paoli has never doubted the findings of Walker's report, *Breadlines in Boomtown*.

She tells us that the emergency food network is high on her list of priorities but that the federal law is a reality, and that the city can't make up for those massive cuts. But, she tells us, the "mayor is sympathetic now, and if we do a lot of work we can get him there. He understands the basic injustice to immigrants."[29]

She warns us: "If you choose to focus on the ills of welfare reform, we will get no sympathy from City Hall. When you talk about $122 million leaving the economy because of the loss of immigrant aid, well, your demand of $9 million seems cheap to me. I want this all in place by August 22. Let's start with the immigrants, where we all agree. The immigrant issue has caught the city's imagination, everyone's on board."

We have other issues—workfare, fundraising, storage space, and feeding an increasing client population. And there are a few dissenters from the immigrant strategy—directors of soup kitchens, who have a concern for immigrants but whose main population is African American and Puerto Rican. It seems to them that the mayor is making the old distinction between the "deserving" (immigrant) and the "undeserving" (black and Puerto Rican) poor. This is, of course, unacceptable, and yet we are being told that immigrants have to be privileged if we are to have a chance of getting more money for EFAP. Some anger is expressed. The commissioner responds: "There is a rule of engagement—you don't shoot the one friend you have in town." Ultimately it doesn't matter: Jason Turner will soon replace Commissioner Barrios-Paoli, and we won't have any friends in HRA.

I found Commissioner Barrios-Paoli charming and intelligent. I never doubted that she understood our problems, even if she sounded overly optimistic about the workfare program. Nor did I doubt that she was a functionary in Mayor Giuliani's welfare program and thus more concerned about the impact of federal legislation on immigrants than on the nonimmigrant poor. The nonimmigrant poor vote for Democrats, when they vote, and thus were not the mayor's concern.

We were co-opted because of the constant crisis that emergency food providers face. We bought into the Barrios-Paoli/Giuliani program because we could not reject the possibility of raising more money for our programs. As a result, we were on board with Giuliani, who had actually helped to create our predicament and who in the years to come would develop programs that were even harsher on our clients.

Through all of this—the meeting, the discussion between the advocates and the commissioner—the poor were absent. The advocates represent the poor, our programs are for the poor, but the poor are still absent. The advocates do good work, but they have failed at getting the poor to represent themselves. What had we gained by getting on board with Giuliani's regime because it was the practical thing to do? We were now on board with Jason Turner, the workfare czar of Wisconsin, and we were on board with a regime that didn't trust Paoli because she is a Mexican. As Wayne Barrett tells us in *Rudy!*—

> A year after Paoli's departure, Rudy told the *Times* that she and her African-American predecessor at HRA, Marva Hammonds, "did not have the same strong philosophical commitment I have."
>
> "My philosophy has been," he said, "first make the changes and have them moving in a very, very strong way—then announce them. At that point, there isn't terribly much that people that oppose it can do."
>
> In the closed circle of an administration that had no real experience with poverty and listened to virtually no minority voices, the blessing of ignorance is certitude and the surest consequence of certitude is decisive action. Who gets hurt in the outer reaches of a centralized media city is an abstraction, a rumor, a bias, an antiquated ideology. His welfare charts on the other hand—with multicolored lines diving by hundreds of thousands—were the hard stuff of practical life, the only snapshots the broader world would see. A Mayor could freeze the frame, define the visible city, invent his own legend.[30]

Mayor Giuliani was ignorant of the actualities of poverty in New York City, without real expertise but armed with a successful, national ideologue on workfare, Jason Turner. He controlled the debate, the media, and the facts. He did this because he was willing to engage in ideological struggle; he transformed poverty into welfare, thus emptying the concept of poverty of all of its meaning, and slashed welfare, which was meaningful and won the debate. Rudolph

W. Giuliani tells us in *Leadership* about the success of his Welfare Reform Initiative:

> When I ran for reelection in 1997, there were about 300,000 fewer people on the welfare rolls than in 1993. Had I announced when I first ran that I was going to reduce the welfare population by such a figure, *The New York Times* would have written an editorial saying I was crazy, and that if I somehow did do that the city would be in chaos. The reality is that I thought I probably could do it—if not predicting the exact numbers, I certainly believed in the concept. . . .
>
> Well the numbers turned out to be impressive. More than 600,000 people left the city's welfare rolls during my administration—from 1,112,490 to 497,113. . . . Our programs constituted a major social realignment, restoring for many the dignity of the work ethic.[31]

The advocates are armed with the facts and real expertise, but they are not willing to engage in ideological struggle and are in fact prevented from doing politics for fear of losing their nonprofit status. Where conservatives like Mayor Giuliani are ready for action, armed with the certitude of ideology, the advocates are armed with practical concerns that limit their political possibilities. Consider the demographics of New York as described by Andrew Beveridge:

> There are more than a million and a half people in New York City who are living "below the poverty line," according to official statistics. The poverty line for a family of four was about $18,000 in the year 2000. . . . But by any measure poverty in New York City has increased. Almost 300,000 more people in New York City's population lived below the poverty line in 2000 than in 1990, according to data from the census. In 1990, some 1.38 million New Yorkers—or 19.3 per cent of the population—were living below the poverty line. By 2000, the number had increased to 1.67 million or, 21.2 percent.[32]

Beveridge's figures make it clear that Mayor Giuliani was throwing officially poor people off the welfare rolls, without concern for the chaos that he was causing in their lives. He labeled the hardships of the low-wage jobs he found for these ex-welfare-recipients "the dignity of the work ethic." Turning the debate from the hardships of the poor to the reduction of the welfare rolls guaranteed his victory in the war against the poor. It didn't matter that he would lose the legal battles, or that his facts were problematic. It didn't matter that the advocates always did better research, or that the facts were on their side. Mayor Giuliani always won the battle. His attack on people in need, instead of being ammunition for a victory of antipoverty advocates, became part of the basis for the legend of Rudolph W. Giuliani as the greatest mayor of New York City. The mayor won the ideological struggle on workfare, and the antipoverty advocates lost again.

How can we make sense of advocates' limited impact on poverty policies? At no point do I question advocates' good intentions or hard work. Nor do I disagree with Kathy Goldman, the director of the Community Food Resource Center, who told me, "I really believe that without our advocacy for all these years, things would be much worse and food stamps and the safety net would be completely gone." Advocacy has made a difference, but it hasn't created a new language of possibility or facilitated the self-organization of the poor.

Over the last 20 years, advocacy has replaced activism and the goal of building a social movement of the poor to end poverty. Now advocacy represents the poor politically in an attempt to maintain the public services that were the result of the legislative struggles of the 1930s and 1960s and came to be known during the Reagan years as the safety net. The advocates are also involved in providing direct services to the poor as an adjunct to public service shortfalls: soup kitchens and food pantries, for example, were first viewed as a temporary, emergency development in response to Reagan's cuts. The emergency network of pantries and soup kitchens has now become permanent.

As privatization and the end of entitlements reduced public services for the poor, direct services have been emphasized and advocacy efforts played down. Professional, corporate-structured nonprofits are replacing advocacy organizations. The poor receive direct services, but without political representation and without new policy initiatives. The nonprofits are adopting the universal, corporate managerial structure that is increasingly emphasized by their executive directors and their boards, and required by foundations.

This current corporate structure is a result of a paradigm shift. It belongs to an economic model of organization that mirrors the capitalist free market. It assumes utility-maximizing behavior by rational actors who opportunistically try to increase their assets and reduce their costs. The old behavioralist model, which valued long-term incentives and loyalty to the firm, has been denigrated because competitive advantage in a global free market demands flexibility and accomplishing the immediate task at hand as quickly as possible. In opposition to the behavioralist model, we have "the economic approach" in which "[o]utput is optimized . . . by conceiving of all relationships as short run only, or in terms of future returns calculated at present discount rates. This applies at every level of the hierarchy, from CEO on down. If an employee serves your purpose today, 'hire 'em'—if not, 'fire 'em.' "[33]

At the center of a universal organizational culture that is modeled around free market profit maximization as an objective condition, the importance of accounting is maximized as well. In the world of the nonprofit, this corporate culture is focused on fundraising and writing foundation grants. These programs are in constant competition for scarce funds. Their ability to initiate programs to help the poor is determined by accounting decisions. In terms of these budgetary constraints, Anthony Tinker calls accountants the "architects of unequal exchange."[34] For Tinker, though it is masked as an objective process, accounting is really an ideological process steeped in power relations and inequalities. In the context of antipoverty nonprofits, accounting decisions that are made in the name of responsibility, necessity, and efficiency are in actuality auditing social justice and social change. In the same vein Robin Roslender writes, "Accountancy is invoked to legitimate decisions about expanding or contracting operations, committing or withdrawing funds, introducing more stringent financial controls, paying out dividends or retaining earnings, etc."[35]

When decisions are made in terms of accountancy, they are viewed as objective decisions in which there is no room for political interest. For Tinker and Roslender, these decisions are in reality not objective but political and ideological. But for the accountant, they are not ideological; they are made in the interest of preserving the organization, and political decisions that threaten fundraising and foundation grants are seen as debits. Politics and social change must be budgeted cautiously. In antipoverty nonprofits, where advocates should be focused on creating possibilities to end or reduce poverty and empower the poor, the corporate structure and the procedures and ideology of accountancy greatly limit the possibilities of doing this. This limitation can be seen in the human resources practices of these nonprofits. They speak the language of living wages and democratically managed workforces but look like corporations in terms of their actual practices. The logic of accounting forces them to try to increase the productivity of their workforce and lower costs at every turn. Their meager budgets often require everyone, from their executive director on down, to work at relatively low wages and salaries and often at reduced hours (or with uncompensated overtime). Here the executive directors of antipoverty nonprofits differ from CEOs: they do not receive exorbitant salaries, stock options, or golden parachutes. Their dedication is commendable, but it is not a good model for the overworked and underpaid working poor.

THE END OF ADVOCACY

At first antipoverty and welfare activists believed that Reaganomics represented a temporary crisis. They believed that the country would come to its senses and vote out Reagan and his "voodoo" economic policies. Instead, Reagan's policies became institutionalized: privatization of the safety net, lower and lower taxes for the upper classes, and a permanent reduction in federal services. No class felt the burdens of this policy more than the poor. It is in this context that programs that were originally constructed as emergency and temporary have now been made permanent, with the bureaucratic and institutional consequences described above. As activists ran emergency programs such as homeless shelters and food pantries, the organizational requirements of maintaining even these "temporary" programs required raising funds and the logic of accountancy. These activists were forced to work within the constraints of bureaucratic regulations and mainstream politics. These constraints severely limited activism, and they became advocates who were now involved in providing for the poor and in representing them. Advocacy displaced the movement building of activism. The ending of poverty through a self-managed movement of the poor became an unrealistic fantasy. Advocates began to privilege institution building as the method for providing for the poor.

It is through this process that, as advocacy organizations became permanent organizations, they increasingly developed corporate management practices favored by funders, and this led to a decline in political representation and an increase in the amount of direct service.

As advocacy fades and the representation of the poor is reduced as well, the advocates are increasingly replaced by a permanent professional administration trained in universal corporate management practices. I often hear from executive directors and members of the boards of antipoverty organizations about the management practices they have picked up from CEOs like Jack Welch and Bill Gates or management consultants like Jim Collins and Stephen Covey. At one medium-sized social justice organization, the executive director required his professional staff to read Jim Collins' *Good to Great*, in which greatness is "measured by cumulative stock returns of over three times the general market in a fifteen year period."[36] Collins' great companies are the likes of Pitney-Bowes, Nucor, Philip Morris, and Walgreens. For this executive director, the corporate world has clearly become the model for his social justice organization. Of course building a great social justice or antipoverty organization is commendable, but is organization building overshadowing the needs of the poor? And what about advocacy?

Organization building requires a professional, academically trained staff with management expertise. These criteria are believed to be objective and based on the efficiencies needed to build an organization that can provide more services for the poor. Expertise in the large and broad field of welfare and poverty is viewed as a plus, but not a requirement. Management expertise is viewed as a universal skill applicable to all organizations. Add professional accounting by a CPA or, even better, a professional financial manager, because it is now believed that all social problems, including poverty, can be resolved by accountants and managers. Politics are too subjective; all problems have managerial solutions. Leadership and a good management team are all that it will take. The logic of accounting has the appearance of objectivity, reducing everything to a simple mathematical calculus of profit and debit. For executive directors, boards, and administrative staff, this mathematical calculus has the warrant of a science in which the facts speak for themselves. Organizational decisions based on accountancy seem independent of subjective interest and power relations; instead, they are based on organizational necessities and what is objectively best for the poor. These corporate, free market, managerial strategies, tied to the objective methods of accountants, create universal competencies that are necessary for both organization building and providing "world-class service" to the poor. It is in the name of these universal competencies that advocacy is being terminated.

This new ethos prompted me to interview executive directors and advocates in the nonprofit sector. Fred is a long-time administrator for AHAP, a medium-sized nonprofit that has been very successful at developing new programs for the poor and getting foundation grants. "As your organization has gotten larger, has your organization increased its emphasis on the political mobilization of the poor?" I ask.

"No, there's less and less work in mobilizing poor people. There's much more on doing the mechanics of fulfilling grants, so that you can get more grants. It's not in mobilization at all. There's no money in mobilization. There's no money in activism."

I ask Fred if this is the end of advocacy. "Yes," he responds. "It's not going to happen overnight. It's the end of advocacy, as we know it. . . . When I started in this advocacy field, I honestly felt in my heart that all of us were working towards ending hunger, ending welfare, ending homelessness, and that's what we worked towards. That was our goal. Our goal wasn't to make it more comfortable. And now we are institutionalizing the very soup kitchens and food pantries."

Fred, like many advocates, is uncomfortable with the professional, corporate-style managers who now run antipoverty nonprofits. They are concerned with providing a better quality of service for the poor, "to make it more comfortable." They are not concerned with the political struggles that must be made to end poverty, homelessness, and hunger in the United States. For Fred, the end of advocacy is occurring at two levels: first, the reorganization of advocacy groups on a corporate, private-sector model, and, second, the failure of the professional managers to understand power relations within the city, state, and federal governments. "From an advocacy point of view," he says, "advocacy is not taught at the university level, there's no course work on it. But there's also no history courses, governmental courses. So what happens as university students who are professionalized come into the sector? They don't even understand the structure of the city they're living in, in this mobile world we live in. And if they don't understand the structure from a historical perspective of how the city functions, then it's the death of advocacy on another level of professionalization. I had interns who needed one month more for their masters in nutrition or public administration and all kinds of things. And because I'm an advocate, the work that I did was their community service, and they didn't get it because they didn't understand the structure of the city. They didn't understand the power and how it would play out."

Fred sees advocacy dying because these university-trained administrators were trained to be postmodern managers. They could provide world-class service if only they lived in a world without history and without differential power relations. This is the world in which advocacy dies: "It's not going to happen overnight," as Fred says, but it is happening.

He works on developing food programs with interns who have no knowledge of the city or the state. He says, "I try to get them where their interest level is—to try and get them to understand from an educational point of view that you can't work in a vacuum. That you have to learn the structures; you have to learn what power is. . . . The new wave of young people come into the workforce with very, very tunnel vision. They have specific, limited skills. There is no strategic kind of thinking. There is no broad, deep way of working. . . . Nobody looks at the longer, broader role of any of the areas that we work in." Fred's concern that no one looks at the big picture, that there isn't a long-term strategy for making significant reductions in poverty and hunger, led him to ask for a strategic conference. "I just asked for it on a regional level. I said we need a strategic conference. 'Do you know how much work that would take?' they said. So there's no time."

For Fred, the organization's work is about creating programs that will give poor adults and children more educational opportunity, jobs with living wages, and a better life. The work is political. It's not just about building a better organization and fundraising and using status quo politics to accomplish these internal goals. But the organization is now concerned with efficiency and not with the empowerment of the poor: "It's time management. Time management is about efficiency. Efficiency has nothing to do with the work. Time management is like the computer, like the robot, but ultimately the robot has to be programmed by somebody, and it's still a narrow tunnel vision. Robots are programmed for a particular skill; they are not programmed for the broader strategic way of thinking." Advocacy requires a broader political vision, and this is being destroyed by the new professional administrators' emphasis on the narrow, specific tasks required to develop fundable direct-service programs for the poor.

The executive director of another antihunger/antipoverty program talks about this problem: "It would be nice if the foundations looked to see what is really at the root of the problems they're trying to address. And really figure out that it's really not about . . . putting all your funds into service and Band-Aid work. But it is about groups that really have a mission and agenda, a project that addresses more substantial long-term changes. But I think that really involves the government in terms of having the responsibility for ending hunger and poverty." This ED is involved in both the mobilization of poor people and influencing government on issues from TANF to food stamps to state and city budgets. She is not against the direct service of food pantries, soup kitchens, and homeless shelters but understands the importance of political struggle and the difficulty of raising money to wage it.

"Right now," she continues, "it seems like most of the foundations are doing the service part of the work. Many of the foundations are falling into the 'deserving poor' issues." She adopts a foundation persona, changing her voice: "We fund children's issues, seniors' issues. We fund disabled issues, but you don't fund the gosh-darn family that's just working poor. . . . Or the single man or woman who is poor, or the single parent who is poor." Back to her own voice: "Those are the categories—the foundations are definitely sticking to the deserving poor element."

She would like to see foundations change their structure so that they could fund more political work. "So that they can actually fund more direct organizing, and fund much more lobbying, direct lobbying with less restrictions . . . the foundations actually, really develop a plan—maybe they have to develop a separate wing, a baby foundation. . . . They should do it because I think some of the reasons these foundations do fund safer work, nonlobbying work, is because . . . 501(c)3 restricts their donations. As well as who is on their board; if their board is more conservative . . . it understands giving food to people, but it doesn't understand organizing the people."

An administrator from another antipoverty/social justice organization tells me that her board no longer wants to do advocacy, as it has done in the past, but is concerned with getting large direct-service grants and with training new managers to expand the scope of the organization. This administrator says, "I don't understand— the chair of the board . . . seems no longer concerned with the politics of poverty."

I ask if foundations do not want to fund political work because poverty in the United States exposes the flaws in the system.

The executive director responds: "I think that's true—not so much for foundations as for individual donors. I think individual donors acknowledge a certain degree of fault in the system, but they want the money to go to hunger programs you know. If we were to solicit money for welfare rights organizing, we probably wouldn't get a dime. . . . People just don't like that idea. People want service. . . . I think that you're right to the degree that foundations don't want to see the systemic flaws in the system, the social and economic justice flaws. They understand that some people fall into bad times—those flaws are sort of more temporary. It wouldn't be systemic, it wouldn't be because of the color of your skin . . . everybody has their tough days. So they understand that level of problems, and that's why they fund service work. But I think that you're right—the more a group says, 'No, this is systemic, we want it to end, we don't just want Band-Aids work,' that's a problem—that's what the foundations do not want to fund."

It is more and more difficult to get grants to fund advocacy or even voter registration drives. "One of the foundations that we receive funds from, the North Star Foundation, real big grassroots funders, and some small grants. We received funding from them for about seven or eight years, and last year I noticed in their form that you have to sign when you get the check, an acknowledgment form, it said something like, 'We agree that we will not use any part of these funds to do any type of voter education or registration.' And to me that was a brand new restriction. In the past we have been able to use foundation funding as long as we didn't tell people how to vote."

This problem has to be understood in context. Many small to medium-sized advocacy organizations are competing for a shrinking pot of foundation funding. This, combined with the current emphasis on professionalized administration concerned with organization building, dampens antipoverty advocacy. "Very few foundations, only a handful of foundations, fund advocacy work on poverty or hunger issues. And there are so many people competing, so many groups competing, for that same small pot of money. And some of the foundations that you would think would focus on advocacy work aren't doing it, aren't prioritizing it. It's surprising."

This executive director is under tremendous pressure. Resources are always difficult to raise, but if advocacy and organizing are your primary work, fundraising is even harder. Grants are based on the viability of the organization and its track record in getting grants because advocacy organizations are always near the edge financially. This makes it even more difficult to raise the money to support a staff to do the difficult political and legislative work that is necessary to keep the poor from falling through the cracks. At the same time, your staff works long hours at relatively low pay. This includes the executive director who tells me: "Actually, I'm trying not to work past eight [P.M.] more than a couple of days a week. Last night I was here until 8:15." This ED is typical.

Another problem is that organizations and foundations have fragmented the problem of poverty into the subcategories of homelessness, living wages, hunger, and welfare rights. The advocates have divided and conquered their own antipoverty organizations. And, as the ED says, "We are all under-resourced . . . "

"Is there ever a time when there is no pressure on you to raise funds?" I ask.

"Absolutely none, no."

The executive director explains how the money from a grant is used. "Most of the funds go to the staff, the actual staff that's doing the work. Then you get 10 percent for the management, which is myself. And then I'd say about 15 percent goes to overhead, rent, and supplies.

"A different issue," she notes, "is that foundations like to fund new projects. And then foundations like to fund you only for a certain amount of time. . . . So basically . . . right now we have a good shot at a grant . . . a three-year policy/advocacy grant. But we can't use that money to fund a current policy person. We actually have to hire a new staff person. We could be in the weird position of laying off a policy person from an old grant. . . . the weird thing about how these foundations work is that it always comes to a point where in three or so years you're going to run out of funding for current staffers. And the only thing foundations fund is new projects, and usually that means new staffers."

Organizations are forced to repackage their old grants in new ways so that they can continue doing their valuable work. The executive director worries about losing experienced staff members who have made political contacts and have expertise on the issues—certainly more expertise than the foundations who are funding projects. But for the executive director there is also the problem of job security, paying living wages, and keeping skilled and reliable staff. She is always looking for foundations that fund antipoverty and antihunger advocacy. "The other place we are looking for funding is hunger grant foundations. They don't care about the welfare piece, about living-wage jobs. It's like, 'OK, we'll just address hunger.' Well, that's a place where we can try to get some policy/advocacy money. . . . What I quickly found out is that all the hunger foundations are all talking about direct services, direct-delivery provision of meals. Phillip Morris specifically said no to advocacy, Robin Hood Foundation is like no to advocacy. The Starr Foundation said something about they wanted to fund human services.

"There are no hunger foundations that are interested in the fair-wage piece . . . the New York Foundation, the Rockefeller Foundation—they're doing some of this funding for economic policy stuff. It just seems to be that the hunger foundations in particular seem completely disconnected to the root causes of hunger. For some reason the hunger foundations seem to think if they just feed people, that's enough. They're being super-aggressive about not funding advocacy."

Foundations that fund antipoverty organizations are doing important work that is essential for the lives of the poor. The problem is that foundation grants address only one part of the dialectic of Sister Bernadette. As usual, the real roots of poverty are not dealt with, only some of the consequences. The Robin Hood Foundation claims to "attack the source" of poverty: "Our philosophy is simple: to significantly affect people living in poverty you have to attack it at the root causes. That's why Robin Hood focuses on poverty prevention through programs in early childhood, youth, education, jobs, and economic security. And, because we can't turn our backs on those living and suffering in poverty, we also fund basic survival programs in health care, hunger, housing, and domestic violence."[37]

The problem here is that the foundation confuses root causes with consequences. To find the root causes, you must, at a minimum, look at poverty in the context of the whole society and its cultural, political, and economic relations. Of course, hunger and inadequate education must be dealt with, and Robin Hood is attempting to deal with them. But these problems will continue because our society seems to be mass-producing poverty and material and cultural hardship in the lives of tens of millions of people.

In the same vein, The New York Community Trust states, "The goals of The Trust's hunger and homeless program are to improve the institutions serving people who are homeless and hungry, and to promote the independence and reintegration into society of homeless families and adults."[38]

Again, the goal of ending poverty or getting at its root causes is absent. The work of The New York Community Trust is crucial; we could use a hundred more foundations like it in New York City alone. But it too deals only with the direct-service piece and rarely with advocacy and organizing work, apart from "advocacy to increase public understanding of hunger and homelessness and to improve funding and services."[39] This is advocacy to help create better direct service—not advocacy to enable the poor to struggle politically at the local, state, and federal levels.

We academics doing research in this area often reify the consequences of poverty and describe them endlessly, whether our methodologies are ethnographic or quantitative. We, too, rarely deal with the premises of poverty in the richest free market capitalist country in a global world. We also keep applying analytic Band-Aids while the cultural, political, and economic conditions that mass-produce poverty go unchanged.

The problem of ending poverty, as another executive director tells me, "is humongous." At the same time, she believes that this is the task that has to be accomplished. I ask about her successes as the executive director of an advocacy-oriented antihunger program. Her answer captures the difficulty of being an advocate. "It's very hard to talk about successes at all. When you come in at a poverty rate in NYC of 28 percent and you leave with a poverty rate of 23 percent, and you had nothing to do with it. You know what I mean—it's just the economy."

I ask the ED of a similar organization about the national "Welfare Made a Difference" campaign. She responds, "It's not where I would put my energy, that's for sure. It's just a lost cause. Sure we should acknowledge that it helped. First of all, I wouldn't use the word anymore. I mean, how many people in America will listen to you when you use the word *welfare*? Yeah—like 10. . . . It's the wrong fight; it's absolutely the wrong fight."

What does she think about attempts by ACORN and Community Voices Heard (CVH) to organize WEP workers? "That's a little bit different to me," she says. "There really is a constituency there and they really want to organize. . . . My argument is that you should talk about them as unemployed workers and mothers of small children, and talk about childcare issues. I think when poor people switched from being workers, like in Marx, to welfare recipients, they lost. So the ones that you are talking about are workers. That's a much more positive battle. They have chances, and they're fighting with dignity . . . and that people will fight for and that people will have sympathy for."

THE LIMITS OF WORLD-CLASS SERVICE AT ST. JOHN'S BREAD AND LIFE

The Mobile Soup Kitchen: "The idea really stemmed from John. He used to work as a volunteer here and what he used to do, he used to live in an abandoned building, he was homeless himself. And he used to live with a couple of families, with children, and mothers and husbands in this abandoned building, somewhere in Brooklyn.

"So every day at the end of the day . . . one of the buildings, that I know, it's on Stuyvesant between Willoughby and Hart. And he lived there for at least several months. So every day I would watch John asking Sister Bernadette, saying that I live with these people, can I get some food for them? As you know, she's a nun. She would prepare packages for the dinner, and he would take that to them. So I used to talk with John, and he used to tell me that, well, some of these families are embarrassed to come to the soup kitchen. Some of them physically are not able to come because they have infant children. They don't have the transportation money. It costs an arm and a leg to get here. That's the reason he'd actually take food to them. So I thought of, back then, how can we reach out to these people? . . . So that thing stuck in my head—how can we go to them, rather than they come to us? So that's how the idea came—how do we move out of here and go somewhere else? And part of it really has to do with this development attitude that we have as a manager."

Hossein Saadat has been explaining how he got the idea for the Mobile Soup Kitchen project. In the ideology of nonprofits, a good manager keeps increasing the services provided. This requires not only developing new ideas for providing services but also developing new ways of funding. Hossein tells me that fundraising is about 40 percent of his job: individual donors, foundation grants, public-sector grants, and corporate funding. He makes it clear that fundraising doesn't end with grant writing or developing a special fundraising event but includes networking with potential donors, figuring out programs that can be funded, and even gaining access to the discretionary funds that most foundation can distribute to successful programs. For Executive Director Hossein Saadat, the most important variable is always success. "Everyone wants to be part of a successful program," he tells me. For him, achieving the success required to gain the funding that is the lifeblood of any program means continually running a program with a good staff and an active board of directors and providing fine services that are always being improved and perfected—which in turn is the basis for getting more funding. Hossein and the board of directors raised hundreds of thousands of dollars to build the Mobile Soup Kitchen and operate it at two sites for the first two years.

The Mobile Soup Kitchen is the kind of project that foundations prefer over advocacy work. It provides world-class service to poor neighborhoods in East New York, Brooklyn, where there are relatively few soup kitchens and food pantries. Sister Madeline Cavanaugh does excellent work providing meals and social services in both the rundown schoolyard at St. Gabriel Church and at Our Lady of Presentation. Often neighborhood gang members from the Bloods or the Crips walk through St. Gabriel's schoolyard when we serve the food. I have served food to two Bloods, who wanted to pay for it. (We didn't charge them, of course.) We have never had trouble with any of the neighborhood gangs. After we are finished at St. Gabriel's, which is a very poor parish, we drive to Our Lady of Presentation, which is less poor, and serve food for an hour and a half. The pastor there takes care of a homeless man who lives in a bush in front of the church. The pastor allows him to use the church bathroom and continually tries to find him a better place to live.

We serve the food out of the counter, a window cut into the side of a remodeled Winnebago. Sister Madeline and a social worker also provide various social services from an office inside the kitchen, finding housing, or jobs, or schooling, or treatment facilities. She has amassed a very competent paid staff and volunteers from each site. The mobile kitchen feeds on average over 450 meals a day at both sites and provides social services and job counseling for 100 people a month.

The Mobile Soup Kitchen is a model program, as are all the programs at St. John's Bread and Life. Hossein Saadat raised over $300,000 to build and run it, mostly from the Starr Foundation. St. John's Bread and Life is now a well-funded, multiservice, one-stop-shopping program for the families of Bedford-Stuyvesant, Williamsburg, and, thanks to the Mobile Soup Kitchen, East New York as well.

It wasn't always as fiscally sound as it is now. In August 1993 Brooklyn Catholic Charities stopped funding the soup kitchen, and Robin Hood did not renew a $41,000 grant, and our individual donations were insufficient to keep the program running. Sister Bernadette vowed that she would go begging from door to door. One day Hossein and I sat on the steps near the parish's New Horizons educational program, and he told me his tale of woe. "Financially we are down to $11,000 to $12,000 in the bank. We desperately need more money to continue.... Last year we raised $16,000 to $17,000 for the HIV Support Group. This year we haven't been able to raise anything. I mean, the Foundation Corporation didn't give us anything... and it's a model program. I think what we are lacking most is going after big government grants. Even though they have a lot of restrictions. They actually have a lot of mandates. They literally tell you how to manage your program at the beginning. At the end they solve your financial problem.... I think what we have to do—we really have to do different types of fundraising. We have to focus more on fundraising than anything else.... In terms of funding we're going to pull it off.... It creates a lot of stress on all of us."

With the help of his assistant, Anne (Anmati) Sukhan-Ramdhan, Hossein saved the program. An emergency grant from Robin Hood got them through the immediate financial crisis. Sister Bernadette did not have to go begging. They formed a board of directors, as required by law. A fundraising team consisting of Hossein, the board's president, Father James Maher, and board members Neil Sheehan and Joseph Martino developed special fundraising events such as the Run Against Hunger during the New York Marathon and the Johnny's Angel Awards, which helped to put St. John's Bread and Life on a solid fiscal base. Hossein became very successful at getting foundation grants. But he understands the price of this success. Here Hossein tells me how much things changed between the early 1990s and February 2001: "Back then it was generic; now it's specific. That's what they're looking for. They've become smarter."

"They only fund new programs?" I ask.

"Not necessarily, if you have a successful program. The thing is that funders, as I said, want to be part of a successful project, whether it's new or not. The reason they sort of go after new is because, now since they've become smarter, they know how to control it. They know how to impose expected outcomes. If you have a successful program . . . they want to be part of it."

"You think that success is the key variable?"

"Absolutely!" he answers. "If I give you money, whether I'm a corporation or a foundation, I want to know, and then, based on my individual philosophy, I want to indirectly impose on your process. If I hate people to stay home and I hate people on public assistance and I'm working on self-sufficiency [he raises and deepens his voice as he impersonates a funder]: 'GET THEM OUT THERE! PEOPLE HAVE TO WORK!' So what am I saying to you? I'm imposing my philosophy, and it would be your real obligation if you want to be refunded, you follow. And if not, you get a letter, 'I cannot continue your funding.' "

Anne Sukhan-Ramdhan worries about the structural changes in the program that are the result of the funders' provisions, mandates, and controls: "It's forgetting the heart. The funders' demands may be more efficient, but Bread and Life is always the heart of the community. That must be genuine. We can be both—the heart and efficient too. They're forgetting the heart; this isn't genuine anymore."

The structural changes in both direct-service and advocacy organizations have resulted in the professionalization of staff and an increase in administration—often in the creation of a whole new administrative level. Credentials have become important, including Ph.D. degrees and academic publications. Some organizations require their professional staff to account for every 15 minutes of work; others require a grant a month. The danger is, as Anne says, that professionalization will remove the staff's connection with the community, and thus the organization's mission. Fred, the AHAP administrator, says: "We used to hire a lot of grassroots people who lived the life that they were working in. Therefore they had an innate understanding of the people's needs. They may not have degrees, not be professional. They may not even speak in complete sentences, but they really cared about making change. It was possible for them to go out and do outreach. It was possible for them to provide information."

For Fred, it is also important to hire poor people who are competent so that they can build a resume around their job experience in the organization and possibly go on to real living-wage employment in the community. The current professionalization has forgotten that function of antipoverty organizations.

If Fred and Anne are right, the dialectic of Sister Bernadette must be seen in terms of Lukacs' crisis in capitalist rationality. In the world of antipoverty nonprofits, will the corporate model in managerial and accounting decisions, the fetishism of fundraising, and the delivery of world-class services occur independent of a real understanding of the everyday lived experience of poor people? In a society that emphasizes wealth and endless consumption, will the delivery of services take the place of a real reduction in poverty? Delivering world-class services at best makes poverty slightly more palatable to providers while sustaining the permanence of poverty. Advocacy itself was never up to task of ending poverty in the richest society in world, but the end of advocacy seems to leave the poor with almost nothing—only the slight possibility that some few will move into the lesser hardships of lower-middle-class life. The professionalization of antipoverty programs functions to maintain poverty.

For sociologists the macro, the large institutional sphere of society, and the micro, the face-to-face interactional sphere, are like East and West in the famous poem by Rudyard Kipling: "and never the twain shall meet." But in this book the macro and the micro are intertwined. Three macro events—the welfare reform legislation of 1996, the economic boom of the mid-1990s–2000, and the current global dominance of free market capitalism and its "material and mental production"—dominate the everyday micro lives of the poor. The consequences of these events include the increased ideological emphasis on work and self-reliance and the second managerial revolution, with its universal emphasis on corporate management methods. This sociological antinomy of macro and micro is not only false; it prevents us from looking at daily life in terms of the impact of global and national conditions. It gets in the way of an important condition of change: the creation of the new common sense and the new ordinary life that a world without poverty would require.

I conclude this chapter with another duality. Father James Maher, chair of the board of directors of St. John's Bread and Life, often worries about the tension between charism and bureaucracy. By *charism* he means "gift, or core beliefs." The "core belief" of the Vincentians (his order) "is service to the poor," he says. Father Maher here means that service to the poor could get lost in the minutiae of bureaucratic rules and regulations. For him this is always a potential problem. In this chapter about advocacy and charity, the secular and the sacred, we can see the tension between charism and bureaucracy as in part the result of the crisis of capitalist rationality. The requirements of bureaucracy and the domination of the commodity form create indifference to the needs of people. Just as human social life is dominated by the commodity form, the church's mission to the poor can become secondary to fundraising and its formalistic rules and regulations. We have seen throughout this chapter how, even for antipoverty organizations, both direct-service and advocacy-oriented, the ordinary misery of poor people has become secondary. This is the result of not taking the dialectic of Sister Bernadette seriously. If we take it seriously, then the ultimate goal of both direct-service and advocacy groups is to put themselves out of business—because there should no longer be any need for them.

Though advocacy organizations continue to involve themselves in legislative struggles and continue to educate and organize the poor, their tendency to be continually underfunded and unable to take on broader struggles is directly linked to their failure to preserve the safety net. The best that they can do is slow down its destruction. Charity may still work for direct service, even if it's only a Band-Aid, but it no longer works for advocacy and the mobilization of the poor.[40] In fact, the corporate model and the dependence on charity and foundation money has in the long run been a disaster for advocacy. It is time to think of an alternative model that isn't exclusively dependent on charity and foundation money. This is a model that enables the political work of antipoverty activists to be independent of corporations and their inability to create living-wage jobs with benefits—which, after all, is one of the root causes of poverty.

5   Forgetting Poverty
A Seder for Everyone

THIS CHAPTER IS ABOUT what is absent from most studies of
poverty, and that is a larger theoretical picture. Poverty is not just a
problem for a community; it is a problem for the whole society and
for all Americans. Social scientists have been very good at describing
the practical conditions of poverty in a local sense, but these empirical studies are too narrow, and they miss the broader global trends.
The only way to understand these trends is to engage the theoretical
discourses that can help us make sense of them. We must understand
poverty in the global, postmodern world that we live in; we cannot
be empirically provincial.

Up to now I have also been guilty of this narrow empiricism, describing the poor only in their local environment. It is now time to expand this locally grounded view and put local poverty in a global,
postmodern context. Thus in this chapter we will engage theories of
both the postmodern and global capitalism to understand what we
have to do to end poverty in the richest country in the world, the
United States of America.

At a Passover Seder I attended, one of the guests at the table said
how lucky we were to live in a country where there was no longer
any poverty and hunger. This was a very privileged group, upper-
middle-class, white, both Jews and non-Jews. What must it be like to
be poor in a world where you are continually judged by the nonpoor
in almost all of your everyday situations, from the welfare office to
work, from housing to school? This privileged and well-meaning
guest knew the right politically correct things to say on issues of sex-
ism, racism, and nutrition, but he had no sense of hunger or poverty.
The Seder deals with the misery of the powerless Hebrews and their
decision to flee in the face of overwhelming power, but here and now,

for the poor in the United States, there is no possibility of flight and nowhere to go; only the privileged can afford to flee. Ironically, the well-meaning guest seems to know all the details of the Seder but misses its point. Elijah is still waiting outside the door, still without anyone to listen to his prophecy of the coming of the Messiah.

The well-meaning guest is like mainstream economists and businessmen who talk about all the new opportunities of global capitalism but forget that it still forces billions of people in the world to live on less than two dollars a day.[1] Currently, conservative, neoliberal economists believe that all economic problems can be resolved just by reducing the involvement of government in the free market.[2] They believe that the private interest of global capitalism is the same as the general interest. They believe that there are no such things as political and social problems, only problems seeking technical economic remedies. But these neoliberal economists are forgetting that democracy isn't necessarily beneficial for the specific individual interests of corporate capitalism. Though armed with their science, they can never answer a simple question about the U.S. labor force: why can't the capitalist economy produce middle-class jobs for over half of the population in the United States? These "dismal" scientists ignore the class hardships of an enormous number of working people while producing optimistic economic forecasts for the few who can take advantage of them. Are neoliberal economists just ignorant of the lives of the majority of Americans, or do they really believe that "trickle-down economics" will make "all boats float"? Has their fetishism regarding their mathematical models blinded them to the real struggles of ordinary people?

Even as poverty in the United States has been both racialized and feminized, it is also still an issue of class. This means that it is about the resources that are required to live a normal life in society, what Weber called "life chances": that is, the opportunities for jobs, wages, education, health care, housing, and access to culture. But the ignoring of these class issues has spread, not abated, even though fully half of the population lives below the median family income and about 60 percent are living in hardship and significant debt in order to maintain their lifestyle.[3] To put it succinctly, the oppressors cannot see the impact of their oppression on the oppressed. The powerful are unable to see the poor and the powerless through their own eyes; thus the poor are seen as incompetent or mentally challenged or constitutionally lazy. Their poverty is their own fault.

This willful ignorance about the hardships of life is seen at almost every point in this society. Economists parade their statistics about corporate profits and economic growth as if unaware of their failures. First, they fail to understand the actual human relations that lie behind their statistics. They are cynical about descriptions of the daily lives of the have-nots by ethnographers and journalists; these positivists call such reports "anecdotal." Second, they fail to understand that their statistics are not absolutes but representations—approximations of reality. They allow for heuristic understanding but suffer from the crisis of representation. Alfred North Whitehead called it the "fallacy of misplaced concreteness": that is, "mistaking the abstract for the concrete."[4]

The Seder story is a way to get to the key question for this chapter: how can the privileged guest be ignorant of the tens of millions of poor people who live in the United States and billions more who live around the world? This is a society in which everyone is assumed to be middle-class and the poor are regarded like the terminal patients in David Sudnow's *Passing On*, whom the doctors treat as dead before they actually die.[5] The poor are forgotten, ignored, and, some say, invisible.

MEMENTO AND PURPOSEFUL FORGETTING

Forty years ago Michael Harrington told us about the poor who live in the other America: "The millions who are poor in the United States tend to become increasingly invisible. Here is a great mass of people, yet it takes an effort of the intellect and will even to see them."[6] Today, David Shipler tells us how to see the working poor: "The first step is to see the problems, and the first problem is the failure to see the people. Those who work but live impoverished lives blend into familiar landscapes and are therefore overlooked. They make up the invisible, silent America that analysts casually ignore."[7] After all these years, the poor still can't be seen.

Harrington's description of the poor as invisible, though seemingly valid at the time, is too passive an explanation of how poverty came to be ignored by most Americans and why the poor are overlooked. Ignoring the poor is actually a much more active and purposeful process: they are intentionally forgotten and willfully ignored. Jean-Paul Sartre would say that those to whom the poor are invisible are in bad faith. For Sartre, bad faith is a form of willful ignorance that makes the denial of truth and the flight from freedom possible: "the first act of bad faith is to flee what it cannot flee, to flee what it is."[8] Over all these years, the impact of many excellent academic studies of poverty has been forgotten, and bad faith has been dominant. The poor are forgotten and their aid is continually cut. Thus the war on poverty is forgotten or deliberately misremembered as a failure that should be forgotten. Poor people are undercounted, and the fact that we have the most poverty of any of the richest countries of the world is also ignored.[9] This purposeful forgetting has a very important impact on social policy, limiting what can be done not only about poverty but also about the hardships of the middle class in terms of taxes, medical care, and other issues. Moreover, we have also forgotten how to be critical, so most people fail to notice that American capitalism isn't working for most of the population and that poverty is just the most extreme illustration of its failure. Only minor reforms (at most) are practical. We are not allowed to dream of alternatives to the free market.

How can the poor be invisible when they are everywhere? They are the workfare workers cleaning the parks, the busboys, the Polish, Mexican, and Colombian men and women shaping up for construction work or sewing knockoffs of designer clothes in the sweatshops of your neighborhoods in Brooklyn, Queens, or Los Angeles. They live in public housing projects, trailer parks, rundown tenements, and abandoned buildings. They shop with food stamps in the supermarket and use the emergency ward for their medical care. There are officially 35 million in the United States, more in both absolute and percentage terms than in any of the other 19 richest countries in the world. The

Organization for Economic Cooperation and Development (OECD), in its comparisons of the rich countries, "measures poverty as 50 percent or less of the median income in each country."[10] The OECD standard points to a much higher number of poor Americans than the official Census Bureau count: 16.9 percent[11] versus 13.3 percent in 1997.[12] Statistical manipulations based on outdated poverty thresholds keep the numbers down, but the 35 million officially poor people in the United States exceed the population of Canada and are more than half the population of Italy or France or the United Kingdom.[13] Harrington and Shipler tell us that all these people are unseen. An intentional and purposeful forgetting seems to be a better explanation.

Sigmund Freud's notion of purposeful forgetting, combined with Sartre's notion of willful ignorance, provides another perspective. The poor can't be seen because Americans are not motivated to see them. When unavoidably confronted with poverty, they willfully and purposely forget what they have seen.

"Forgetting impressions, scenes or experiences nearly always reduces itself to shutting them off," Freud says. "When the patient talks about these 'forgotten' things he seldom fails to add: 'as a matter of fact I've always known it; only I never thought of it.' "[14] Analyzing his own forgetting, he observes, "In every case the forgetting turned out to be based on a motive of unpleasure."[15]

Are Americans forgetful, willfully ignorant, or just "innocent"? Sartre tells us in *Truth and Existence* that "there exists a true knowledge in the ignorance of the innocent person. Through a dialectical reversal, not knowing is the best way of knowing."[16] For Sartre, innocence involves both "an intuitive grasp of the world," an ability to see past evil and grasp possibility, and also a certain irresponsibility. Sartre uses the example of the young virgin who is unaware of her sexuality and unknowingly puts herself in danger: "When a bourgeois decides to ignore the conditions of the working class or the origin of steak, he thus becomes like a young virgin. Historically, moreover, in Genesis knowledge is presented as a fall. The tree of knowledge was a trap."[17]

In biblical times the price of truth was human freedom. Only God provided truth, and humans were limited to passive reception. In the world after the Fall, when humans are on their own, being is always at risk, and truth and freedom are difficult to achieve. Willful ignorance becomes a way to avoid the conflicts of choice: "ignoring is fear of being."[18] It is also the fear of freedom because "freedom exists only in and through its efforts to make others free."[19] Willful ignorance allows one to ignore responsibility and freedom as active choices: "As a bourgeois I want to ignore the proletariat's position in order to ignore my responsibility for it."[20] *Necessary* ignorance, however, is crucial for knowing; it's "the starting point for truth."[21] Necessary ignorance is the beginning of the questioning and curiosity that are essential to knowing. In contrast, the seductive desire of willful ignorance may lead to bad faith. This makes the denial of truth and the fleeing of freedom possible at the same time. Bad faith is a self-deception in which the world is understood as if there are no other choices and no alternatives. It is a flight from freedom of choice and the responsibility of consciousness and action.

The existence of poverty in the richest and most successful capitalist country in the world is about the victory of bad faith. We see a similar dialectic of necessary and willful ignorance being played out tragically in the film *Memento*. *Memento* can help us understand the ordinariness of the bad faith of Americans, whose willful ignorance and purposeful forgetting are necessary for the continuance of poverty in their country.

The protagonist of *Memento*, Leonard Shelby, has a short-term memory problem, and we are told that it's not amnesia. The narrative of the film is structured by Leonard's identity problem, which is also a memory problem. He is trying to solve his wife's murder, but he cannot remember anything that happened since her death. The main narrative of the film is told in reverse, while the flashbacks move forward to the present. Leonard's documentary evidence, like Foucault's archaeology, consists of notes on paper and labeled Polaroid photos, with the most important facts tattooed on his body. These "facts" lead him and the audience on a murderous journey. He calls his fragments of evidence his "system," and he believes that ultimately it will lead him to avenge his wife's murder. In fact at the beginning of the movie he accomplishes his revenge with the killing of Teddy. The system has worked; his archaeology is completed. Still, the movie proceeds from the end to the beginning, with episodic mementos of evidence.

At the beginning of the film, Leonard describes his problem: "I have this condition. . . . I have no short-term memory. I know who I am, I know all about myself. Since my injury . . . I can't make new memories. Everything fades. If I talk too long, I'll forget how we started, and the next time I see you I'm not going to remember this conversation. I won't even know if I met you before."[22]

Throughout the movie Leonard tells his story over and over again. An important figure in this endlessly repeated narrative is Sammy Jankis, who serves as Leonard's role model. In Leonard's first important case as an insurance investigator, he denied Sammy's insurance claim because he concluded that Sammy's problem was mental and not physical. As a result of a car accident, Sammy can't remember anything for more than a few minutes. He cannot work and sits at home all day with his wife, who is an insulin-dependent diabetic.

After the insurance company rules against Sammy, his wife gives him his "final exam," saying, "It's time for my [insulin] shot." She knows that he loves her, and asking for an extra shot will reveal whether he is faking. But he isn't faking, and he continues to give her shots of insulin. She dies, and Sammy is placed in a home, not even knowing that his wife is dead.

Eventually Leonard tells us how his wife was murdered. One night he wakes up and finds that she has left their bed. As he starts to look for her, he hears a muffled scream. He loads his gun and continues into the bathroom. There he finds a hooded man raping his wife, who is bound and gagged, with a plastic bag over her head. Suddenly Leonard is hit on the head from behind and knocked out. He awakes with a brain injury and finds his wife dead. The police do not believe his story about the second man, so his quest to find his wife's killer, "John G.," "J. G.," begins.

In the final scene of the movie—which shows the beginning of this story told in reverse—Leonard kills the drug dealer Jimmy Grant, "J. G." Afterward he takes a Polaroid photo and hauls the body into an abandoned building. As he drags the body down the basement steps, he believes he hears the dead man say, "Sammy." Leonard looks at his Polaroids; confused, he asks, "What have I done?"

His helper, Teddy, arrives and tells Leonard that he is a cop—in fact, the cop who was originally assigned to Leonard's case. From Teddy's account we learn that Leonard's wife survived the assault but refused to believe in Leonard's short-term memory condition. It was Leonard's wife who had diabetes. Sammy Jankis didn't even have a wife, and he *was* a faker. It was Leonard who unknowingly killed his wife.

As Freud says: "[W]e may say that the patient does not *remember* anything of what he has forgotten and repressed but *acts* it out. He reproduces it not as a memory but as an action; he *repeats* it, without, of course, knowing that he is repeating it."[23]

Here we find out that Teddy helped Leonard find the real John G. and kill him over a year before. Leonard was happy for a moment but soon forgot and started to search again for John G. So Teddy helped him find a new John G., whom Leonard has just killed. Knowing that Leonard will soon start searching for John G. again, Teddy tells him, "You want to have a puzzle that you can never solve."

The cop now reveals that "Teddy" is a nickname; his real name is John Gammel. As the movie ends, Leonard tells himself: "You're John G., you can be my John G. Do I lie to myself to be happy? In your case, Teddy, yes, I will." He takes the Jaguar of the man he just killed and drives away, as Teddy yells after him. He stops at the tattoo parlor. We know he will kill Teddy and then forget. The movie ends, but the story seems to be an endless, repetitive loop.

Leonard goes beyond Sartre's avoiding and ignorance of the truth. When he finds out that he killed his wife by giving her too much insulin, he kills the truth teller and changes the evidence to disguise the truth teller's identity. This active forgetting and purposeful disguising of the truth are the keys to understanding how the possibility of change, especially in terms of ending poverty, has been forgotten in the United States. The premises and the conditions of capitalism that reproduce and maintain poverty are purposely forgotten. As in *Memento*, the poor are degraded and the truth tellers are metaphorically killed, in the sense that their effectiveness is canceled. This is why so many good academic studies of poverty are routinely forgotten.

Memento seems to end without resolution—or is the resolution Leonard's complicity with the purposeful forgetting of the killings? Remember that the crime is difficult to solve because Leonard doesn't want to remember that it has already been solved. His willful ignorance of this crucial fact leads him to create an endless and deadly puzzle that can never be resolved even when it has been. He also forgets his own guilt in degrading and killing his wife. In the United States we engage in the same kind of willful ignorance about poverty. Are we as sick as Leonard is? We have forgotten the poor, are complicit in the maintenance of poverty, and continue to "blame the victims." We forget to remember that a solution to poverty in the United States is already available. The "unpleasure" that leads to forgetting in this instance is generated by what poverty indicates about the United States and its free market capitalist regime. Poverty is a major indicator of the limits and failures of capitalism to provide for all. We are in bad faith, compulsively blaming the poor for their poverty instead of blaming American capitalism. Here Freud is helpful again, explaining the importance of forgetting when national identity is attacked: "It is universally acknowledged that where the origin of a people's traditions and legendary history are concerned, a motive of this kind, whose aim is to wipe from memory whatever is distressing to national feeling, must be taken into consideration."[24]

In bad faith we forget the realities of poverty in the richest country in the world while the political-economic verities that maintain the society are safe. We deny the existence of the poor, especially the working poor. We ignore all of the studies of social scientists and advocates and believe that the free market, or the new economy, will lift all boats. We falsely believe that poverty is a marginal phenomenon in the United States and that the few who are poor have some moral or genetic problem.

But it cannot be overlooked, ignored, or forgotten how overwhelming the lives of the poor are and how difficult it is to struggle for even simple changes in their misery. It cannot be forgotten that policy changes that provide more resources for the poor are not enough to end poverty in the United States. Nor can we forget that the conservatives who currently run the country continue to cut antipoverty programs. The first step in ending poverty is to begin remembering how ordinary poverty and economic and social hardships are in the United States. We need to remember that even during liberal administrations, poverty, though reduced, still existed for tens of millions of Americans. These are difficult issues that require both significant changes in our understanding of American society and the hard work of facing up to its failures. If we cannot stop being willfully ignorant of the poor, then, as in *Memento*, American poverty will remain on an endless, repetitive loop.

Here I want to broaden the context to our current postmodern condition. Like the screenplay of *Memento*, the postmodernists uncover truth only to disguise its origins and any real possibility of overcoming it. Bureaucracy deflects truth with practicality and the logic of accountancy, and willful ignorance takes the form of asserting that class power is no longer important and that social movements are independent of class struggle. We have forgotten class rules. Have we also forgotten that we cannot understand poverty and the possibility of ending it unless we understand power in the context of the narratives of our time?

THE POSTMODERN AND THE LAST MASTER NARRATIVE

Michel Foucault's critique of modernism and his analysis of power have had a profound effect on postmodern and poststructuralist social theory. Foucault describes

> [t]he omnipresence of power: not because it has the privilege of consolidating everything under its invincible unity, but because it is produced from one moment to the next, at every point, or rather in every relation from one point to another. Power is everywhere not because it embraces everything but because it comes from everywhere.[25]

Further: "Where there is power there is resistance, and yet, or rather consequently, this resistance is never in a position of exteriority in relation to power."[26]

Foucault theorizes about the micro-level of power in opposition to the tyranny of all totalizing discourses: the grand narratives of history composed by Marx, Freud, the sciences of man. Thus he opposes Marxism as a project in which the continuity and singularity of its great truth dialectically explains history as an inevitable contest between classes ending with the defeat of the bourgeoisie. Power is not to be understood in terms of these grand schemes of history, culminating in the myth of scientific truth. It is not to be understood as continuous and the result of history, but as a break that constitutes both individuals and knowledge. Struggles here occur at the level of micro-politics, at the capillary level: "the point where power reaches into every grain of individuals, touches their bodies and inserts itself into their actions and attitudes, their discourses, learning processes and everyday lives."[27]

Foucault's notion of power equalizes instead of creating hierarchies. Power is everywhere; it is equal, circulating, multiple, constituting discourses, fomenting micro-struggles. This allows an insurrection of subjugated knowledge to surface: "the historical contents that have been buried and disguised in a functionalist coherence or formal systematization."[28] Disqualified knowledges display themselves, and individuals are constructed by the power of these discourses. Many struggles come to the surface; a whole "politics of identity" is constituted everywhere from gays and lesbians to the Taliban to Serbs and Croatians. Here knowledge is power—the power to define others.

Power/knowledge at the micro-level is liberation; as it is institutionalized, it becomes *panoptic*, a word conveying domination, judgment, surveillance, discipline, and control. Foucault appropriates Jeremy Bentham's Panopticon, the circular prison in which the prisoners in their cells were all visible from a central watchtower while the guards themselves remained invisible. For Foucault, the Panopticon was a form that could increase control and surveillance in a multiplicity of institutions: "Is it surprising that prisons resemble factories, schools, barracks, hospitals, which all resemble prisons?"[29]

Here we seem to have a description of the world of poverty. Advocates, professionals, the homeless, the hungry, the HIV-positive, poor women, engage all kinds of micro-struggles for benefits and programs, which, as they become successful, become panoptic. Foucault's description has real relevance for understanding poverty, but he cannot offer an alternative analysis, or a vocabulary that can nourish a movement to change all of this misery. The micro-struggles help to define a situation, and even provide some innovations for ending poverty. But they are pluralist, as if power competes equally. To end poverty these micro-struggles must unify. Unification is necessary for power as a force that moves the world. This is not happening, Foucault is right, and as long as he is, the misery of the poor will increase.

Only micro-politics is possible at this postmodern moment. The old grand narratives offer no alternatives, and micro-politics is a reformist alternative. Thus we live in an endless present in which there is no possibility of reinventing the world. Women's voices, lesbian and gay voices, African American voices, postcolonial voices—a multiplicity of formerly marginalized voices are now heard, but the emancipatory project of modernism seems exhausted, its voice reduced to the language of domination and oppression. Between Foucault's pluralism and his equalization of power and all these micro-struggles and micro-histories, we can't see the forest for the trees. The big picture is ruled out by his privileging of control over disciplinary regimes of power. Thus change is minimized at every point because of the success of this regime of bio-power. He tells us that the power regime of control is about the administration of the life of whole populations: "one would have to speak of *bio-power* to designate what brought life and its mechanisms into the realm of explicit calculations and made knowledge-power an agent of transformation of human life."[30] Of course people resist, and conflicts are everywhere, but there seems to be no way out, "no exit," from the bio-politics of control. The postmodern seems to be a trap.

With this complete rejection of totality, the poor have been unintentionally deconstructed as agents. I say "unintentionally" because they are not part of the postmodern gaze. They are absent in their discourse, as are class agents, women agents, racial agents, gay and lesbian agents. We have a series of fragmented presents; we have difference, but we do not have a way out of the present immiseration. There is no alternative to the ubiquitous present, no riots, no movement—only poverty professionals and advocates structuring the lives of the poor.

Micro-struggles are real, as are their limits. I am part of those limits. I am a professional social scientist and poverty advocate. I am on the board of directors for St. John's Bread and Life program, New York City Coalition Against Hunger (NYCCAH), and Hunger Action Network New York State (HANNYS); I was on the steering committee of the Same Boat Coalition and a member of the WEP Workers Organizing Committee (WWOC) of ACORN. I also lobby for these groups and participate in the three-minute democracy of public hearings. The following example is drawn from that experience.

A few years ago, there was a continuous and concerted effort to lobby the New York City Council in opposition to Mayor Rudy Giuliani's relentless cuts in education and poverty programs. Council member after Council member told NYCCAH advocates and members of the Same Boat Coalition that they were against these cuts. One told us: "You have to understand that Giuliani is a nightmare. . . . [W]e are on your side." Though NYCCAH and HANNYS are primarily oriented to hunger issues, they lobbied for more services and benefits for all of the poor. Thus, NYCCAH lobbied to add $4 million to the Emergency Food Assistance Program (EFAP), and also for $2 million for the eviction prevention program, legal services for the poor, and an educational outreach program to help people in danger of losing their housing. In the end, the City Council crumbled and approved Giuliani's budget. Poverty and education programs were cut. The antihunger advocates were relatively successful and got about half of what they wanted for EFAP, but the poor received none of the other benefits.

Here is an example of the limits of micro-politics, where many interest groups struggle against each other for pieces of a shrinking pie—not for a larger pie or an alternative to this insidious structure. The rules of the game are determined beyond the world of the advocates, in the back rooms of government, where the political meets Wall Street, the corporations and the banks that are the real power.

Micro-struggles at best can fight for reforms. Only a social movement can change the rules of the game. The postmodern condition is a reformist and pluralist moment in a time that requires great change. Thus, the micro-struggles of the poor take a Foucauldian turn: they cheat, rob, and steal. Crime becomes a major form of resistance, and domination, judgment, and surveillance increase in response. The endless loop of the immiseration of the poor continues.

Ernesto Laclau and Chantal Mouffe resist the Marxist privileging of the agency of a single subject.[31] Their analysis denies any agency to the proletariat and reduces the poor to silence: the poor are even excluded from their pluralist game. Laclau and Mouffe allow the working-class struggle as a discursive formation, but this struggle takes the form of a transformation that will occur without any human agents. As a result, their argument denies the autonomy of the plurality of the oppressed groups they are defending. They deny the subjectivity of groups that have only recently displayed their subjectivity, whether they are women struggling for equal rights, lesbians, or the Brazilian working class. This is particularly important for the poor who remain outside the power of discourse. What Laclau and Mouffe have unintentionally posited is a new vanguardism of "intellectual and moral leadership." Their claim that domination and oppression do not exist until a discursive formation labels them as such negates the actual experience of ordinary people. Nor can these people struggle to formulate their own discursive formations, according to Laclau and Mouffe. If true, this explains why there are no poor people's movements and why radical discourse seems to exist independent of their lives. A truly radical democracy would have to create the conditions of active participation for all, based on the guarantee of a middle-class standard of living for everyone. This is the basis for a new class project: one that understands the demands of women, gays, and racial minorities and also the centrality of knowledge-based high-tech production regimes. Here class is not to be understood as a reified category but as a project that is formed in a movement. Class then is not to be excluded; it is central to the formation of an alternative to the current pursuit of piecemeal reforms.

Laclau and Mouffe seem to be correct—like Foucault—in explaining why social movements fail to develop. They are all pluralists; they equalize power, and in this equalization of power ordinary people lose their struggles before they begin. But it is in Foucault that this is most important because his bio-politics misses the inequality of power in his dichotomous definition of power. The power of the Group of Eight and of multinational corporations increasingly defines the world and its local politics. It is not an either/or but both/and more. It is not the development from a disciplinary society to a society of control, but both disciplinary and control are simultaneous and global. Power is used by the powerful in the ways that are necessary for the maintenance of their power. As a result, both wars and police violence are still required. It is global in a new sense: that local is only an option to the extent that it is part of a global system. This global system is pluralist in form but really about financial domination by the powerful—that is, the dominant nations and their corporations.

Thus global capitalism is more centralized and increasingly concentrated. All countries have to play by the same rules; the welfare state must be privatized, and workers must become more flexible. "More with less" is a global strategy. Here one hopes that the "Specter of Marx" is haunting the beginning of a global social movement.[32] Such a movement would understand that global poverty is maintained by the powerful, who say they are trying to eliminate it but really mean that they are trying to contain it. Poverty is about the race to the bottom caused by this strategy. The global middle class is not exempt from this race; they are increasingly losing their resources and power. As global capital forces privatization and shrinks the welfare state, wages and salaries continue to decline, and health care and housing become more expensive. The global free market whose invisible hand will raise all boats is merely the ideological apparatus of the managers of global policy and their institutions: the Group of Eight, the World Trade Organization, the International Monetary Fund, the United Nations.

There is more forgetting on the global level. The economists, the managers, and the global corporate elite have forgotten the realities of their own zero-sum games in which the free market really benefits only the few. They have forgotten the universal management strategy of "more with less": that is, higher productivity and fewer workers. They have purposely forgotten that they still need cheap labor in a world of virtual economic games. Global corporations still require workers because they are still involved in capital accumulation. They have purposely forgotten that their version of global development means global immiseration for billions and a jobless future for too many. They have purposely forgotten that this current regime of global power has a lasting impact on the poor and the middle class and that, simply put, the free market always means "less for more." In a world of commodity fetishizers, this means that the middle and lower classes will pay more for fewer goods and services. In an increasingly "Wal-Martized" world, even the charm of a Macy's or a Bloomingdale's department store is lost as the middle class, in its downward spiral, looks for cheaper and cheaper products. Here Wal-Mart delivers the goods by not paying its employees real living wages and benefits and by being the number-one U.S. market for clothing manufactured by China's low-waged labor force. In these cheap prices, based on exploiting labor in both China and the United States,[33] we see the direct impact of the global economy.

We see the same relationship between global competition, the deregulation of the garment industry, and the increasing immiseration of the poor in Barbara Ehrenreich's *Nickel and Dimed*. Ehrenreich and her coworkers were paid $7.00 per hour at the Wal-Mart in Minneapolis, "putting clothes away" in the women's clothing section. They can barely find affordable housing, are forced to work overtime, and are continually degraded by Wal-Mart's "corporate miserliness."[34] Even in the postmodern world, there seems to be a continuum of exploitation and oppression. There is still a master narrative, and it is still capital accumulation.

The Secret Narrative of Postmodernism

The grand narratives no longer work, but there is nothing to take their place—certainly not micro-politics or radical democracy, because neither is attached to a social movement, and therefore they remain abstractions. But even with all of the postmodern discourse against the master narrative, the signs and spaces of the postmodern world are flooded by an unspoken signifier: global capital. Computer-aided postmodern capitalism is the signifier of this world and its last master narrative.

Computer-aided capitalism meets the postmodern at the point of flexible, just-in-time, post-Fordist production regimes. These production regimes have been made possible because of the new knowledge-based computer technologies. They depend on the computer in the same way that Fordist mass production regimes were dependent on the mechanical technologies of industrial capitalism: the moving assembly line and the enormous factories in which the mass production of commodities took place. The postmodern is the cultural sensibility that enframes the commodity production of computer-aided capitalism. This new form of capitalism enables the commodification of knowledge in endless and instantaneous simulations. It reduces all signifieds to its free market script. It has annihilated space and time. Space is transformed into controllable cyberspace, where Wall Street and banks become unnecessary as physical places and exist only in the ever-increasing power of the World Wide Web. Time is compressed to automatic turnover in an endless excess of profit. This immediate capitalism no longer has to legitimate itself because there aren't any competing grand narratives now that history is obsolete. It sounds like science fiction, but it has become our world. William Gibson defines it in his science fiction novel *Neuromancer*: "Cyberspace. A consensual hallucination experienced daily by billions of legitimate operators, in every nation, by children being taught mathematical concepts. . . . A graphic representation of data abstracted from the banks of every computer in the human system. Unthinkable complexity. Lines of light ranged on the nonplace of the mind, clusters and constellations of data. Like city lights receding."[35]

Computer-aided capitalism is global and multicultural in the sense of being a truly hegemonic domination. Capitalism in its modernist stage was oppressive, but it needed a strong nation-state to facilitate accumulation and social programs to pacify its citizens and buffer capital's excesses: Social Security, AFDC, and unemployment benefits helped legitimate nationally based corporate capital. Under computer-aided capitalism, as it morphs into cyber-capitalism and knows no space, such as a nation state, its only allegiance is to excessive profits, and as a result all welfare state benefits are now at risk. With faster and faster turnovers, profits multiply in cyberspace, the economic nonplace without boundaries. Capitalism has always been global and in that sense de-territorialized, but this quality has now become dominant in cyber-capitalism. As Gilles Deleuze and Felix Guattari tell us, "Today we can depict an enormous, so-called stateless, monetary mass that circulates through foreign exchange and across borders, eluding control by the States, forming a multinational ecumenical organization, constituting a de facto supranational power untouched by governmental decision."[36]

So far, the state still regulates when necessary and provides unprofitable services that citizens require. President George W. Bush uses the word *compassionate* (as in "compassionate conservatism") to legitimate privatization and the further hollowing out of the state. "[G]overnment seems to be disappearing before our very eyes," according to "The Post-Work Manifesto":

> In the era of the roaring return of the once discredited idea that everyone is on her or his own . . . and its role as an adjunct to the interests of large corporations, the legacy of the era of the "compassionate state" is being erased as fast as the corporations and their political allies can manage. They are hollowing out these compassionate functions, leaving intact only the tasks associated with fighting crime, deploying the army to police the world and negotiating international business deals often coded as government diplomacy.[37]

The free market, increasingly free of state regulation, is now in a hyper form, beyond anything Adam Smith imagined. It creates profit at every itch and scratch. Public space implodes, and politics is reduced to a sideshow for capitalism's expansion beyond space and time. The hollow state is concerned with balancing budgets and eliminating taxes; this is how the public good is now defined.

First on the agenda of the hollow state are the entitlements of the poor. Advocates for the poor fight back, not through social movements but through attempts to rebuild the modernist functions of the nation-state and nostalgia for the New Deal and the Great Society. They try to maintain local programs that the hollow state must cut to balance the budget. Some of these battles are won. But the postmodern state's tendency is toward deregulation and privatization; that is the accumulation function for computer-aided capitalism. The poor are the greatest victims, but the lives of working-class and middle-class people are also being sacrificed. The middle class is angry, aware of their wage stagnation and job insecurity, but they can be appeased by tax cuts. The poor are silent.

The irony of this postmodern world is that everything has been deconstructed except computer-aided capitalism. All this postmodern politics ignores the hegemony of computer-aided capitalism and takes this reformist moment of history and universalizes it. Foucault, Laclau and Mouffe, Deleuze and Guattari have all created their own grand narrative of multiplicity, difference, and contingency. At this point in the present they are right, but we must not forget that this is but a moment. Even the hegemony of computer-aided capitalism is a moment. Ordinary people, as subjects of their own lives, reflect on, create, and produce their own cultural worlds, their own communities of resistance, their own alternatives to this moment of increasing immiseration. They still live in everyday life. They must do this both materially and discursively. Even when they are fragmented as a class and there seems to be no alternative to the world of global, computer-aided capitalism, there is the possibility of the beginnings of an alternative narrative—radical democracy. This is not an abstraction. It is based on a guaranteed income and a shorter work week without any reduction in wages and benefits. There is both time and space for resistance and change even in the face of a global cyber-capitalism. But this is always contingent on the willingness to struggle and build a social movement.

Here alternatives to the free market are often deflected by reference to the changes and complexities, the new processes and structures, that occur in global capitalism. As Michael Hardt and Antonio Negri point out in *Empire*:

The activities of corporations are no longer defined by the imposition of abstract command and the organization of simple theft and unequal exchange. Rather they directly structure and articulate territories and populations. They tend to make nation-states merely instruments to record the flows of the commodities, monies, and populations that they set in motion. The transnational corporations directly distribute labor power over various markets, functionally allocate resources, and organize hierarchically the various sectors of world productions. The complex apparatus that selects investments and directs financial and monetary maneuvers determines the new geography of the world market, or really the new biopolitical structuring of the world.[38]

In the bio-political structuring of postmodern capitalism, Lukacs' contradiction between the rationality of capitalist accumulation and the irrationality of its structure for human beings still has not been resolved. Hardt and Negri do not resolve this contradiction because for them the world has bypassed it. But are they wrong? Is Lukacs' contradiction still relevant? This question is crucial to the ordinary lives of the poor. To answer it, we must understand what Hardt and Negri mean by *Empire* in their controversial—and theoretical and conceptual—work. They define it as follows:

> [T]he concept of Empire posits a regime that effectively encompasses the spatial totality, or really that rules over the entire "civilized" world. No territorial boundaries limit its reign. . . . [It] suspends history and thereby fixes the existing state of affairs for eternity. . . . [T]he object of its rule is social life in its entirety and thus Empire presents the paradigmatic form of biopower. Finally, although the practice of Empire is bathed in blood, the concept of Empire is always dedicated to peace—a perpetual and universal peace outside of history.[39]

Hardt and Negri have constructed an Empire that is over-competent. They have suspended time and unified space, and there seems to be no convincing counterforce to this Empire. It exists as singularity, without an outside, without the contradictions that might have provided the necessary cracks in the bloc. But they have suspended the dialectic of technology so that the computer matrix provides the information that governs production and the immaterial labor that dominates the workplaces of Empire. Even the bio-politics of desire just provides new spaces for production, not for freedom. Here, information becomes dominant in the economy, and immaterial labor becomes the major productive force.[40]

Even the dialectic of domination has been suspended, and the administrative apparatus just smoothes over conflicts. This suspension of the dialectic of domination in the context of the move to immaterial labor has special meaning for the poor because the informational labor required for postmodern capitalism requires at least some higher education. The multitudes of poor and lower-class people in the world do not have sufficient access to the education that Empire requires. Thus they are doomed to be cheap labor, paid below the social wage. They are forced to compete in the rush to the bottom as their living standards decline and the gap between the rich and the poor increases. As the free market continues to dominate and de-territorialize the workplace, forcing workers to become nomads, there is no place for this mobile workforce to escape to. Empire has suspended values as well, and the contradictions in desire have been resolved through corruption.

Lukacs' contradiction of rationality is not resolved; it is ignored and reduced, like all contradictions, to a singularity. The dialectic of domination is also reduced to the smoothness of the multitude, a diffuse agent that is the hope and contradiction of Empire. But an Empire that is in constant crisis doesn't seem to be in any real danger. Its imperial power seems to have become an iron cage for the multitude. Hardt and Negri tell us that the multitude exists in a world where revolution is more possible than ever before. For them the multitude is a de-territorialized spatial movement whose labor power is a mobile and spatial commodity. "Through circulation the multitude reappropriates space and constitutes itself as an active subject."[41]

The singularity of the multitude exists only because Hardt and Negri ignore the real cleavages of nationalism, religion, class, race, and gender. These cleavages would fragment the already too diffuse multitude. In the best-case scenario, multitude seems to be another case of postmodern reform that is endorsing a global citizenship; and at its worst, it is a political trap. Even though Hardt and Negri call for "a social wage and a guaranteed income for all,"[42] it is a political trap because they have created an Empire in which domination is complete. Their suspension of the dialectic of inside and outside has disarmed the multitude's ability to struggle because it forces them to discard the terrain of national and local politics. Discarding the terrain where ordinary people could struggle for themselves is disastrous and leaves only the global as the terrain of struggle—a terrain that is a nonplace, too diffuse for any serious agency. Here we see that Hardt and Negri, as much as they claim to have discarded their past, have just reasserted the young Marx's argument in "On the Jewish Question."[43]

In that essay Marx argued about the limits of a purely political struggle, viewing the struggle specifically for Jewish emancipation as too particular and declaring that the real struggle is for total human emancipation. Though I agree with the spirit of Marx's argument, these are not revolutionary times. As a result, local, national, and international cultural and political struggles are all important. In the spirit of the dialectic of Sister Bernadette, which always reminds us of the difficulties of even simple struggles, we all must do what we can to fight for our freedom. Sartre reminds us of the attractiveness of the flight from freedom, and we have to recognize that it is both difficult and dangerous to struggle against the ruling powers. The struggle for Jewish emancipation was a fight that led to more struggles, just as the Civil Rights Movement led to other struggles in the 1960s and 1970s, from the antiwar movement to feminism.

Thus there are both strategic and theoretical dangers in Hardt and Negri's emphasis on this diffuse multitude. In their arguments for the multitude, they may have decapitated agency. The "creative imagination" that they call for in the multitude is too abstract; it has none of Bloch's creativity and boldness, nor does it create the theoretical space that Adorno does with his negative dialectic (see Chapter 2). Here, in the present, theory can become a political strategy. The danger that always exists in theory is that it can have no possible relation to action, when both theory and action are needed to create progressive change and wage a real war on poverty. Throughout *Empire* Hardt and Negri create an either/or logic that disguises the complexities of the world. Is the either/or a form of willful ignorance that does away with the unpleasure of the dialectic and the difficult contradictions of the global world? To struggle against the behemoth of Empire that they have created would call for the best and most radical elements of modernity, postmodernity, and whatever else is coming. They end that possibility, as all postmodernists do, by suspending history and creating a world that is stuck in eternity. They defeat themselves in their political postmodern theoretical purity. They have forgotten that nothing in the world is as competent as the Empire they have formulated. They flee before the unpleasure of the uncertainty of global capitalism. But the dialectic and its unending contradictions are not really suspended. There is no inviolable Empire. Class, race, and gender struggle and real social changes are still possible.

A VALUE SYSTEM FOR GLOBALIZATION: HUNTINGTON AND HAYEK

When I was in graduate school, my political sociology professor, Feliks Gross, often told the class, "You cannot understand domestic policy without understanding the foreign policy of a country; they are a continuum." In fact, they must be understood as codetermining. Gross's teachings have at least two implications for this book. One is that poverty in the United States must be understood in terms of the power structure—hence the discussion in the previous section of Hardt and Negri's analysis of power, and the discussion of Samuel Huntington and F. A. Hayek below. The other is that poverty in the United States is related to global poverty. My emphasis in this book on income solutions to U.S. poverty is ultimately not that different from Edward Muller and Mitchell Seligson's arguments for the use of income solutions to reduce global poverty.[44] In the race to bottom that the new global economy has forced on people all over the world, local poverty must be understood globally.

Choices for the Poor: Lessons from National Poverty Strategies, published by the UN Development Programme, reports "that falling incomes and rising poverty are eroding the capacity of poor people to be part of social networks of support, leaving them unable to engage in and maintain social exchange. By cutting people off from vital sources of support, social isolation...makes them even more vulnerable to adverse shocks and crises."[45] The study demonstrates that a reduction of social isolation and participation in governance will help with "poverty alleviation":

> The PSI [Poverty Strategies Initiative] studies confirm the findings of others which show how genuinely participatory governance at the local level can yield benefits in terms of both efficiency and equity, by giving people a sense of ownership, by allocating resources according to people's preferences and by utilizing their skills and knowledge. But the goal of genuine participatory decentralization remains a distant one in most developing countries despite the efforts made during the last half century.[46]

Such calls for more participatory governance for the poor are viewed by the global power blocs as both unrealistic and impractical. After all, world politics and the global economy increasingly require the expertise of scientists, scholars, policy experts, and politicians. Real "of the people and for the people" mass participatory democracy cannot be allowed. The future of the world is at stake, and real-world citizenry is out of the question. The demands of global capitalism and the free market must deny mass participatory democracy. Paramount among studies of expertise and global policy is the work of Huntington and Hayek.

The Clash of Civilizations by Samuel P. Huntington is a powerful statement about current global conflicts. After the events of 9/11, it defined the global crisis for many. It actually conceals as much as it reveals. More important, it has become a model for American foreign affairs, including an expanding military budget and continued active military aggression in a post-cold-war world. Huntington privileges cultural conflict and masks political and economic conflict. Cultural conflict exists at the racial and ethnic levels, but class struggle is relegated to the past because capitalism has delivered the goods. Thus problems of class, such as poverty, are no longer crucial. With the end of the cold war, conflicts between civilizations now dominate the globe. The great majority of the world's population is still poor, and one could argue that their hopeless and miserable lives are behind much of the strife in the world, but Huntington doesn't make this argument. Instead, he tells us, "In this new world the most pervasive, important and dangerous conflicts will not be between social classes, rich and poor, or other economically defined groups, but between people belonging to different cultural entities."[47]

Huntington is not questioning the hegemony of liberal democratic capitalism, but he is worried that the contradictions between civilizations will undermine that hegemony. His real concern is with the dominance of Western Civilization and what he defines as the "American Creed"—the principles "[o]n which Americans overwhelmingly agree: liberty, democracy, individualism, equality before the law, constitutionalism and private property."[48]

In Huntington's view, this American Creed has come under attack by the multiculturalists, who pose a threat not only to the United States but to the whole of Western Civilization. Huntington seems to be reacting to the current wave of immigration to the United States from Asia and South and Central America and its resulting diversity. He attacks the policies of President Clinton, and specifically his "encouragement of diversity,"[49] which Huntington sees as the cultural Achilles heel of liberal capitalism and a danger to Western hegemony.

Ellen Willis reminds us of what is left out of the "clash of civilizations" imagery: these opposing civilizations have in common patriarchy and its violence and control of women and children.[50] She explains the limits of his version of the "personal is political" in the narrowness of his vision of the patriarchal singularity of "American Identity" embedded in an "Anglo-Protestant Culture." Here the patriarchal American Creed is threatened not only by the liberal policies of multiculturalism, affirmative action, and bilingual education, but specifically by the sizable Hispanic migration that refuses to assimilate and that threatens to make Anglo-Protestant Americans a minority. Thus Huntington tells us that for Hispanics the American dream is conditional: "There is only the American dream created by an Anglo-Protestant society. Mexican-Americans will share in that dream and in that society only if they dream in English."[51]

Anglo-American culture demands that everyone be a white male of (at least) upper-middle-class background, have an advanced professional degree, work hard, speak English, and go to church on Sunday. Here the poor have been written out of America's identity, as have immigrants and people who are not Christian or not white. Manning Marable and Robin D. G. Kelly, among others, argue that the price of political equality should not be giving up your own distinct cultural identity.[52] But for Huntington it is: you must give up your ethnic or racial identity to become an American and participate in Anglo-Protestant culture. The patriarchal structure of the American Creed is believed to be a positive norm, required of all citizens as a core condition for America's proper dominance of the world.

The world of globalization is a world in which prosperity as a result of market capitalism is now taken for granted. Huntington's cultural conditions are necessary but not sufficient for global domination. Thus, the dominance of free market capitalism is the result not of the end of ideology, but really of the success of ideology. At the heart of this success is the work of F. A. Hayek. His economic principles are basic to capitalism in its computer-aided and global form. Here workers' movements for higher wages and the existence of the poor are not just ignored; they are viewed as impediments to a "free economy."

Hayek is probably the thinker most responsible for the current emphasis on free market principles. Central to this development is his stress on the importance of knowledge for a "rational economic order." He argued that collectivism and planning (not just communism, which was for him the pure embodiment of these two principles) were leading the world down the road to totalitarianism. Planning, even armed with a sophisticated social science methodology, could not accomplish a rational economic order. The requirements of knowledge were just too great, not only for governments but for science as well. In Hayek's epistemology, humans are just not up to the task. This may seem strange because he also emphasized individualism, but what he really meant was individual competition—the economic activity to which he reduced all human behavior. But his economic individuals had only a partial and thus insufficient knowledge: Hayek referred to "the unavoidable imperfection of man's knowledge and the consequent need for a process by which knowledge is constantly communicated and acquired."[53]

His economic epistemology is an automatic system that overcomes the problems of both government planning and even individual inadequacies. In a world of imperfect knowledge, the "marvel" of the price system provides the solution.[54] For Hayek the price system provides the automatic machinery for understanding liberal capitalism as a rational economic order. The problem has always been too much government intervention, too much economic planning, too many monopolies, and too much egalitarianism. Everything that restricts practical competition, markets, and prices causes problems for a free economy.

A complete interrogation of Hayek's work is outside the scope of this book, but some description is important for understanding this work as part of the ideological foundations of current global capitalism, including its real opposition to participatory democracy and its tolerance of economic hardship for the lower classes. It is especially important to look at Hayek's position on the rich and the poor.

As Hayek saw it, all attempts to remedy poverty that involve planned redistribution are doomed to failure. These policies will only increase the misery of the poor and those who receive low wages. Trade union struggles for higher wages and full employment only lead to more inequality. If unions resist lower wages, then they will have to be "coerced," through unemployment, to take low-waged jobs.[55] Economic redistribution to help the poor just alienates members of other classes and leads us down the "road to serfdom." Minimum-wage legislation just makes the worker more expensive and prices him out of the world market: "Minimum wage legislation, supposedly in his interest, is frequently no more than a means to deprive him of his only chance to better his conditions by overcoming natural disadvantages by working at wages lower than his fellows in other countries."[56] The only opportunity for the poor worker is to continue to work at low wages. This is not the road out of poverty, but that doesn't seem to bother Hayek, any more than it bothers today's global capitalist. Hayek is concerned only with the rights of the rich. This position can be seen clearly in his view of redistribution through progressive income taxation as merely a hindrance to the successful man, both economically and politically.[57]

Here in a nutshell, in the work of Huntington and Hayek, is the logic of the current globally organized world. It is a world where poor people and low-wage workers are not only denied a decent standard of living; they are excluded from democracy as well—not just in the sense of self-governance, but even in the sense of voting in contested elections. It is a world of serious cultural conflicts but also a world in which there is an "end of ideology." This is because free market capitalism is believed to have delivered on its promise. Hayek's work provided the rationale for free global markets and for hollowing out nation-states so that they provide fewer and fewer protections and services for their citizens. Huntington justifies the West's control of global capitalism. The world that these theorists have helped to create does not nurture either the poor or democratic participation in society. It is a grim world in which the great majorities are excluded and most still live at the margins. With six-sevenths of the world's population left out of middle-class prosperity, the failure of market capitalism is massive.[58]

Global capitalism has in fact failed to deliver on its promise. The poor in the United States and the world seem to be stranded in their lives of economic and cultural deprivation. Even in the richest countries, the comfortable lives of the middle class are threatened. As the welfare state is hollowed out throughout the world, wages and benefits do not keep up. The returns of global capital are diminishing for all but the wealthiest.

This chapter has investigated the theoretical and ideological framework of global capitalism and its relations to global and local poverty. It is my contention that they are bound together. It is in this context that I now turn to the possibility of ending poverty in the United States. One would think that this would be unnecessary and that in the richest capitalist country in the world poverty would be on the verge of extinction. But, as we have seen, this isn't the case: half of the population endures continual hardship, which is actually increasing because the massive costs of globalization in its corporate and military forms make traditional domestic programs unaffordable for the middle and lower classes. We see this in the destruction of entitlements during the Clinton years and the continuing threats by

President George W. Bush's administration to privatize Social Security, which would be disastrous for the middle class as well as the working class and the poor. Thus I turn to the simple struggles that are the minimum requirements for building a social movement to end poverty in the United States of America.

6   Conclusion

Making Poverty Extraordinary

WE HAVE SEEN THAT the poor did not benefit from the economic boom during the Clinton years, when public policy was guided by the conservative politics of the *Contract With America.* Similarly, during the economic boom of the 1960s, public poverty policy was heavily influenced by Moynihan's *Negro Family* study. Good economic times do not necessarily lead to significant changes in public policy in favor of poor people. In fact, as Piven and Cloward make clear in *Regulating the Poor*, only periods of struggle and social movement seem to benefit the poor in any substantial way, fostering antipoverty legislation and social programs like food stamps. Moreover, as I argue throughout this book, the incremental reforms of liberal public policy have continued to fail the poor.

This failure of liberal policy is the context for this exploration of poverty in Brooklyn from 1988 to 2000. Throughout this period, the number of people who are poor or living in hardship has stagnated at one half the population of the United States—a failure that is willfully ignored by liberals and at the same time thrown in their faces by conservatives. Meanwhile, *The Negro Family* and *The Contract With America* are still used to justify society's meager care for the poor.

I have tried to convey how overwhelming the lives of poor people are and how difficult it is to struggle for even simple changes in their lives. There are some victories: WWOC has won some of its simple struggles for better conditions for workfare workers; the poor and their advocates, using all the legal forms of resistance that are available to them, won increased funding for soup kitchens and food pantries. As we saw in Chapter 4, however, advocacy organizations, even if they are successful, tend to become more bureaucratic and increasingly alienated from the lives of the poor whom they serve, while doing very little to reduce poverty overall. For the great majority of poor people, hardship is a permanent condition.

Here the dialectic of Sister Bernadette offers some hope. Sister Bernadette's dialectic is the practical expression of Lukacs' crisis of capitalist rationality, which I have examined in terms of the irrationality of capitalist expansion for the lives of the poor. Simply said, even good times are bad times for poor people. The economic growth of free market capitalist society means the creation of more misery for them. They become more dependent just as welfare programs are cut, the number of low-wage jobs increases, and housing and health care become more expensive. Private charity expands to meet the needs of the poor but is unable to provide the same levels of compensation as the public programs of the past. This increasing immiseration makes political action even more important for the poor, while, in terms of Sister Bernadette's dialectic, at the same time it becomes more difficult to maintain the mixture of public and nonprofit programs that they depend upon.

The years of George W. Bush have been increasingly bad for both the lower and middle classes, with no end in sight to their hardships as long as he is president. Throughout this book I have argued that the poor have not created a social movement to end poverty, nor have advocates helped to create one. As long as this is true, their poverty is permanent. In the penultimate chapter I added a global context for the conditions of the poor in the United States. The present chapter explores what it will take to build a social movement to end poverty in the richest country in the world—within this global context and at a time of conservative triumph.

Here I turn to Karl Marx. Why? Not because his analysis succeeded in building a Communist movement that negated capitalism and achieved universal human emancipation. Clearly it didn't. In this postmodern period there seems to be no class with "radical chains." But there are still lessons to be learned from Marx, who always reminds us that real social change requires struggle in the context of a social movement. If there is any hope for the poor, it is that the simple struggles that are explained in this chapter can lead to the development of a new social movement that benefits both the poor and the middle class, whose hardships are increasing as well.

er gives up hope, even
d the Paris Commune.
y and understands that
he originally thought.
ut they do not make it
r circumstances chosen
ectly encountered and
rong about proletarian
rong about the impor-
wrong about men and
tion I focus on Marx's
e working day, as pre-
ucial point of struggle,
is a struggle that the
together.
t the relative unimp-
l trying to increase the

working day. Lukacs' crisis of capitalist rationality can still be seen in the introduction of flexible specialization into the workplace, where the increased productivity of workers is part of capital's managerial strategy to do "more with less." The global exploitation of the workforce is still alive and healthy, while Lukacs' contradiction is all but forgotten.

Spatially, class is about a worker's location in the labor process. There are four possible locations: you can own or control the labor process; you can be involved, directly or indirectly, in the production of value (from scientists to factory workers); you can manage or provide necessary services for the maintenance of the labor process; or you can be excluded from the labor process (housewives, the unemployed). Class exists in a continuum, and race and gender always play a role in terms of spatial location, and in terms of profits, salaries, wages, and benefits. Class, gender, and race must be understood as simultaneous and mutually determining. In terms of racial designations, for example, there is a crisis in the employment of black men throughout this society and particularly in New York City, where only 51.8 percent of black men were employed in 2003.[2]

Class also exists as a historical phenomenon. As Stanley Aronowitz argues: "[C]lass occurs when insurgent social formation(s) make demands that cleave society and engender new social and cultural relations. Needless to say, rulers may, with varying success, incorporate or integrate elements of these demands in order to thwart their class-producing consequences."[3]

Jacques Derrida tells us that Marx's ghost still haunts the world.[4] More than that, the struggle over the working day still cleaves the world. In *Capital* Marx poses the struggle over the working day and the exploitation of labor as an argument between the capitalist and the worker in the workplace: "Suddenly,... there arises the voice of the worker, which had previously been stifled in the sound and the fury of the production process.... You and I know on the market only one law, that of the exchange of commodities. And the consumption of commodities belongs not to the seller who parts with it.... The use of my daily labor power, therefore, belongs to you."[5]

In the workplace the class struggle is both writ large and specific to all workers, in all different occupational pursuits. It is the struggle for daily survival because people must pay their rent or mortgage; they must pay for food, clothing, education, and entertainment. They need time to interact with their family and friends; they need to eat, relax, and sleep. But to survive, most must work and make a wage or salary that allows them to maintain their standard of living. The struggle over labor time and pay continues, just as the need of capitalists to accumulate capital continues, even into these postmodern times. Even in the world of cyber-capitalism, with its myriad of changes, this struggle over wages and labor time still cleaves the society. Marx, concluding his discussion of the working day, has the worker address the capitalist as follows: "but the thing you represent when you come face to face with me has no heart in its breast. What seems to throb there is my own heartbeat. I demand a normal working day because, like every other seller, I demand the value of my commodity."[6]

The poor people all over this country who work for their benefits through workfare (WEP in New York City) have a practical under-standing of Marx. Though they deal with welfare bureaucrats, not capitalists, for them there is little difference. They work as many hours as they are required to for $1.86 per hour plus Medicaid benefits. They are also subject to the tyranny of the working day. On July 13, 2000, Eliot "Skip" Roseboro and Jose Nicolau were interviewed about WEP on the *CityWatch* segment of WBAI's *Wake-up Call* radio show.[7] Eliot defines the program for the listeners: "Basically WEP workers are previous welfare participants that as of a few years ago were asked to start working for their benefit checks. We've replaced approximately 2,200 positions that used to be regular city positions. That the mayor [Giuliani] moved out, forced people off, when he first came into office. Basically we are doing jobs for our welfare benefits."

Eliot Roseboro and Jose Nicolau are the co-chairs of ACORN's WEP Workers Organizing Committee (WWOC). They have both or-ganized and taken part in actions to democratize WEP. They helped get the New York City Council to pass legislation to give WEP workers the right to grieve, even though Mayor Giuliani refused to implement the procedures; they fought against the sexual harass-ment of female WEP workers, against unfair and dangerous working conditions, and for real training that will lead to living-wage jobs, as opposed to Job Search's temporary jobs. (When temporary jobs end, the worker must reapply for welfare and start all over again from the beginning. What Job Search really accomplishes is not a transition from welfare to work but a shift from welfare to increased poverty without any benefits.) WWOC also fights against excessive hours and arbitrary sanctioning with lost benefits. WEP workers seem to have been thrown back to a time and place in which working people have no rights or dignity. As members of WWOC, they support each other and struggle to make their conditions better.

Thus, Jose tells WBAI listeners: "We're the forgotten. We're like working in sweatshops. We're getting sweatshop salaries. We're getting intimidated, we're getting harassed, we're getting abused.... That's why I became an ACORN member. What does it matter to them. The supervisor is lousy.... I've seen the threats of sanction. Mothers going Thanksgiving without food. Crying that their kids got nothing for Christmas. It's really inhuman what they're doing to us. . . . It is sad that we as people have to go through this misery and oppression and deprivation."

Jose and Elliot may not be typical WEP workers, but they can help bridge the gap between workfare and the working and middle classes in a simple struggle over the working day. I do not know if a class formation can occur that will make this struggle possible, but it is still a struggle worth making.

POVERTY AND QUANTUM MEASURES FOR A JOBLESS FUTURE

Ulrich Beck states: "Capitalism is doing away with work. Unemployment is no longer a marginal fate. It affects everyone potentially, as well as the democratic way of life."[8]

Beck's position is at odds with the analysis Stanley Aronowitz and I present in *The Jobless Future*. He confuses work with employment. Aronowitz and I never argue that capitalism is ending work; we say that global, computer-aided capitalism is doing away with good jobs that offer good wages and benefits:

> [I]f the tendency of most investment is labor-saving in comparison to the part played by machinery in production, then the jobs created will be reduced relative to the unit of invested capital. So from the construction of buildings and the production of machinery the number of workers— intellectual as well as manual—is reduced by *quantum measures* in computer-mediated labor.[9]

By *job*, we, mean paid labor that has security and pays a real living wage (that is, is not contingent, temporary, or part-time). This very definition seems to run counter to the contemporary trend in the labor market. The massive destruction of jobs is not just the result of new technologies; it is also the result of a managerial ideology which views the increase in productivity as both efficient and necessary for the accumulation and reproduction of capital. This managerial ideology seeks to increase productivity by getting fewer workers to do more work for less pay and benefits and by exporting jobs to countries where labor is cheaper. Here is a danger for big capital. First, replacing living labor with machinery always involves a threat to the rate of profit;. Second, countries where cheap labor predominates are often ripe for a struggle for a higher standard of living. Most recently, for example, the rate of profit has been threatened in Brazil and Venezuela, where the poor have waged unremitting combat for higher wages, jobs, and income supports from the government.

The problem is that new jobs at living wages and with benefits for all workers are not being created in capitalist societies, either in the more technologically advanced countries or in the less developed world. Yet there is plenty of work to be done, from cleaning up the environment to caring for the sick and the elderly. In our perspective, *work* comprises physical and intellectual activity, both paid and unpaid, and noneconomic activity in which humans reproduce their relationship to nature and form themselves. There is work that isn't reified as labor but is productive activity for creating the conditions of human freedom. One of the basic conditions for human freedom is the shortening of the working day and the provision of more free time. Thus work is a continuum whose parameters include everything from paid labor to productive activity for human freedom. A guaranteed annual income that ensures at least a middle-class cultural and economic living standard also facilitates the possibility of human freedom.

In *The Jobless Future,* Aronowitz and I never separate wages from employment; we emphasize the importance of the historically necessary level of income for maintaining freedom and a good life for all. Thus the current notion of unemployment is incorrect not only because it is not correctly calculated but because a real living wage is not factored into the calculation. If workers are not being paid a real living wage, they do not really have jobs. (Recall my criticism in an earlier chapter of "job solutions" to poverty that do not specify living wages and benefits.) Simply put, the true minimum wage is not some arbitrary $5.15 per hour that maintains workers at a poverty level but a wage that enables them to meet a basic middle-class living standard. It is not jobs but incomes that must be changed. A guaranteed annual income is the basis for a simple struggle that poor people can make to end poverty.

Jobs as we define them also entail the right of workers to collectively determine the conditions of their work, including the introduction of new technology. We do not oppose technology per se; rather, we see the introduction of labor-saving technology as an opportunity to democratize the workplace and shorten the workday. In the current workplace, capitalists and their servant economists use technology to replace workers, keep wages at artificially low levels, and maintain tens of millions of workers in conditions of hardship. Aronowitz and I see the new technologies as an opportunity to reduce the number of hours worked and increase free time without a reduction in income, keeping wages at levels high enough to guarantee, at a minimum, a self-sufficiency income.

The *self-sufficiency* standard, developed by Diana Pearce, measures "how much income is needed, for a family of a given composition in a given place, to adequately meet its basic need—without public or private assistance."[10] In 2000, for example, in Queens County of New York City, that level of income would be $46,836 per year for a family with one parent, one preschooler, and one school-aged child. Compare the official figures for the same family: the U.S. federal poverty line of $14,150, and full-time earnings at the minimum wage of $16,476 (with adult and child tax credits). The self-sufficiency standard of $46,836 represents 93 percent of the median family wage in Queens of $50,600.[11] These figures give us a sense of what the economic boom of the 1990s in the United States has meant. It was not a boom for the poor or the various strata of the working class, but it did benefit the top one-fifth of the population. How was it possible to have a nine-year economic boom without inflation? The answer is that wages remained stagnant for the majority of working people. Further, as Holly Sklar, Laryssa Mykyta, and Susan Wefald show us, profits outpaced wages during the 1990s: "Adjusting for inflation, profits increased by 67 percent during the 1990s while average hourly earnings only increased by 4 percent and the minimum wage rose 3 percent."[12]

The only "trickle down" in income was statistical: analysts averaged the increasing income of the top quintile, which included the 400 Forbes billionaires, into the total incomes of the whole workforce. For the middle class the economic boom was mainly smoke and mirrors; that is, their apparent affluence was the result more of increased debt than of a truly better economy. The following statistics are illustrative: "[I]n 1973, mortgage debt on 1–4 family houses was 36.6% of total personal income. In 1999, the figure was a whopping 61.5%."[13] This debt spending by the middle class continues to prop up a declining economy in the United States at the beginning of the twenty-first century.

The more one investigates the economic boom, the more smoke-and-mirror effects are found. Thus the Economic Policy Institute has developed basic family budgets based on twice the poverty line for 400 communities in the United States:

> Nearly 30% of families with incomes below twice the poverty line faced at least one critical hardship such as missing meals, being evicted from their housing, having their utilities disconnected, doubling up on housing or not having access to needed medical care; and over 72% of such families had at least one serious hardship, such as worries about food, missed rent or mortgage payments, reliance on the emergency room as the main source of medical care, or inadequate child care arrangements.[14]

Since George W. Bush began his term, post-boom America has lost 65,000 jobs a month. By the end of 2002, it got worse: "The nation continued to bleed jobs in December, the Labor Department reported yesterday.... Payrolls in non-farm businesses, adjusted to account for normal seasonal variations, dropped by 101,000 and the unemployment rate stayed at 6 percent. The Labor Department also revised the number of jobs lost in November to 88,000 from 40,000."[15]

As political analyst Kevin Phillips tells us: "Ordinary families gained amid the late nineties boom, but even in 1999, analysts found that the average real after-tax income of the middle 60 percent of the population was lower than in 1977.... [T]he U.S. census of 2000 created a stir by showing median family incomes in New York and California ... declining 5 to 6 percent between 1990 and 2000."[16]

Meanwhile, the income and wealth gap between the rich and the poor became greater than at any time since the "great depression."[17] But even more shocking than the explosion of inequality in the United States is the absence of any "trickle down," not only to the poor, but to the middle class as well. Jobs were actually eliminated, Phillips argues: "As the five hundred largest corporations eliminated almost five million US jobs between 1980 and 1999, they tripled their assets and their profits and enlarged their market value eight-fold as measured by stock prices."[18] This affects not only the poor and the working class, who have seen manufacturing greatly reduced in the United States, but also the supposedly privileged workers in the new high-tech economy. Thus the cover of the February 3, 2003, issue of *Business Week* boldly asks: "Is Your Job Next? A new round of globalization is sending upscale jobs offshore. They include chip design, engineering, basic research—even financial analysis. Can America lose these jobs and still prosper?"[19] This *Business Week* article is perfectly consistent with *The Jobless Future* and even deals with some of the high-tech professionals in engineering and basic scientific research whom Aronowitz and I discuss there.

Economists' and businessmen's belief in the magical ability of the free market to solve all economic and social problems has led to an overemphasis on privatization. Instead of offering a panacea, privatization has led to massive fiscal crises, with crippling budget deficits for states and local governments that have resulted in layoffs, cuts of essential services from education to health care, and increases in taxation. On a global scale, privatization has led to a world economy that provides services only where they are profitable and eliminates them where they are not. Governments that attempt to run like businesses diminish services for those who cannot pay their way, so that economic hardship increases as jobs that pay well and provide good benefits become scarce.

Just as the top one-fifth of earners reaped most of the benefits from the economic boom of the 1990s in the United States, the advanced countries earn the lion's share of global income. In the new global, high-tech, information economy, the diffusion of new technology continually favors the advanced countries. *World Employment Report*

2001, by the International Labor Office (ILO), finds "that nearly 90% of all Internet users are in industrialized countries, with the United States and Canada accounting for 57% of the total. In contrast, Internet users in Africa and the Middle East together account for only 1 per cent of global Internet users. Where ICT [information and communications technology] is most in use, changes in economic relations and behavior are occurring."[20]

Apart from technology, the *UN Human Development Report 2001* finds that "[a] third of the world's extremely poor—those living on less than a dollar a day—live in countries that are lagging behind or slipping further away from the goal of halving such poverty by 2001."[21] The world continues to get harsher for the less advanced countries and their people. According to *The World Employment Report 2001*, "As of 2001, as much as one third of the world's workforce of three billion people are unemployed or underemployed. Of these, about 160 million people are openly unemployed, 20 million more than before the outset of the Asian financial crisis in 1997."[22]

A society where everyone would enjoy at least a middle-class standard of living because of a guaranteed annual income would require vast changes. It would be a society in which everyone would have good housing, education, and health care, and everyone would live in a clean and nonpolluted environment. This will not happen as a result of the kindness of the powerful and the wealthy. A social movement to struggle for a world where the utopian would be normal and not deviant is beginning—at least, that is one way of understanding the new struggles against globalization. From Seattle, Washington, to Genoa, Italy, hundred of thousands have demonstrated in the streets against the Group of 8, the World Trade Organization, and the U.S. war in Iraq. Ordinary people are contesting the policies of the powerful countries that control the globe. The protests have forced changes in the agendas of international meetings, which now at least include the global problem of debtor countries, war, health care, the environment, and poverty. The press frames the protestors as irresponsible anarchists, but in fact they represent the beginning of a worldwide social movement, not only against the World Trade Organization and the Group of 8, but for a new world with democracy and affluence for all.

Thus it is important to view *The Jobless Future* as the beginning of a discussion for a world that no longer privileges the economy of global corporate wealth, built on global impoverishment and the elimination of middle-class jobs. A world that is democratic and concerns itself with human freedom must end inequality by guaranteeing jobs that pay at least middle-class incomes with benefits for all as the primary condition of globalization. Ending poverty in a jobless future is contingent on income solutions—that is, a guaranteed income that will provide a living standard meeting the real requirements of a good life for all.

A NEW ACTIVISM TO END POVERTY: SIMPLE STRUGGLES

In the last two sections I have started to speak about ways to end poverty. Two different but related suggestions involve simple struggles: first, to shorten the working day without any decrease in wages and benefits, and, second, to secure a guaranteed annual income. I have not mentioned a increase in welfare benefits because that is no longer a struggle worth making. At the same time, remembering the dialectic of Sister Bernadette, we must continue to keep welfare benefits as high as possible while these simple struggles are waged. Success is never guaranteed, and the poor must not bear any more misery than they already have. The struggle for a shorter working day has had a setback in Europe, as the European Union has become less competitive in the global market because of its higher-paid workers, shorter workday, and longer vacations (compared with the United States). Klaus F. Zimmerman, the president of the German Institute for Economic Research, says: "We have created a leisure society, while Americans have created a work society. But our model doesn't work anymore. We are in the process of rethinking it."[23]

Similarly, problems related to taxes and debt make the struggle for a guaranteed annual income difficult to undertake. While the rich and the super-rich are fleecing American taxpayers, the rest of us, from the upper middle class to the working poor, are paying much more than our fair share to subsidize their tax cuts. In the last two decades, progressive taxation has basically disappeared and a flat tax has been imposed in the United States. This would seem like a good time to protest against this "trickle up" tax policy. Instead, Americans are quiet. As David Cay Johnston tells us:

> The tax system is becoming a tool to turn the American dream of prosperity and reward for hard work into an impossible goal for tens of millions of Americans and into a nightmare for others. Our tax system is being used to create a nation with fewer stable and viable jobs and less secure retirement income. The tax system is being used by the rich, through their allies in Congress, to shift risk off them and onto everyone else. And perhaps worst of all, our tax system now forces most Americans to subsidize the lifestyles of the very rich, who enjoy the benefits of our democracy without paying their fair share of the price.[24]

My assumption throughout this book is that global free market capitalism forces most working people in the United States into competition with a global workforce, causing them to accept lower and lower wages with increasingly bad benefits: the race to the bottom. In the United States the median family income is \$43,300.[25] If you include the tax burden of this family and its mortgage and credit debt, its members are all struggling to keep their heads above water. Such families may not be poor, but they are not middle-class; in fact, they are just a few paychecks and missed mortgage payments away from being poor. Their debt load is at a record level: "In 1946, just after World War II, consumer debt amounted to 22 percent of household after-tax income, reports the Federal Reserve. (That is, for every \$10,000 of income, there was \$2,200 of debt.) Now debt is almost 110 percent of income. More families borrow, and debtors have more debt in relation to income."[26]

You would think this society would be crying out for a solution to its debt and tax problems, but this is not happening. Although Americans complain about taxes, they don't complain much about the high interest rates on their credit cards, and they see their mortgage debt as normal. And when they complain about taxes, they are much more likely to mention the welfare that goes to the impoverished, not subsidies for the wealthy and for corporations. The goal of the simple struggle for a guaranteed annual income is to provide the poor and all those who receive a family income below the median level with a chance to be middle-class. The start of such a simple struggle could be the adoption of a "universal living wage."

To the self-sufficiency standard mentioned above, I want to add the standard of the universal living wage indexed to housing costs: "No more than 30 percent of a person's gross monthly income should be spent on housing."[27] The universal living wage is based on HUD's fair market rents and therefore would vary throughout the country according to local housing and utility costs. Both the self-sufficiency standard and the universal living wage deserve to be included in the simple struggles made by ordinary people. With successes in these struggles, goals may become broader. In fact, they must become broader because the global free market has created a worldwide race to the bottom in terms of wages and benefits. Ultimately, the struggles for a shorter workday and a guaranteed annual income may become part of the antiglobalization and antisweatshop movements.[28]

Though it would be counterproductive to create an endless list, there is one more simple struggle that is crucial in the context of patriarchy and can be made by people in the rhythms of their daily lives. That is the struggle for "comparable worth," once a central demand of the women's movement, an attempt to deal with the undervalued and underpaid nature of female labor. It called for a reevaluation of the occupational structure to show the centrality of women's work for society. Today this reevaluation makes even more sense as a response to changes in the occupational structure caused by cyber-capitalism. In *The Jobless Future* we argued for the radicalism of this demand:

> In demanding comparable worth, the women's movement is demanding a total redefinition of the class structure. The reconstitution of the occupational structure is conditioned by other developments as well, including the high-tech revolution, and the increasing centrality of knowledge and knowledge workers in the production process, the restructuring of world capitalism and struggles for liberation in Eastern Europe and the "third world."[29]

Of course, this is the basis for a simple struggle, not a revolutionary demand. It will not end patriarchy but it is the kind of struggle that people can make, and that can lead to more struggles if they succeed.

Simple struggles occur within the repetitive rhythms of lived time. They relate to the kinds of struggles that ordinary people can make and consist of theories that they can understand because they are part of the logic of their world. They are struggles that go to the heart of power, but understand that speaking truth to power is never enough. By *simple* I mean that they are basic and that they will change the power relations within society. They will create not just discomfort, but structural change as well. They are not revolutionary in the sense of changing all relations of power and creating an "of the people, for the people" mass democracy. But they may be the starting points of such struggles in everyday life. Though simple, they will always be struggles in which people's reach will exceed their grasp.

Aronowitz has told us that the poor live in "ontological insecurity."[30] They may not know what that phrase means, but they understand the experience of the continuing struggle for survival and the compromises that they too often make. They understand that they are ruled over and that they often have too little say about their own lives. Their lives have too much work, desperation, and anger, but not enough of anything else. This is no guarantee that they will be willing or able to take on the difficulties of simple struggles. Even if they make these simple struggles, there are no guarantees that they will be successful. We should remember that when the powerful feel threatened they will, as Hegel tells us, "be willing to fight to the death."

Besides the examples I have already provided, more simple struggles are possible: for universal health care, quality education, and good housing for all. Unlike Hardt and Negri's multitudes, these struggles are not diffuse and abstract but focused. They make sense for the lives of those willing to take on an increasingly powerful national and global ruling class. And they are made in the simultaneity of class, race, and gender.

Here, after all these years, we turn to W. E. B. DuBois, who reminds us of our "two-ness." Confronting his "blackness" in *The Souls of Black Folk*, he tells us: "One ever feels his two-ness,—an American, A Negro; two souls, two thoughts, two unreconciled strivings; two warring ideals in one dark body, whose dogged strength alone keeps it from being torn asunder."[31]

It is this two-ness that all oppressed ordinary people must call on. They must remember how they are oppressed and treated as less even though it is painful. It is what helps them to overcome their domination in society. This is especially true for the poor. Luce Irigaray reminds us of the two-ness caused by patriarchy: "What if women were not constituted on the model of the one (solid, substantial, lasting, permanent...) and its base of contradictions, both effective and occulted within a proper hierarchy. What if women were always 'at least two,' without opposition between the two, without reduction of the other to the one, without any possible appropriation by the logic of the one."[32]

The powerful can exist in singularity and can take their power for granted. The oppressed can take little for granted and are forced to confront their two-ness. But two-ness enables the oppressed to be both reflexive and critical. If an oppressed person fights against willful ignorance and forgetting, he or she can comprehend both the big picture and the limits of the practical. Two-ness questions the nature of the real and gives us the strength to struggle against it and redefine it.

The real is not set in stone, as I argue in Chapter 2. The real is discontinuous, nonidentical, and full of two-ness, though the powerful present it as certain and disguise its contradictions, encouraging us to forget its limitations. This uncertainty causes unpleasure, but we must deal with it: our freedom and our simple struggles are contingent on remembering. If people are capable of making their own histories through the social formation of themselves as political actors, they constitute the simple struggles that they take on. Then they also constitute what is real. In doing this, they constitute both the conditions that make their domination possible and the possibility of ending that domination. This is the case with poverty as well. Ending poverty is possible—contingent on making at least the three simple struggles that I have outlined.

At the beginning of this book I asked why the poor do not struggle to end poverty. It is through simple struggles that those who have forgotten how to fight for themselves can learn to fight again and engage in the struggles that are necessary to make poverty extraordinary in the United States of America.

Notes

CHAPTER 1

1. George Bush, *Public Papers of the President of the United States: George Bush, 1989, Book 1, January 20 to June 30, 1989* (Washington, D.C.: Government Printing Office, 1990).

2. "Clinton's Economic Plan: The Speech; Text of the President's Address to a Joint Session of Congress," *New York Times*, February 18, 1993.

3. Wallace C. Peterson, *Silent Depression* (New York: Norton, 1994), p. 75.

4. "In 2001 the National Bureau of Economic Research published an exhaustive study documenting what economists and government statisticians had long suspected. From 1980 to 1998 most of the benefits of economic growth in the United States flowed to the very wealthiest families. Although the U.S. economy grew, average wages fell during the 1980s and through much of the 1990s. Middle income families maintained their living standards—barely—and only because women worked more hours outside of the home. Yet the most affluent 1 percent of families nearly tripled their incomes—to an average $515,000. Most of this ended up in the richest thirteen thousand families, whose earnings averaged $17 million. U.S. income had not been concentrated in so few hands since the 1920s." Ellen Frank, *Raw Deal: How Myths and Misinformation About the Deficit, Inflation, and Wealth Impoverish America* (Boston: Beacon Press, 2004), p. 1. And see Thomas Piketty and Emmanuel Saez, "Income Inequality in the United States, 1913–1998," Working Papers, no. 8467 (Cambridge: National Bureau of Economic Research, September 2001).

5. For Richard Rorty, vocabularies are contingent rather than true: "a recognition of that contingency leads to a recognition of the contingency of conscience and . . . both recognitions lead to a picture of intellectual and moral progress as a history of increasingly useful metaphors rather than of increasing understanding of how things really are." Richard Rorty, *Contingency, Irony and Solidarity* (New York: Cambridge University Press, 1989), p. 9.

6. Gwendolyn Mink, *Welfare's End* (Ithaca: Cornell University Press, 1998).

7. "Citing Drop in Welfare Rolls, Clinton to Seek Further Cuts," *New York Times*, January 25, 1999; see also *Daily News*, January 25, 1999. President Clinton in his autobiography speaks about the successes of his administration: "I judge my presidency primarily in terms of its impact on people's lives. That is how I kept score: all the millions of people with new jobs, new houses and college aid; the kids with health insurance and after school programs; the people who left welfare for work; the families helped by the

family leave law; the people living in safer neighborhoods—all those peoples have stories, and they're better ones now." Bill Clinton, *My Life* (New York: Knopf, 2004), p. 955. That these jobs were temporary and that they were low-waged is forgotten, as is the fact that Clinton made Bush II look bad because of an economic boom created by the artificial maintenance of extremely low interest rates by Alan Greenspan. This led inevitably to a bad economy in 2001, which was then exacerbated by President George W. Bush's tax breaks for the rich. In any case the poor missed the boom in places like Bedford-Stuyvesant and Harlem.

8. U.S. Census Bureau, *Statistical Abstract of the United States 1999*, 119th ed. (Washington, D.C.: Government Printing Office, 1999), p. 485.

9. Randy Albelda, "What Welfare Reform Has Wrought," *Dollars and Sense*, January/February 1999, pp. 16–17.

10. Rorty, *Contingency, Irony and Solidarity*, p. 73.

11. HR 2460, May 23, 1991.

12. Karen DeWitt, "Teachers' Union Chief Faults Bush School Plan," *New York Times*, July 12, 1991.

13. National Commission on Children, *Beyond Rhetoric: A New American Agenda for Children and Families* (Washington, D.C.: Government Printing Office, 1991).

14. Ibid., p. xxxv.

15. Charles Murray, *Losing Ground: American Social Policy, 1950–1980* (New York: Basic Books, 1984). Other influential books of the 1980s and 1990s were: George Gilder, *Wealth and Poverty* (New York: Basic Books, 1981); Lawrence Mead, *Beyond Entitlement: The Social Organization of Citizenship* (New York: Free Press, 1986); Mickey Kaus, *The End of Equality* (New York: Basic Books, 1986); Michael Tanner, *The End of Welfare: Fighting Poverty in Civil Society* (Washington, D.C.: Cato Institute, 1996).

16. M. B. Katz, *The Undeserving Poor* (New York: Pantheon, 1989), p. 152.

17. Tanner, *End of Welfare*.

18. Murray, *Losing Ground*, p. 9.

19. Katz, *Undeserving Poor;* Christopher Jencks, "How Poor Are the Poor?" *New York Review of Books*, May 9, 1985, pp. 41–49. David T. Ellwood makes a different argument than Murray, stating that the problem isn't only the welfare system but economic growth. "It is largely a picture of families who are struggling to provide for themselves and who are sharply affected by the availability of jobs and the wages being paid." David T. Ellwood, *Poor Support: Poverty in the American Family* (New York: Basic Books, 1988), p. 96. Jill Quadagno also points to the racial issues that Murray ignores: "Segregation systematically builds deprivation into the residential structure of black communities and increases the susceptibility of the neighborhood to spirals of decline." Jill Quadagno, *The Color of Welfare: How Racism Undermined the War on Poverty* (New York: Oxford University Press, 1994), p. 177.

20. Murray, *Losing Ground*, pp. 156–57.

21. Ibid., p. 162.

22. Ibid., p. 175.

23. Ibid., pp. 173, 177.

24. Representatives Newt Gingrich and Dick Armey and the Republican National Committee, *Contract With America* (New York: Times Books, 1994).

25. Kaus, *End of Equality* (New York: New Republic, 1992), p. 18.

26. Ibid., p. 102.

27. Ibid., p. 105.

28. Ibid., pp. 106–7.

29. Stephen M. Rosoff, Henry N. Pontell, and Robert Tillman, *Profit Without Honor: White Collar Crime and the Looting of America* (Upper Saddle River, N.J.: Prentice-Hall, 1998), p. 16.

30. Ibid., p. 17, and Federal Bureau of Investigation, *Uniform Crime Reports for the United States, 1992* (Washington, D.C.: Government Printing Office, 1993).

31. Kristin Luker, *Dubious Conceptions: The Politics of Teenage Pregnancy* (Cambridge: Harvard University Press, 1996).

32. Mark Robert Rank, *Living on the Edge: The Realities of Welfare in America* (New York: Columbia University Press, 1994).

33. Kaus, *End of Equality*, p. 137.

34. Robert Polner, "A Welfare Mess: Fed Report, State Official Fault City's Food-Stamp Policy," *Newsday*, January 21, 1999.

35. Nina Bernstein, "New York City Plans to Extend Workfare to Homeless Shelters," *New York Times*, February 20, 1999.

36. Jason DeParle, "Symbol of Welfare Reform, Still Struggling," *New York Times*, April 20, 1999.

37. Andrew Hacker, *Two Nations: Black and White, Separate, Hostile, Unequal* (New York: Scribner's, 1992).

38. William Julius Wilson, *The Truly Disadvantaged* (Chicago: University of Chicago Press, 1987), p. 7.

39. Ibid., p. 50.

40. Bob Blauner, "Black Workers and the Underclass," *New Politics* 2, no. 4 (Winter 1990), pp. 12–20.

41. Wilson, *The Truly Disadvantaged*, p. 8.

42. Ibid., p. 94.

43. Ibid., pp. 100–101.

44. Ibid., p. 83.

45. Ibid., pp. 153, 150.

46. Ibid., p. 153.

47. William Julius Wilson, *When Work Disappears: The World of the New Urban Poor* (New York: Vintage, 1996), p. 23.

48. Ibid., p. 87.

49. Ibid., p. 106.

50. Ibid.

51. Ibid., p. 107.

52. Ibid., p. 207.

53. Ibid., p. 214.

54. Ibid., p. 226.

55. Ibid., pp. 221–22.

56. Sheldon H. Danziger and Peter Gottschalk, *America Unequal* (Cambridge: Harvard University Press, 1995).

57. *When Work Disappears*, pp. 228–29.

58. Ibid., p. 234.

59. Herbert J. Gans, *The War Against the Poor* (New York: Basic Books, 1995).

60. Henri Lefebvre, *Critique of Everyday Life*, vol. 2 (New York: Verso, 2002), pp. 41–63, 193–206, 340–58.

61. "As soon as this active life-process is described, history ceases to be a collection of dead facts, as it is with the empiricists (themselves still abstract), or an imagined activity of imagined subjects, as with the idealists." Karl Marx and Friedrich Engels, *The German Ideology* (Amherst, N.Y.: Prometheus, 1998), p. 43.

62. Frank McCourt, *Angela's Ashes* (New York: Touchstone, 1996); Alex Kotlowitz, *There Are No Children Here: The Story of Two Boys Growing Up in the Other America* (New York: Doubleday, 1991). Theodor Adorno, Walter Benjamin, Ernst Bloch, Bertolt Brecht, Georg Lukacs, *Aesthetics and Politics* (New York: Verso, 1977), is the basic work for understanding this debate. Although the debate may seem obscure and not directly connected to descriptions of the lives of poor people in the United States in the 1990s and 2000s, the issue of "the real" that is central to it is still important. Its specific importance to African Americans is demonstrated by the work of Robin D. G. Kelley on surrealism and social change: *Freedom Dreams: The Black Radical Imagination* (Boston: Beacon Press, 2000), pp. 157–94.

63. Daniel Patrick Moynihan, *The Negro Family: The Case for National Action* (Washington, D.C.: Department of Labor, Office of Policy Planning and Research, 1965).

64. Georg Lukacs, *History and Class Consciousness: Studies in Marxist Dialectics*, (Cambridge: M.I.T. Press, 1971).

65. Michael Harrington, *The Other America: Poverty in the United States* (New York: Penguin, 1962).

66. Michel Foucault, *The History of Sexuality*, vol. 1: *An Introduction* (New York: Vintage, 1978).

67. Michael Hardt and Antonio Negri, *Empire* (Cambridge: Harvard University Press, 2000).

68. Stanley Aronowitz and William DiFazio, *The Jobless Future: Sci-Tech and the Dogma of Work* (Minneapolis: University of Minnesota Press, 1994).

CHAPTER 2

1. Frank McCourt, *Angela's Ashes* (New York: Touchstone, 1996), pp. 22–23.

2. Alex Kotlowitz, *There Are No Children Here: The Story of Two Boys Growing Up in the Other America* (New York: Doubleday, 1991), p. 40.

3. Siegfried Krackaur, "The Biography As an Art Form of the New Bourgeoisie," in *The Mass Ornament: Weimar Essays* (Cambridge: Harvard University Press, 1995), p. 105.

4. Loic Wacquant, "Scrutinizing the Street: Poverty, Morality and the Pitfalls of Urban Ethnography," *American Journal of Sociology* 107 (2002), p. 1501. Wacquant's devastating critique of street ethnography points out what is important in Elijah Anderson, *Code of the Street: Decency, Violence and the Moral Life of the Inner City* (New York: Norton, 1999).

5. Michel Foucault, *The Order of Things: An Archaeology of the Human Sciences* (New York: Vintage, 1973), pp. 344–55.

6. Willard Van Orman Quine, *From a Logical Point of View: Nine Logico-Philosophical Essays*, 2d ed. (Cambridge: Harvard University Press, 1980), p. 45.

7. Georg Lukacs, Theodor Adorno, Walter Benjamin, Ernst Bloch, Bertolt Brecht, *Aesthetics and Politics* (New York: Verso, 1977) p. 33.

8. Ibid., pp. 47–48.

9. Ernst Bloch, *The Principle of Hope*, vol. 1 (Cambridge: M.I.T. Press, 1995), p. 116.

10. Ernst Bloch in Lukacs et al., *Aesthetics and Politics*, p. 22.

11. Theodor Adorno in Ibid., p. 163.

12. Theodor W. Adorno, *Negative Dialectics* (New York: Seabury Press, 1973), p. 53.

13. Ibid., p. 148.

14. W. J. Grinker, *Unfinished Business: Report on the Interagency Task Force on Food and Hunger* (New York: Human Resources Administration, 1989), pp. v–vi.

15. Ruth Sidel, *Woman and Children Last* (New York: Viking, 1986), p. 3.

16. Grinker, *Unfinished Business*, p. 11.

17. Ad Hoc Coalition on Housing, "Housing New York: A Coalition Platform," *City Limits* 15 no. 1 (January 1990), p. 22.

18. Robert F. Wagner, Jr., Chair, *New York Ascendant: The Commission on the Year 2000* (New York: Commission on the Year 2000, 1987), pp. 131–32.

19. Coalition for the Homeless, *100 Days of Neglect: Mayor Dinkins and the Homeless* (New York: Coalition for the Homeless, 1990), p. 19.

20. U.S. Department of Housing and Urban Development, *Report to the Secretary on the Homeless and Emergency Shelter* (Washington, D.C.: HUD, 1984), pp. 6–7.

21. Joel Blau, *The Visible Poor: Homelessness in the United States* (New York: Oxford University Press, 1992), p. 8.

22. Robin D. G. Kelley, *Yo' Mama's DisFunktional: Fighting the Culture Wars in Urban America* (Boston: Beacon Press, 1997), pp. 40–42.

23. Cornel West, *Race Matters* (Boston: Beacon Press, 1993), p. 2.

24. Henri Lefebvre, *Critique of Everyday Life*, vol. 1 (New York: Verso, 1991), pp. 167–69.

CHAPTER 3

1. Lester C. Thurow, *Building Wealth: The New Rules for Individuals, Companies and Nations in a Knowledge Based Economy* (New York: Harper Business, 1999), pp. xi–xii.

2. Eric Lipton, "Mayor Eases Reins on City's Spending As Economy Booms," *New York Times*, July 13, 2000.

3. William J. Clinton, "The State of the Union," *New York Times*, January 28, 2000.

4. New York City Welfare Reform and Human Rights Documentation Project, "Hunger Is No Accident: New York and Federal Welfare Policies Violate the Human Right to Food" (New York: New York City Welfare Reform and Human Rights Documentation Project, 2000), p. 4.

5. Representatives Newt Gingrich and Dick Armey and the Republican National Committee, *Contract With America* (New York: Times Books, 1994), p. 65.

6. Ibid., pp. 189–90.

7. James K. Galbraith, *Created Unequal: The Crisis in American Pay* (New York: Free Press, 1998).

8. Daniel Patrick Moynihan, *The Negro Family: The Case for National Action* (Washington, D.C.: Department of Labor, Office of Policy Planning and Research, 1965), p. 43.

9. Oscar Lewis, *La Vida* (New York: Panther Press, 1965).

10. Quoted in Moynihan, *The Negro Family*, p. 130.

11. Ibid., p. 83.

12. Ibid., p. 20.

13. Ibid., p. 94.

14. President Clinton was for welfare-to-work programs and sanctioned many; he ultimately signed the welfare reform legislation after delaying it for a time. As Clinton writes about his veto of the legislation in January 1996: "The next week I vetoed the Republican welfare reform bill because it did too little to move people from welfare to work and too much to hurt poor people and their children. The first time I vetoed the Republican welfare reform proposal, it had been a part of their budget.... Meanwhile, Donna Shalala and I had already gone far in reforming the welfare system on our own. We had given fifty separate waivers to thirty-seven states to pursue initiatives that were pro-work and pro-family. Seventy-three percent of America's welfare recipients were covered by these reforms, and the welfare rolls were dropping." Bill Clinton, *My Life* (New York: Knopf, 2004), p. 694.

15. Moynihan, *The Negro Family*, p. 91.

16. Frances Fox Piven and Richard A. Cloward, *Regulating the Poor: The Functions of Public Welfare*, rev. ed. (New York: Vintage, [1971] 1993).

17. Robert K. Merton, "Social Structure and Anomie," in *Social Theory and Social Structure* (New York: Free Press, 1967).

18. Piven and Cloward, *Regulating the Poor*, p. 195. They are citing Irene Lurie's study, *An Economic Evaluation of Aid to Families with Dependent Children* (Washington, D.C.: Brookings Institution, 1968), p. 131.

19. Ibid., 196.

20. Ibid., pp. 3–4.

21. Edward C. Banfield, *The Unheavenly City Revisited* (Boston: Little Brown, 1974).

22. Richard J. Herrnstein and Charles Murray, *The Bell Curve: Intelligence and Class Structure in American Life* (New York: Free Press, 1994).

23. Frances Fox Piven and Richard A. Cloward, *Poor People's Movements* (New York: Pantheon, 1997).

24. Ibid., pp. 272–73.

25. Ibid., p. 274.

26. Alexis de Tocqueville, *Democracy in America* (New York: Vintage, 1945), pp. 208–9.

27. Community Studies of New York, Inc./Infoshare and The City Project, *City of Contrasts 2000: 51 New York City Council Districts* (New York: Community Studies of New York, Inc./Infoshare and The City Project, September 2000). This data gives a sense of the socioeconomic conditions in the immediate location of the soup kitchen. But the guests come from neighboring areas in Brooklyn and Manhattan as well.

28. Lisa Sandberg, "Thanksgiving Comes a Day Early for Some: Bed-Stuy Soup Kitchen Serves 1,500," *Daily News*, November 28, 1996.

29. Liz Krueger, Liz Accles, and Laura Wernick, *Workfare: The Real Deal II* (New York: Community Food Resource Center, July 1997), p. 3.

30. Judith Walker and Beverly Cheuvront, *Poor in the Land of Dollars: Hunger Arises Amid Prosperity, 2000 Survey of New York City Emergency Food Programs* (New York: New York City Coalition Against Hunger, 2000).

31. Woman's Center for Education and Career Advancement, *The Self-Sufficiency Standard for the City of New York* (New York: Woman's Center for Education and Career Advancement, September 2000). Also see Working Poor Families Project, *Between Hope and Hard Times: New York's Working Families in Economic Distress* (New York: Center for an Urban Future, November 2004).

32. Walker and Cheuvront, *Poor in the Land of Dollars*, pp. 8, 2.

33. Ibid., p. 2.

34. "The welfare queen is an oxymoron—a queen of welfare; she cannot be and is not real. She is an it; an artifact of text , a condition whose possibility is made plausible by the discourse of personal responsibility with its implied debts to gender, race and class." Sanford F. Schram, *After Welfare: The Culture of Postindustrial Social Policy* (New York: New York University Press, 2000), p. 52.

35. Kathryn Edin and Laura Lein, *Making Ends Meet: How Single Mothers Survive Welfare and Low-Wage Work* (New York: Russell Sage Foundation, 1997), p. 43.

36. The text of Sharpton's speech was provided by ACORN.

37. Joyce Shelby, "Sharpton Leads Salary Protest Against Atlantic Mall Developer," *Daily News*, May 10, 2000.

38. The text of Eliot "Skip" Roseboro's speech was provided by ACORN.

39. "By May [1997], it had recruited a third of the WEP workers into the WEP Workers Organizing Committee, formed committees at some three hundred sites, and conducted dozens of job actions, including sit-ins to settle grievances because none of the city departments were willing to establish a grievance procedure. By July, it had over 15,000 authorization cards." Stanley Aronowitz, *From the Ashes of the Old: American Labor and America's Future* (Boston: Houghton Mifflin, 1998), p. 133. They eventually won the right to grieve, but Mayor Giuliani refused to enforce it, even after his veto was overridden by the New York City Council.

40. Linda Gordon, *Pitied but Not Entitled: Single Mothers and the History of Welfare, 1890–1935* (New York: Free Press, 1994), p. 6.

41. Valerie Polakow, *Lives on the Edge: Single Mothers and their Children in the Other America* (Chicago: University of Chicago Press, 1993), p. 48.

42. Rudolph W. Giuliani, "The Welfare Reform Battle Isn't Over Yet," *Wall Street Journal*, February 3, 1999.

43. Community Studies of New York, Inc./Infoshare and City Project, *City of Contrasts 2000*, p. 9.

44. Rachel L. Swarns, "Judge Delays Giuliani Plan on Welfare: 'Urgent Needs' of Poor Must Be Met, City Is Told," *New York Times*, January 26, 1999.

45. Polakow, *Lives on the Edge*, p. 41.

46. Arlie Russell Hochschild, *The Time Bind: When Work Becomes Home and Home Becomes Work* (New York: Metropolitan Books, 1997), p. 27.

47. U.S. Census Bureau, *Statistical Abstracts of the United States: 1999*, 119th ed (Washington, D.C.: Government Printing Office, 1999), tables 355, 162.

48. Mark Robert Rank, *Living on the Edge: The Realities of Welfare in America* (New York: Columbia University Press, 1994), p. 85.

Chapter 4

1. Theresa Funicello, *Tyranny of Kindness* (New York: Atlantic Monthly Press, 1993), p. 252.

2. Julian Wolpert, *What Charity Can and Cannot Do: A Twentieth Century Fund Report* (New York: Twentieth Century Fund, 1996), p. 26.

3. Peter Swords, "Advocacy Without Fear" (New York: Nonprofit Coordinating Committee of New York, Fund for the City of New York, 1996).

4. For a different view on political work and private and government funding for nonprofits, see Mark Chaves, Laura Stephens, and Joseph Galaskiewicz, "Does Government Funding Suppress Nonprofits' Political Activity?" *American Sociological Review* 69 (2004), pp. 292–316. Chaves and his coauthors have a much narrower notion of the political than I have

and very little understanding of the importance of the politics of everyday life. Moreover, the kinds of nonprofits they studied cannot prove or disprove their point (p. 295): "We focus on nonprofit organizations whose primary purpose is something other than political activity or advocacy, but this restriction still leaves substantial variation in organizational types and political goals and tactics."

5. Janet Poppendieck, *Sweet Charity: Emergency Food and the End of Entitlement* (New York: Penguin, 1998), p. 19.

6. Karl Marx, *Critique of Hegel's 'Philosophy of Right'* (Cambridge: Cambridge University Press, 1970), p. 47.

7. Max Weber, *Economy and Society* (Berkeley: University of California Press, 1978), p. 223.

8. Ibid.

9. Robert K. Merton, "Bureaucratic Structure and Personality," in *Social Theory and Social Structure* (New York: Free Press, 1967), p. 254.

10. Ibid., p. 253.

11. Weber, *Economy and Society*, p. 987.

12. Robert Michels, *Political Parties* (New York: Dover, 1959), p. 40.

13. W. Richard Scott, *Institutions and Organizations*, 2d ed. (Thousand Oaks: Sage Publications, 2001), p. 51.

14. Ibid., p. 54.

15. Ibid., p. 58.

16. Ibid., p. 53.

17. Georg Lukacs, *History and Class Consciousness: Studies in Marxist Dialectics* (Cambridge: M.I.T. Press, 1971), p. 83.

18. Ibid., p. 91.

19. Ibid., p. 102.

20. Ibid., p. 201.

21. Walter W. Powell, "The Capitalist Firm in the Twenty-First Century: Emerging Patterns in Western Enterprise," in *The Twenty-First-Century Firm: Changing Economic Organization in International Perspective*, ed. Paul DiMaggio (Princeton: Princeton University Press, 2001), p. 47.

22. Ibid., p. 40. Quotation from Edmund L. Andrews, "AT&T's Plan for Cuts: Be Gentle but Stay Firm," *New York Times*, February 13, 1996.

23. Philip Hancock and Melissa Tyler, *Work, Postmodernism and Organization: A Critical Introduction* (London: Sage Publications, 2001).

24. Jeffrey E. Garten, *The Mind of the C.E.O.* (New York: Basic Books, 2001), p. 249.

25. Ibid., p. 248.

26. Ibid., p. 24.

27. Scott, *Institutions and Organizations*, p. 77.

28. Judith Walker, *Breadlines in Boomtown: Volunteer Programs Buckle Under Growing Need* (New York: New York City Coalition Against Hunger, 1997).

29. Quotations are from the author's field notes.

30. Wayne Barrett, *Rudy!* (New York: Basic Books, 2000), p. 322.

31. Rudolph Giuliani, *Leadership* (New York: Hyperion, 2002), pp. 162–63.

32. Andrew Beveridge, "The Poor in New York City," *Gotham Gazette* (http://www.GothamGazette.com), accessed April 2003.

33. Richard L. Daft and Arlie Y. Lewin, *Talking About Organizational Science: Debates and Dialogue from* Crossroads (London: Sage, 2000), p. 8.

34. Anthony M. Tinker, *Paper Prophets: A Social Critique of Accounting* (New York: Holt, Rinehart & Winston, 1985).

35. Robin Roslender, *Sociological Perspectives on Modern Accountancy* (London: Routledge, 1992), p. 88.

36. Jim Collins, *Good to Great: Why Some Companies Make the Leap and Others Don't* (New York: HarperCollins, 2001), pp. 3–4.

37. Robin Hood Foundation: http://www.robinhood.org.

38. The New York Community Trust: http://www.nycommunitytrust. org/newsite.

39. Ibid.

40. David Wagner, *What's Love Got to Do with It? A Critical Look at American Charity* (New York: New Press, 2000).

CHAPTER 5

1. World Bank Group, "PovertyNet," Overview, Measuring Poverty at the Global Level. See: http://newsletters.worldbank.org/external/default/main?menuPK=494551&pagePK=64133627&piPK=64133598&theSitePK= 494545.

2. John Maynard Keynes commented in *The General Theory of Employment, Interest and Money* (New York: Harcourt Brace Jovanovich, 1964), p. viii, on the theoretical rigidity of economists: "The ideas which are here expressed so laboriously are extremely simple and should be obvious. The difficulty lies not in the new ideas, but in escaping from the old ones, which ramify, for those brought up as most of us have been, into every corner of our minds." In the same vein but critiquing neoliberalism and the illusions of the new economy, see Ellen Frank, *The Raw Deal: How Myths and Misinformation About the Deficit, Inflation and Wealth Impoverish America* (Boston: Beacon Press, 2004); and Doug Henwood, *After the New Economy* (New York: New Press, 2003).

3. Robert J. Samuelson, "A Sixty Year Credit Binge," *Washington Post*, August 27, 2003.

4. Alfred North Whitehead, *Science and the Modern World* (New York: Free Press, [1925] 1953), p. 51.

5. David Sudnow, *Passing On: The Social Organization of Dying* (Englewood Cliffs, N.J.: Prentice-Hall, 1967).

6. Michael Harrington, *The Other America: Poverty in the United States* (New York: Penguin, 1962), p. 2.

7. David Shipler, *The Working Poor: Invisible in America* (New York: Knopf, 2004), p. 11.

8. Jean-Paul Sartre, *Being and Nothingness* (New York: Washington Square Press, 1956), p. 115.

9. Lawrence Mishel, Jared Bernstein, and Heather Boushy, *The State of Working America: 2002/2003*, An Economic Policy Institute Book (Ithaca, N.Y.: ILR Press, 2003), pp. 414–22.

10. Mishel et al., *The State of Working America*, p. 414.

11. Ibid., p. 416.

12. Lawrence Mishel, Jared Bernstein, and John Schmitt, *The State of Working America: 1998–99* (Ithaca, N.Y.: ILR Press, 1999), p. 279.

13. U.S. Census Bureau, *Statistical Abstract of the United States: 2002* (Washington, D.C.: U.S. Department of Commerce, 2002), p. 824.

14. Sigmund Freud, "Remembering, Repeating and Working Through: Further Recommendations on the Technique of Psycho-Analysis II," in *The Standard Edition of the Complete Psychological Works of Sigmund Freud*, vol. 12 (London: Hogarth Press, 1958), p. 148.

15. Sigmund Freud, *The Psychopathology of Everyday Life* (New York: Norton, 1965), p. 136.

16. Jean Paul Sartre, *Truth and Existence* (Chicago: University of Chicago Press, 1992), p. 54.

17. Ibid., p. 55.

18. Ibid., p. 59.

19. Ibid., p. 68.

20. Ibid., p. 52.

21. Ibid., p. 59.

22. The following quotations are from *Memento* (Columbia Tristar, SONY, 2002), written and directed by Christopher Nolan.

23. Freud, "Remembering, Repeating and Working Through," p. 150.

24. Freud, *Psychopathology of Everyday Life*, p. 148.

25. Michel Foucault, *History of Sexuality*, Vol. 1 (New York: Random House, 1978), p. 93.

26. Ibid., p. 95.

27. Michel Foucault, *Power/Knowledge* (New York: Pantheon, 1980), p. 39.

28. Ibid., p. 81.

29. Michel Foucault, *Discipline and Punish: The Birth of the Prison* (New York: Vintage, 1979), p. 228.

30. *History of Sexuality*, vol. 1, p. 143.

31. Ernesto Laclau and Chantal Mouffe, *Hegemony and Socialist Strategy: Towards a Radical Democratic Politics* (London: Verso, 1985).

32. Derrida implies this when he interrogates the ghostly imagery of Marx's *German Ideology* and *Capital* in *The Specters of Marx* and asserts, "[W]e are privileging here, that 'spirit' of emancipatory Marxism whose injunction we are reaffirming here, however secret and contradictory it appears."

Jacques Derrida, *Specters of Marx: The State of the Debt, the Work of Mourning, and the New International* (New York: Routledge, 1994), p. 167.

33. Guy de Jonquieres, "Clothes on the Line: The Garment Industry Faces a Global Shake-up as Quotas End," *Financial Times*, July 19, 2004.

34. Barbara Ehrenreich, *Nickel and Dimed: On (Not) Getting By in America* (New York: Owl Books, 2001), pp. 121–92.

35. William Gibson, *Neuromancer* (New York: Ace Books, 1984), p. 51. See also Tim Jordan, *Cyberpower: The Culture and Power of Cyberspace and the Internet* (London: Routledge, 1999), pp. 21–22.

36. Gilles Deleuze and Felix Guattari, *A Thousand Plateaus: Capitalism and Schizophrenia* (Minneapolis: University of Minnesota Press, 1987), p. 453.

37. Stanley Aronowitz, Dawn Esposito, William DiFazio, and Margaret Yard, "The Post-Work Manifesto," in Stanley Aronowitz and Jonathan Cutler, eds., *Post-Work* (New York: Routledge, 1998), p. 53.

38. Michael Hardt and Antonio Negri, *Empire* (Cambridge: Harvard University Press, 2000), pp. 31–32.

39. Ibid., pp. xiv–xv.

40. Hardt and Negri tell us that there are three types of immaterial labor. "The first is involved in industrial production and has been informationalized and has incorporated communication technologies in a way that transforms the production process itself.... Second is the immaterial labor of analytical and symbolic tasks.... A third type of immaterial labor involves the production and manipulation of affect and requires (virtual or actual) human contact.... These are the three types of labor that drive the postmodernization of the global economy." Ibid., p. 293. See also Andrew Ross, *No-Collar: The Humane Workplace and Its Hidden Costs* (New York: Basic Books, 2003); Maurizio Lazzarato, "Immaterial Labor," in Paolo Virno and Michael Hardt, eds., *Radical Thought in Italy: A Potential Politics* (Minneapolis: University of Minnesota Press, 1996), pp. 133–46.

41. Ibid., pp. 396–97.

42. Ibid., p. 403.

43. Karl Marx, "On the Jewish Question," in *Karl Marx: Early Writings* (New York: Penguin, 1975), pp. 211–41.

44. Edward N. Muller and Mitchell A. Seligson, "Inequality and Insurgency," in Mitchell A. Seligson and John T. Passe-Smith, eds., *Development and Under-Development: The Political Economy of Global Inequality*, 3d ed. (London: Lynne Rienner, 2003).

45. Mark Malloch Brown and Anne Kristin Sydnes, *Choices for the Poor: Lessons from National Poverty Strategies* (New York: United Nations Development Programme, March 2001), p. 2.

46. Ibid., p. 3.

47. Samuel P. Huntington, *The Clash of Civilizations and the Remaking of the World Order* (New York: Touchstone, 1996), p. 28.

48. Ibid., p. 305.

49. Ibid.

50. "The basic impulse of patriarchy . . . is the drive to dominate nature, a project that requires control over sexuality (nature within us), control of women and children (onto whom the anarchy of nature and sexuality is projected), and social hierarchies that assume people's inability to govern themselves. Desire is equated with unbridled selfishness, aggression and violence. Morality is equated with self-abnegation, repression of desire and submission to authority." Ellen Willis, "The Mass Psychology of Terrorism," in Stanley Aronowitz and Heather Gautney, eds., *Implicating Empire: Globalization and Resistance in the 21st Century World Order* (New York: Basic Books, 2003), p. 97.

51. Samuel P. Huntington, *Who Are We?: The Challenges to America's National Identity* (New York: Simon & Schuster, 2004), p. 256.

52. Manning Marable, *The Great Wells of Democracy: The Meaning of Race in American Life* (New York: Basic Books, 2002); Robin D. G. Kelley, *Freedom Dreams: The Black Radical Imagination* (Boston: Beacon Press, 2002).

53. F. A. Hayek, *Individualism and Economic Order* (Chicago: University of Chicago Press, 1948), p. 91.

54. "The most significant fact about this system is the economy of knowledge with which it operates, or how little the participants have to know in order to be able to take the right action. In abbreviated form, by a kind of symbol, only the most essential information is passed on and passed on only to those concerned. It is more than a metaphor to describe the price system as a kind of machinery for registering change, or a system of telecommunications which enables individual producers to watch the movements of a few pointers as an engineer might watch the hands of a few dials, in order to adjust their activities to changes of which they may never know more than is reflected in the price movement." Ibid., pp. 86–87.

55. As for those who continue to demand higher wages, they "must be allowed to remain unemployed. The point that is relevant to us is that if we are determined not to allow unemployment at any price, and are not willing to use coercion, we shall be driven to all sorts of desperate expedients, none of which can bring any lasting relief and all of which will seriously interfere with the productive use of our resources." F. A. Hayek, *The Road to Serfdom* (Chicago: University of Chicago Press, 1944), pp. 207–8.

56. Ibid., p. 225.

57. Such taxation has "been used for extreme egalitarian ends. The two consequences of this which seem to be the most serious are . . . that it makes for social immobility by making it practically impossible for the successful man to rise by accumulating a fortune and . . . it has come near to eliminating that most important element in a free society—the man of independent means, a figure whose essential role in maintaining free opinion and generally an atmosphere of independence from government control we only begin to realize as he is disappearing from the stage." *Individualism and Economic Order*, p. 118.

58. Immanuel Wallerstein, *The End of the World As We Know It: Social Science for the Twenty-First Century* (Minneapolis: University of Minnesota Press, 1999), p. 70.

Chapter 6

1. Karl Marx, *The 18th Brumaire of Louis Bonaparte* (New York: International Publishers, 1963), p. 15.

2. Mark Levitan, *A Crisis of Black Male Employment: Unemployment and Joblessness in New York City, 2003* (New York: Community Service Society, February 2004), p. 2.

3. Stanley Aronowitz, *How Class Works: Power and Social Movement* (New Haven: Yale University Press, 2003), p. 11.

4. Jacques Derrida, *Specters of Marx: The State of the Debt, the Work of Mourning and the New International* (New York: Routledge, 1994).

5. Karl Marx, *Capital: Volume One* (New York: Vintage, 1977), pp. 342–43.

6. Ibid., p. 343.

7. *CityWatch* segment of *Wake-up Call*, WBAI-New York, 99.5 FM, Deena Kolbert and William DiFazio, hosts, July 13, 2000. Quotations from Eliot "Skip" Roseboro and Jose Nicolau come from a transcript of the show.

8. Ulrich Beck, *What Is Globalization?* (Cambridge: Polity Press, 2000), p. 58.

9. Stanley Aronowitz and William DiFazio, *The Jobless Future: Sci-Tech and the Dogma of Work* (Minneapolis: University of Minnesota Press, 1994), p. 299.

10. Diana Pearce with Jennifer Brooks, *The Self-Sufficiency Standard for the City of New York* (New York: Women's Center for Education and Career Advancement, September 2000), p. 1.

11. Ibid., p. 12.

12. Holly Sklar, Laryssa Mykyta, and Susan Wefald, *Raise the Floor* (New York: Ms. Foundation for Women, 2001), p. 57.

13. Arthur McEwan, "Ask Dr. Dollar," *Dollars and Sense*, July/August 2001, p. 41.

14. Heather Boushey, Chauna Brocht, Bethney Gundersen, and Jared Bernstein, *Hardships in America: The Real Stories of Working Families* (Washington, D.C.: Economic Policy Institute, 2001), pp. 1–2.

15. Daniel Altman, "With Companies Still Gloomy, Payrolls Shrink by Thousands," *New York Times*, January 11, 2003.

16. Kevin Phillips, *Wealth and Democracy* (New York: Broadway Books, 2002), p. 111.

17. James K. Galbraith, *Created Unequal: The Crisis in American Pay* (New York: Free Press, 1998); Edward N. Wolff, *Top Heavy* (New York: New Press, 2002).

18. Phillips, *Wealth and Democracy*, p. 112.

19. Pete Engardio, Aaron Bernstein, and Manjeet Kripalani, "Is Your Job Next?" *Business Week*, February 3, 2003, pp. 50–60.

20. Quoted in "Bridging the Digital Divide: Harnessing ICT for Economic Development, Job Creation and Poverty Eradication," *World of Work: The Magazine of the ILO*, no. 38 (January/February 2001), p. 4.

21. Quoted in Alan Beattie, "UN Snapshot Captures Failure to Hit Poverty Goals," *Financial Times*, July 11, 2001.

22. "Bridging the Digital Divide," p. 5.

23. Quoted in Mark Landler, "Europe Reluctantly Deciding It Has Less Time for Time Off," *New York Times*, July 7, 2004.

24. David Cay Johnston, *Perfectly Legal: The Covert Campaign to Rig Our Tax System to Benefit the Super Rich—And Cheat Everybody Else* (New York: Penguin, 2003), p. 19.

25. Dr. Daniel H. Weinberg, "Income, Poverty and Health Insurance 2003—Press Briefing," August 6, 2004, p. 1, chart 1, http://www.census.gov/hhes/income/income03/prs04asc.html.

26. Robert J. Samuelson, "A 60-Year Credit Binge," *Washington Post*, August 27, 2003.

27. For the campaign for a universal living wage, see: http://www.universallivingwage.org.

28. Andrew Ross, *Low Pay, High Profile: The Global Push for Fair Labor* (New York: New Press, 2004).

29. Aronowitz and DiFazio, *Jobless Future*, p. 273.

30. Aronowitz, *How Class Works*, p. 217.

31. W. E. B. DuBois, *The Souls of Black Folk* (New York: Vintage, 1990), pp. 8–9.

32. Luce Irigaray, *To Speak Is Never Neutral* (New York: Routledge, 2002), p. 231.

Index